Cutting-Edge Artificial Intelligence

Artificial intelligence (AI) is impacting industries worldwide by introducing new methods and altering traditional practices. This book examines AI's diverse effects, providing insights into its applications, challenges, and future prospects across education, healthcare, finance, and more.

The chapters explore how AI technologies, such as large language models, enhance feedback in higher education and influence legal studies while upholding academic integrity. A review of key technical approaches—knowledge-based systems, machine learning, and intelligent optimization—lays the groundwork for understanding AI's potential. Real-world examples illustrate AI's role in medical imaging, presenting new diagnostic methods and the use of language models for image interpretation. The book also discusses financial applications, including techniques for credit card fraud detection and forecasting natural gas prices using innovative models. Additionally, it covers personalized federated learning models, highlighting the importance of data privacy and security in AI's evolution.

This comprehensive guide is valuable for educators, researchers, practitioners, and students interested in AI's current and future developments. By combining theory with practical examples, the book offers readers a clear understanding of how AI affects various sectors, enabling them to engage effectively with this rapidly evolving field.

Cutting-Edge Artificial Intelligence

Advances and Implications in Real-World Applications

Edited by
Walayat Hussain,
Luis Martínez López,
Manoj Sahni,
Zhen-Song Chen,
and Jun Liu

CRC Press
Taylor & Francis Group
Boca Raton London New York

CRC Press is an imprint of the
Taylor & Francis Group, an **Informa** business

Designed cover image: Shutterstock

First edition published 2025
by CRC Press
2385 NW Executive Center Drive, Suite 320, Boca Raton FL 33431

and by CRC Press
4 Park Square, Milton Park, Abingdon, Oxon, OX14 4RN

CRC Press is an imprint of Taylor & Francis Group, LLC

© 2025 selection and editorial matter, Walayat Hussain, Luis Martínez López, Manoj Sahni, Zhen-Song Chen and Jun Liu; individual chapters, the contributors

First edition published by Routledge in 2025

Reasonable efforts have been made to publish reliable data and information, but the author and publisher cannot assume responsibility for the validity of all materials or the consequences of their use. The authors and publishers have attempted to trace the copyright holders of all material reproduced in this publication and apologize to copyright holders if permission to publish in this form has not been obtained. If any copyright material has not been acknowledged please write and let us know so we may rectify in any future reprint.

Except as permitted under U.S. Copyright Law, no part of this book may be reprinted, reproduced, transmitted, or utilized in any form by any electronic, mechanical, or other means, now known or hereafter invented, including photocopying, microfilming, and recording, or in any information storage or retrieval system, without written permission from the publishers.

For permission to photocopy or use material electronically from this work, access www.copyright.com or contact the Copyright Clearance Center, Inc. (CCC), 222 Rosewood Drive, Danvers, MA 01923, 978-750-8400. For works that are not available on CCC please contact mpkbookspermissions@tandf.co.uk

Trademark notice: Product or corporate names may be trademarks or registered trademarks and are used only for identification and explanation without intent to infringe.

ISBN: 978-1-032-63247-6 (hbk)
ISBN: 978-1-032-63246-9 (pbk)
ISBN: 978-1-032-63248-3 (ebk)

DOI: 10.1201/9781032632483

Typeset in Palatino LT Std
by Apex CoVantage, LLC

Contents

Editors...vii

Contributors...ix

1 Utilising Large Language Models for Feedback Generation in
Higher Education: Insights from Student Perceptions...........................1
Mehdi Rajaeian, Penny Wheeler, and Walayat Hussain

2 Balancing Innovation and Integrity: Integration and
Implications of Generative Artificial Intelligence
in Legal Education...16
Anne Pickering, Kunle Ola, and Khorsed Zaman

3 Three Technical Routes of AI 35
*Weisi Chen, Francesco Cauteruccio, Yuan Li, Jiaxin Zheng,
and Wulong Liu*

4 Multi-Criteria Decision-Making for Operating ATM Systems...........55
Reetika Singh, Shivani Kalyan, and LN Das

5 FFP: Robust, Interpretable, and Lightweight Framework
for Medical Image Diagnosis..89
*Shancheng Jiang, Xing Zhang, Kun Xiang, Jiawen Pan,
Wenxiao Zheng, and Jiahao Xu*

6 Grey Prediction Model Based on Fixed-Point Accumulation
and Its Application to Predict Natural Gas Futures
Contract Price 106
Lianyi Liu, Junliang Du, and Sifeng Liu

7 Large Language Models in Medical Image Understanding...............139
Ghada Khoriba, Muhammad Nouman, and Essam A. Rashed

8 **Enhancing Credit Card Fraud Detection with Spatial-Temporal Analysis and Balanced Learning Approaches**.......................................171
Nur Indah Lestari, Walayat Hussain,
José M. Merigó, and Mahmoud Bekhit

Index...189

Editors

Walayat Hussain received his PhD in Computer Systems from the University of Technology Sydney, Australia. He is currently an associate professor and the head of the Information Technology & Systems Discipline at Australian Catholic University, Australia. His research interests include AI, business intelligence, computational intelligence, and service computing.

Luis Martínez López received his PhD in Computer Sciences from the University of Granada, Granada, Spain, in 1999. He is currently a professor in the Department of Computer Science at the University of Jaen, Jaen, Spain. His research interests focus on fuzzy decision-making, linguistic preference modelling, fuzzy systems, decision support systems, and recommender systems.

Manoj Sahni received his PhD in Applied Mathematics from Jaypee Institute of Information Technology, Noida, India. He is currently a professor at the School of Technology, Pandit Deendayal Energy University, Gandhinagar, Gujarat, India. He exemplifies dedication and expertise as a distinguished mathematics educator and researcher, with over 20 years of invaluable contributions to teaching and scholarly inquiry.

Zhen-Song Chen is a senior member, IEEE. He received his PhD in Traffic and Transportation Planning and Management from the School of Transportation and Logistics, Southwest Jiaotong University, Chengdu, China, in 2016. He is currently an associate professor and a Chutian Fellow in the School of Civil Engineering at Wuhan University. He has authored or coauthored more than 190 papers in reputed journals.

Jun Liu received his PhD in Information Engineering from Southwest Jiaotong University, Chengdu, China, in 1999. He is currently a professor of Artificial Intelligence and the director of the Artificial Intelligence Research Centre (AIRC) at the School of Computing, Ulster University. He has been actively working in the field of AI for many years.

Contributors

Mahmoud Bekhit
Peter Faber Business School
Australian Catholic University
North Sydney, Australia

Francesco Cauteruccio
Department of Information
   Engineering,
Electrical Engineering and Applied
   Mathematics
University of Salerno
Fisciano, Italy

Weisi Chen
Xiamen University of Technology
Xiamen, China

LN Das
Delhi Technological University
Delhi, India

Junliang Du
School of Business
Jiangnan University
Wuxi, China

Walayat Hussain
Australian Catholic University
North Sydney, Australia

Shancheng Jiang
Department of Systems Engineering
Northeastern University
Shenyang, China

Shivani Kalyan
Netaji Subhas University of
   Technology
Delhi, India

Ghada Khoriba
Information Technology and
   Computer Science School
Nile University
Giza, Egypt

Zaman Khorseduzzaman
Thomas More Law School
Australian Catholic University
North Sydney, Australia

Nur Indah Lestari
University of Technology Sydney
Sydney, Australia

Yuan Li
School of Computer and
   Information Engineering
Xiamen University of
   Technology
Xiamen, China

Lianyi Liu
Management Science and
   Engineering
Nanjing University of Aeronautics
   and Astronautics
Nanjing, China

Sifeng Liu
Henan University
Kaifeng, China

Wulong Liu
Computer Science and
   Technology
Xiamen University of
   Technology
Xiamen, China

José M. Merigó
School of Computer Science
Faculty of Engineering and Infor-
    mation Technology
University of Technology
Sydney, Australia

Muhammad Nouman
School of Information Science
University of Hyogo
Akashi, Japan

Kunle Ola
Dean of the Thomas More Law
    School
Australian Catholic University
North Sydney, Australia

Jiawen Pan
Sun Yat-sen University
Guangzhou, China

Anne Pickering
Thomas More Law School
Australian Catholic University
North Sydney, Australia

Mehdi Rajaeian
Peter Faber Business School
Australian Catholic University
Melbourne, Australia

Essam Rashed
School of Information Science
University of Hyogo
Akashi, Japan

Reetika Singh
Department of Applied
    Mathematics
Delhi Technological University
Delhi, India

Penny Wheeler
Centre for Learning & Teaching
Australian Catholic University
Canberra, Australia

Kun Xiang
School of Intelligent Systems
    Engineering
Sun Yat-sen University
Guangzhou, China

Jiahao Xu
School of Intelligent Systems
    Engineering
Sun Yat-sen University
Guangzhou, China

Xing Zhang
Shanghai University
Shanghai, China

Jiaxin Zheng
Xiamen University of Technology
Xiamen, China

Wenxiao Zheng
School of Intelligent Systems
    Engineering
Sun Yat-sen University
Guangzhou, China

1

Utilising Large Language Models for Feedback Generation in Higher Education: Insights from Student Perceptions

Mehdi Rajaeian, Penny Wheeler, and Walayat Hussain

1.1 Introduction

Generative artificial intelligence (GenAI) has revolutionised numerous sectors by transforming how we communicate and perform daily tasks. This transformation spans fields such as business, research, education, coding, healthcare, and employment. Users can prompt AI to create human-like text, programming code, images, audio, and video. Unlike traditional conversational AI, which relies on predefined responses, Generative AI produces outputs that surpass its initial programming (Lim et al., 2023), enhancing learning experiences, particularly in education. However, ensuring accuracy, avoiding overreliance, and addressing data privacy are essential for its successful integration (Eke, 2023).

Despite various challenges posed by these Generative AI tools, including concerns about the impact of Generative AI on originality and assessment reliability (Yu, 2023; Dwivedi et al., 2023), such tools hold significant potential to assist in various educational endeavours (Ausat et al., 2023), the role of Generative AI remains significant. Despite challenges, these tools offer considerable promise, particularly for generating personalized feedback on assessments (Kaiss et al., 2023; Baidoo-Anu and Ansah, 2023).

Constructive assessment feedback is critical to improving student learning, though delivering timely, quality feedback for large cohorts remains challenging (Pardo et al., 2019). As a result, students express significant shortcomings in the quantity and quality of the feedback they are provided with (Boud and Molloy, 2013). These challenges have motivated educators to leverage two other sources of external feedback: student peer feedback or automated feedback systems. In student peer review, students evaluate their peers' work, present a means to foster collaborative learning, encouraging active engagement and deeper understanding through interaction with

DOI: 10.1201/9781032632483-1

peers' insights (Lerchenfeldt et al., 2019). Moreover, peer review can nurture a sense of accountability, as students assume responsibility for their evaluations and contributions to the learning process. This approach also holds the potential to alleviate instructors' workload, as students take on a more participatory role in assessment. However, unhelpful feedback, as well as biases and inconsistencies in feedback, provided by peers must be acknowledged as its limitations (Lerchenfeldt et al., 2019).

Traditional automated feedback systems generate feedback based on predefined set of rules for feedback delivery. The source of this rules is either domain experts (expert-driven), student data (data-driven) or both (hybrid) (Deeva et al., 2021). Available automated feedback systems (such as BEETLE II, ActiveMath, SQL-Tutor, and others) offer several advantages over instructor feedback such as speed and scalability (Deeva et al., 2021). However, they have limitations such as low levels of learner control and adaptiveness to student characteristics, as well as focusing more on feedback automation to address teacher's workload, rather than mainly addressing the quality of the feedback given to the students (Deeva et al., 2021). With the increasing use of Generative AI in assessment evaluation and generating feedbacks (Teubner et al., 2023), the question arises as to whether it can be effectively used to generate automated feedback and how the usefulness of AI-generated feedback is compared to other types of feedback. Although some studies (Kochmar et al., 2020; Fui-Hoon Nah et al., 2023) reported the utility of intelligent AI tools for providing automated feedback to students and its impact on learning outcomes, studies on the use of LLM-based for providing student feedback are scarce. To gain an in-depth analysis of the effectiveness of feedback generated by LLM-based AI, it is imperative to assess the usefulness of AI-generated feedback for delivering constructive comment to students.

Building upon the preceding discussion, the research question for the study is:

> *How do students perceive the usefulness of AI-generated feedback compared to peer review feedback?*

To answer these research questions, first we administered a technology-mediated peer review process in which students were tasked to provide feedback on essays submitted by their peers and rate the feedback they receive from their peers. Then we asked ChatGPT to provide constructive feedback on students' essays written in response to an assessment task, provided the ChatGPT-generated feedback to students, and asked them to rate this feedback too. Finally, we conducted a survey asking students to provide their view on different dimension of feedback usefulness for both peer feedback and ChatGPT-generated feedback. Although many existing studies discuss the features and limitations of ChatGPT in academia, to the best of our knowledge, this is the first work that empirically investigates the perceived usefulness of ChatGPT-generated feedback from students' perspective. Also, based on the findings we identify some improvement opportunities for automated feedback and peer review systems.

The rest of the chapter is organised as follows. First, a brief review of related literature on Generative AI in education and students' assessment feedback is presented. Then the research methodology and the results of data analysis are provided. Finally, the results and implications of the research as well as limitations and future directions are discussed.

1.2 Related Research

1.2.1 Feedback for Learning

Feedback is fundamental to the learning process, with various models and theories examining its mechanisms and influence on student engagement, teaching, learning, and assessment (Lipnevich and Panadero, 2021). Despite increased focus and investment in feedback research within higher education, scholars indicate that both educators and students still struggle with understanding and effectively implementing feedback, as highlighted in studies by Dawson et al. (2019), Henderson et al. (2019), and Boud and Molloy (2013).

Although there is broad consensus on feedback's importance, opinions diverge on what constitutes "effective" feedback. Dawson et al. (2019) conducted a qualitative investigation to understand the perspectives of educators and students on the purpose of feedback and their criteria for effective feedback. The study found that both groups consider *improvement* as the primary purpose of feedback. Educators focus on feedback design elements like *timing* and *modalities* and connected tasks, while students emphasize the importance of high-quality comments that are usable, sufficiently detailed, and address their own work (i.e., personalised). Dawson et al. (2019)'s research uncovers some incongruous experiences of effective feedback, with some students valuing tailored feedback while others appreciate generic comments. Dawson et al. (2019) also identified frontier topics that have not been fully explored, such as evaluative judgement, peer feedback, exemplars, and feedback moderation. They advocate for understanding the effects of feedback within the framework of individuals' perceptions of feedback's purpose and effectiveness.

As Henderson et al. (2021) rightly argue, feedback is known to have a powerful influence on learning, only if learners can make use of it. From a learner-centred perspective that recognizes the active role of students in their own learning (Carless and Boud, 2018), feedback should be considered as a learner-centred process, in which learners need to be able to make sense of performance information and then act upon it in order to improve their future performance (Boud and Molloy, 2013). Therefore, the feedback comments must be *useful* to the learner (Henderson et al., 2021).

In this chapter, for measuring the feedback usefulness, we used the measurement instrument developed by Henderson et al. (2016) and used for various studies (e.g. Henderson et al., 2021). Feedback is considered useful if it is understandable, sufficiently detailed, usable personalised, and specific to the assignment (Henderson et al., 2016, 2021).

Feedback can be originated internally from the learner (self-assessments) or come from external sources, including peers, academic educators, or automated feedback systems.

A systematic review of the literature (Deeva et al., 2021) highlights the current state of automated feedback technologies in education and emphasizes the need for a shift towards a more student-oriented approach. The existing technologies are predominantly teacher-oriented, focusing on automating feedback to reduce teacher workload rather than prioritizing the quality of feedback for students. The authors argue that a more student-oriented approach, with increased learner control and adaptiveness to student characteristics, could significantly benefit students. They suggest that data-driven personalization, where no teacher intervention is required, could lead to immediate and tailored feedback for students based on their needs and preferences. Deeva et al. (2021) also discusses the importance of leveraging the abundance of data available through learning analytics to enhance system adaptiveness and support complex knowledge acquisition. The authors encourage future system developers to explore the possibilities offered by the age of data and modern data processing techniques in order to develop more advanced automated feedback systems capable of addressing complex tasks and promoting better learning outcomes.

Although student peer review is recognized as a valuable approach for providing feedback to enhance learning (Mulder et al., 2014), scholars have highlighted various limitations and difficulties associated with its implementation. For instance, in a study by Brammer and Rees (2007) investigating student perceptions of peer review in a master's-level program, some students expressed strong dissatisfaction, considering the exercise a waste of time. They believed their peers were not capable of adequately identifying errors in the submitted work. Similarly, Evans (2015) found that peer review did not yield equal benefits for all students, as the quality of feedback varied among participants. Another study (Mulder et al., 2014) showed that students' expectations of peer review's effectiveness were higher before the experience, but in conflicting findings in another study (Cheng and Warren, 1997), students who initially lacked confidence showed more positive attitudes after completing the review. Another challenge of student peer review, especially in larger classes, is managing the administrative tasks like distributing assignments and collecting reviews. However, these concerns have been largely resolved with the widespread adoption of online learning management tools (Indriasari et al., 2020). In this study, peer review process was facilitated by FeedbackFruits, which is a learning management system integrated tool suite that automates the manual tasks involved in the peer review process.

1.3 Large Language Models

Large language models (LLMs) are deep neural network models with remarkable capabilities in effectively processing and analysing intricate linguistic structures (Teubner et al., 2023). Their capacity to generate human-like text has sparked considerable interest in the realm of natural language processing (NLP), making them a highly promising technology in educational contexts (Dai et al., 2023; Pardos and Bhandari, 2023).

Among the most notable LLMs is the Generative Pretrained Transformer (GPT) series developed by OpenAI. The GPT series, leveraging a Transformer architecture, excels in capturing long-range dependencies and positional information within text. These models combine large-scale architectures with huge amounts of textual training data. This scaling up has allowed LLMs to understand and generate text at a level comparable to that of humans (Teubner et al., 2023). In addition to the ChatGPT application, which provides a chat user interface, an application programming interface (API) is available, which makes it possible to seamlessly integrate ChatGPT with various existing applications, including educational apps.

Considering the relatively brief period since the emergence of ChatGPT, the literature in this area is evolving, and early positive effects resulting from its utilization have been reported in some experiments. For instance, Dai et al. (2023) examined the agreement between ChatGPT and the instructor when assessing assignments of 103 students according to the marking rubric. The results show that, compared to instructors, ChatGPT can generate more detailed feedback on the student proposal reports, which fluently and coherently summarises students' performance. In addition, ChatGPT achieved high agreement with the instructor when assessing the topic of students' assignments and could provide feedback on the process of students' completing the task, which benefits students in developing learning skills. Pardos and Bhandari (2023) compared the efficacy of ChatGPT hints with hints authored by human tutors across two high school algebra topic areas and found 70% of hints produced by ChatGPT passed the manual quality checks and suggested that the technology still requires human supervision in its current form. In another study, Pankiewicz and Baker (2023) randomly assigned students to either the control group ($N = 66$) or the experimental group ($N = 66$) and automated the feedback generation process by employing

OpenAI's GPT–3.5 model to create personalised hints for the experimental group students working on programming assignments. Almost half of the experimental group students (46%) positively rated the usefulness of GPT-generated hints, with a median rating of 4 or 5 on a 5-point Likert scale. In the experimental group where GPT hints were enabled, students relied less on the platform's regular feedback but demonstrated better performance in terms of the percentage of successful submissions across consecutive attempts for tasks where GPT hints were available. For tasks where GPT feedback was not provided, the experimental group required significantly less time to complete assignments. Additionally, when GPT hints were unavailable, students in the experimental group were initially less likely to solve the assignment correctly, indicating a potential over-reliance on GPT-generated feedback. However, they were able to correct their approach rapidly and eventually achieved the same percentage of correct submissions after seven attempts. The study found that the availability of GPT hints did not significantly impact students' affective state (focused, frustrated, anxious, confused, bored) during the learning process.

1.4 Research Method

Our study adopts a quantitative research approach, focusing on the systematic collection and analysis of numerical data to evaluate the effectiveness of AI-generated feedback in comparison to peer-generated feedback within the context of student essay assessments.

We obtained ethics approval from an Australian university and followed the ethical guidelines, including informed consent, confidentiality, and anonymity. The participants in this study were undergraduate students enrolled in a first-year university course on Introduction to Emerging Information Technologies and IT Ethics. As part of their formal assessment requirements, students were required to write a 400-word essay on the ethical aspects of using virtual reality (VR) technology in the context of a case study, participate in a peer feedback review process facilitated by an automated tool and rate the usefulness of the feedback they receive on a scale of 1 to 10 (0 not useful to 10 very useful). The essay writing task was adopted from a publicly available online source (Ramirez, 2022). The FeedbackFruits platform assigned the submissions randomly and anonymously to the reviewers and recorded participants' activity data (e.g., feedback comments, submission and review date/time, ratings on feedback, etc.) throughout the review process. Students were asked to provide feedback based on two criteria: (1) the organization and development of ideas (writing) and (2) response to question writing prompts (content). From the 290 students enrolled in the course,

228 students handed in essays for peer review, of which 156 students rated the feedback received from their peers.

After removing the personal identifiers from the 228 essays, each essay was submitted manually to the free version of Chat-GPT (GPT–3.5), using the prompt: "Please provide constructive feedback on this essay." Then, we added the following disclaimer statement at the beginning of the obtained feedback to avoid misleading students: "This is AI-generated review feedback. Please read the feedback carefully and rate the review feedback (0 not useful <-> 10 very useful). If you think the feedback is not correct/relevant, please explain the issue in the comment section." ChatGPT-generated feedback was provided to students via FeedbackFruits, and 86 students rated AI-generated feedback. The ratings of 81 students who provided ratings for both types of feedback were used for evaluating the difference in their usefulness. As students received and rated multiple peer review feedback, the average rate was used as peer review rate.

1.5 Results

After examining data to ensure the assumptions of normality, homogeneity of variance, and independence, a paired samples T-test performed using SPSS v.29 which indicated significant differences between the student ratings two feedback types based on data obtained from FeedbackFruit. *AI-generated Feedback* was ranked higher than peer feedback ($t = -3.93$, $p = 0.001$), with a *moderate effect size* based on Cohen's *d* (−0.437) and Hedges' correction (−.433) (See Appendix Table A.1 and Table A.2.)

A summary of survey data is presented in Table 1.1, which shows students' perceptions of AI-generated feedback in comparison to peer review feedback.

The analysis of survey data using a paired samples T-test (see Appendix Table A.3) revealed significant differences between the two feedback types with respect to level of details in the feedback but no significant differences across the other four dimensions (see Appendix Table A.4). *AI-generated feedback* was perceived to be more detailed than peer feedback ($395t = -3.212$, $p = 0.001$, with a *moderate effect size* based on Cohen's d (−.395) and Hedges' correction (−.391).

To triangulate, we compared peer feedback and AI-generated feedback across various metrics including the average word count per essay, along with the minimum, maximum, and standard deviation of word counts for both types of feedback. As shown in Table 1.2, the length of AI-generated feedback was indeed significantly higher than peer feedback.

From the five students' comments on AI-generated feedback, four comments were positive, and one completely disagreed with the AI-generated feedback.

TABLE 1.1

Summary of Survey Data

		Mean	N	Std. Deviation	Std. Error Mean
a. I understood the comments.	Peer feedback	4.03	81	1.022	.126
	AI feedback	4.08	81	.997	.123
b. The comments were detailed.	Peer feedback	3.50	81	1.218	.150
	AI feedback	3.94	81	.990	.122
c.	Peer feedback	3.91	81	1.173	.144
	AI feedback	3.94	81	1.201	.148
d. The comments were personalised to me.	Peer feedback	3.68	81	1.139	.140
	AI feedback	3.65	81	1.130	.139
e. The comments included statements about my specific assignment.	Peer feedback	3.88	81	1.103	.136
	AI feedback	3.82	81	1.162	.143

TABLE 1.2

Comparison of Peer Feedback vs. AI-Generated Feedback

	Peer Feedback	AI Feedback
Count	433	228
Average word count per essay	83.99	221.74
Min.	5	75
Max.	1094	472
St. Dev.	90.87	53.48

The AI-generated feedback for the student who perceived it negatively and rated it 1 out of 10 is presented here:

> This is an AI-generated feedback. Please read the feedback carefully and rate the review feedback (0 Not useful to 10 very useful). If you think the feedback is not correct/relevant, please explain the issue in the comment section.
>
> Overall, your writing style is clear and easy to understand. However, it would be helpful to provide some evidence to support your claims, particularly around the potential health impacts of VR and the risks associated with sharing personal information with SuperFly.
>
> When discussing the potential health impacts of VR, it would be beneficial to provide references to studies or research that support your claims. Additionally, you could acknowledge that there may be some benefits to using VR in certain situations, such as for therapeutic purposes.
>
> Regarding the risks associated with sharing personal information with SuperFly, it would be useful to provide specific examples of how this

data could be misused or hacked. This would help to illustrate the potential harm to users and emphasize the importance of strong cybersecurity measures.

Overall, your arguments could be strengthened by providing more concrete evidence and examples to support your claims. Additionally, you may want to consider addressing potential counterarguments or opposing viewpoints to provide a more balanced perspective.

Despite the student comment, the teacher's evaluation of the AI-generated feedback confirmed its validity.

1.6 Discussion

The results of this study demonstrate that students perceive ChatGPT-generated feedback to be more useful overall compared to student peer review feedback. The higher level of detail in ChatGPT-generated feedback was identified as a significant factor contributing to its perceived superiority. This finding aligns with previous research by (Dawson et al., 2019), which highlighted the importance of detailed feedback that is usable and specific to the assignment.

The use of AI-generated feedback has the potential to address some of the challenges associated with traditional teacher feedback, such as the resource-intensive nature of providing personalised feedback to large cohorts of students. The scalability and speed of LLMs like ChatGPT make them a promising technology for automated feedback generation and can simultaneously facilitate the delivery of timely and detailed feedback to a large number of students, thereby enhancing the learning experience.

However, it is crucial to acknowledge the limitations of AI-generated feedback. While students appreciated the detailed nature of ChatGPT-generated feedback, it may produce invalid comments, lack nuanced judgement that human instructors can provide. As feedback plays a significant role in shaping student learning and motivation, it is essential to strike a balance between the efficiency of automated feedback and the personalized support that human instructors can offer. One promising approach could be cooperation between instructors and AI as an intelligent assistant (Dhiman et al., 2022) by embedding LLMs in learning management systems to generate a draft feedback for the instructors to be provided to students after instructor's review and revision.

The study also revealed no significant differences between ChatGPT-generated feedback and student peer review feedback in other dimensions of usefulness, such as understandability, personalisation, and specificity. This suggests that both forms of feedback can be valuable in certain aspects, and a combination of AI-generated feedback and peer review feedback may complement each other to offer a well-rounded feedback experience for students.

1.7 Limitations and Future Research

The study's findings are based on a specific essay writing task and a limited sample of students and may not fully represent the diverse assessment types and population of learners in higher education. Also, the availability of the case study used for the essay writing task online raises the possibility that it could have been incorporated into the training data for ChatGPT, potentially influencing the responses generated by the chatbot. In addition, the prompt we used for obtaining feedback from Chat-GPT could have impacted the quality of the provided feedback. Future research can explore the impact through examining various prompt engineering techniques. The perceptions and preferences of students from different disciplines, educational backgrounds, or cultural contexts might vary, limiting the generalizability of the results. The study focuses on comparing ChatGPT-generated feedback with student peer review feedback. However, it does not investigate the usefulness of AI-generated feedback in various learning domains or assess its adaptability to different types of assignments or assessments. To advance educational AI, it is crucial to conduct comprehensive research that explores AI feedback across various disciplines and assessment types, while also addressing bias and promoting transparency.

The integration of AI-generated feedback into educational settings raises a number of ethical considerations, such as transparency and data privacy, that need to be carefully addressed.

Transparency is key when it comes to information provided by AI. Students have the right to know whether the information they receive was generated by AI or by human teachers. Clear communication of sources helps students understand the nature of the input they receive and manage their expectations accordingly. Failure to identify the source of feedback can lead to confusion and undermine trust between students and educational institutions. This includes being transparent about limitations in AI-driven feedback, such as potential gaps in nuanced understanding.

Data privacy is another important ethical consideration. When students interact with AI systems for feedback, their data is collected and processed. Educational institutions must implement strong data protection measures to protect student information and to, safeguard data storage, transmission, and processing to prevent unauthorized access and possible breaches. Institutions must also clearly communicate how student information will be used and stored and that it may be shared with third parties, in order to obtain informed consent from students. As an example, the process of submitting assessments could include providing students with guidelines to ensure that their assessment reports do not contain any personal data intended to be fed into the AI system.

Additionally, potential biases in data provided by AI must be addressed. ChatGPT and other AI models learn from large datasets, which can inadvertently introduce bias in the training data. These biases can lead to inappropriate responses or discrimination. It is important for educational institutions to conduct frequent audits and mitigate AI-generated biases.

Further research is needed to explore the long-term effects of different feedback types on students' academic performance and engagement. This study primarily captures student perceptions of feedback. Including instructor perspectives on AI-generated feedback could offer a more comprehensive understanding of the challenges and benefits of its implementation in higher education.

1.8 Conclusion

In conclusion, this study sheds light on the potential of using of AI-generated feedback as an effective strategy for enhancing the feedback process in higher education, especially by using large language models such as ChatGPT. The study reveals that students consider ChatGPT-provided more useful overall compared to student peer review articles, mainly due to its increased detail. This finding aligns with previous research highlighting the importance of detailed and usable feedback. The flexibility and efficiency of the information provided by AI offers a promising solution to address the resource-intensive nature of providing personalized feedback to large groups of students.

However, while the information generated by AI offers advantages in terms of speed and scalability, it is important to acknowledge its limitations. The information provided by AI may lack the nuanced judgment, empathy, and personal touch that human instructors can provide. Thus a balanced approach that combines the strengths of AI-provided feedback with human teacher feedback can provide students with a comprehensive and effective feedback experience.

The study also highlights the need for ongoing research and analysis of AI-driven feedback. It emphasizes the importance of analysing the data generated by AI in different learning environments, considering different applications and assessments, and understanding its appropriateness in student populations.

References

Ausat, A. M. A., Massang, B., Efendi, M., Nofirman, N. & Riady, Y. 2023. Can chat GPT replace the role of the teacher in the classroom: A fundamental analysis. *Journal on Education*, 5, 16100–16106.

Baidoo-Anu, D. & Ansah, L. O. 2023. Education in the era of generative artificial intelligence (AI): Understanding the potential benefits of ChatGPT in promoting teaching and learning. *Journal of AI*, 7, 52–62.

Boud, D. & Molloy, E. 2013. Rethinking models of feedback for learning: the challenge of design. *Assessment & Evaluation in Higher Education*, 38, 698–712.

Brammer, C. & Rees, M. 2007. Peer review from the students' perspective: Invaluable or invalid? *Composition Studies*, 35, 71–85.

Carless, D. & Boud, D. 2018. The development of student feedback literacy: Enabling uptake of feedback. *Assessment & Evaluation in Higher Education*, 43, 1315–1325.

Cheng, W. & Warren, M. 1997. Having second thoughts: Student perceptions before and after a peer assessment exercise. *Studies in Higher Education*, 22, 233–239.

Dai, W., Lin, J., Jin, F., Li, T., Tsai, Y.-S., Gasevic, D. & Chen, G. 2023. Can large language models provide feedback to students? A case study on ChatGPT. *2023 IEEE International Conference on Advanced Learning Technologies (ICALT)*. IEEE.

Dawson, P., Henderson, M., Mahoney, P., Phillips, M., Ryan, T., Boud, D. & Molloy, E. 2019. What makes for effective feedback: Staff and student perspectives. *Assessment & Evaluation in Higher Education*, 44, 25–36.

Deeva, G., Bogdanova, D., Serral, E., Snoeck, M. & De Weerdt, J. 2021. A review of automated feedback systems for learners: Classification framework, challenges and opportunities. *Computers & Education*, 162, 104094.

Dhiman, H., Wächter, C., Fellmann, M. & Röcker, C. 2022. Intelligent assistants. *Business & Information Systems Engineering*, 64, 645–665.

Dwivedi, Y. K., Kshetri, N., Hughes, L., Slade, E. L., Jeyaraj, A., Kar, A. K., Baabdullah, A. M., Koohang, A., Raghavan, V. & Ahuja, M. 2023. "So what if ChatGPT wrote it?" Multidisciplinary perspectives on opportunities, challenges and implications of generative conversational AI for research, practice and policy. *International Journal of Information Management*, 71, 102642.

Eke, D. O. 2023. ChatGPT and the rise of generative AI: Threat to academic integrity? *Journal of Responsible Technology*, 13, 100060.

Evans, C. 2015. Students' perspectives on the role of peer feedback in supporting learning. *Journal of Cognitive Education and Psychology*, 1, 110–125.

Fui-Hoon Nah, F., Zheng, R., Cai, J., Siau, K. & Chen, L. 2023. *Generative AI and Chat-GPT: Applications, challenges, and AI-human collaboration*. Taylor & Francis.

Henderson, M., Boud, D., Molloy, E., Dawson, P., Phillips, M. & Ryan, T. 2016. *Feedback for learning survey [measurement instrument]*. https://feedbackforlearning.org/wp-content/uploads/Feedback_for_Learning_Survey.pdf

Henderson, M., Ryan, T., Boud, D., Dawson, P., Phillips, M., Molloy, E. & Mahoney, P. 2021. The usefulness of feedback. *Active Learning in Higher Education*, 22, 229–243.

Henderson, M., Ryan, T. & Phillips, M. 2019. The challenges of feedback in higher education. *Assessment & Evaluation in Higher Education*, 44, 1237–1252.

Indriasari, T. D., Luxton-Reilly, A. & Denny, P. 2020. Gamification of student peer review in education: A systematic literature review. *Education and Information Technologies*, 25, 5205–5234.

Kaiss, W., Mansouri, K. & Poirier, F. 2023. Pre-Evaluation with a personalized feedback conversational agent integrated in Moodle. *International Journal of Emerging Technologies in Learning*, 18, 177–189.

Kochmar, E., Vu, D. D., Belfer, R., Gupta, V., Serban, I. V. & Pineau, J. Automated personalized feedback improves learning gains in an intelligent tutoring system. *Artificial Intelligence in Education: 21st International Conference, AIED 2020*, Ifrane, Morocco, July 6–10, 2020, Proceedings, Part II 21, 2020. Springer, 140–146.

Lerchenfeldt, S., Mi, M. & Eng, M. 2019. The utilization of peer feedback during collaborative learning in undergraduate medical education: A systematic review. *BMC Medical Education*, 19, 321.

Lim, W. M., Gunasekara, A., Pallant, J. L., Pallant, J. I. & Pechenkina, E. 2023. Generative AI and the future of education: Ragnarök or reformation? A paradoxical perspective from management educators. *The International Journal of Management Education*, 21, 100790.

Lipnevich, A. A. & Panadero, E. 2021. A review of feedback models and theories: Descriptions, definitions, and conclusions. *Frontiers in Education*, 6.

Mulder, R. A., Pearce, J. M. & Baik, C. 2014. Peer review in higher education: Student perceptions before and after participation. *Active Learning in Higher Education*, 15, 157–171.

Pankiewicz, M. & Baker, R. S. 2023. Large language models (GPT) for automating feedback on programming assignments. *arXiv preprint arXiv:2307.00150*.

Pardo, A., Jovanovic, J., Dawson, S., Gašević, D. & Mirriahi, N. 2019. Using learning analytics to scale the provision of personalised feedback. *British Journal of Educational Technology*, 50, 128–138.

Pardos, Z. A. & Bhandari, S. 2023. Learning gain differences between ChatGPT and human tutor generated algebra hints. *arXiv preprint arXiv:2302.06871*.

Ramirez, E. 2022. *SuperFly a VR ethics case study*. https://www.scu.edu/ethics/focus-areas/internet-ethics/resources/superfly-a-vr-ethics-case-study/ [Accessed 30/08/2022].

Teubner, T., Flath, C. M., Weinhardt, C., Van Der Aalst, W. & Hinz, O. 2023. Welcome to the era of ChatGPT et al. *Business & Information Systems Engineering*, 65, 95–101.

Yu, H. 2023. Reflection on whether Chat GPT should be banned by academia from the perspective of education and teaching. *Frontiers in Psychology*, 14, 1181712.

Appendix: Statistical Analysis Results

TABLE A.1

Paired Samples Test Results

Paired Samples Test

| | | | | Paired Differences | | | | | Significance | |
| | | | | 95% Confidence Interval of the Difference | | | | | One-Sided | Two-Sided |
	Mean	Std. Deviation	Std. Error Mean	Lower	Upper	t	df		p	p
Peer—AI	−.8272	1.8943	.2105	−1.2460	−.4083	−3.930	80		<.001	<.001

TABLE A.2

Paired Samples Test Effect Size

Paired Samples Effect Sizes

| | | | Standardizer[a] | Point Estimate | 95% Confidence Interval | |
					Lower	Upper
Pair 1	Peer—AI	Cohen's d[b]	1.8943	−.437	−.663	−.207
		Hedges' correction[c]	1.9123	−.433	−.657	−.205

a. The denominator used in estimating the effect sizes.
b. Cohen's d uses the sample standard deviation of the mean difference.
c. Hedges' correction uses the sample standard deviation of the mean difference, plus a correction factor.

TABLE A.3

Paired Differences Analysis

| | | | Paired Differences | | | | | | |
| | | | | | 95% Confidence Interval of the Difference | | | |
		Mean	Std. Deviation	Std. Error Mean	Lower	Upper	t	Df
a. I understood the comments.	PF*—AIF**	−.045	.935	.115	−.275	.184	−.395	80
b. The comments were detailed.	PF*—AIF**	−.439	1.111	.137	−.713	−.166	−3.212	80

TABLE A.3 (*Continued*)

Paired Differences Analysis

			Paired Differences					
				Std.	95% Confidence Interval of the Difference			
		Mean	Std. Deviation	Error Mean	Lower	Upper	*t*	Df
c. I will use/ have used the comments to improve subsequent work.	PF*—AIF**	−.030	1.052	.129	−.289	.228	−.234	80
d. The comments were personalised to me.	PF*—AIF**	.030	1.095	.135	−.239	.299	.225	80
e. The comments included statements about my specific assignment.	PF*—AIF**	.061	1.108	.136	−.212	.333	.444	80

* *PF:* Peer feedback; ** AIF: AI-generated feedback.

TABLE A.4

Significance Results

		Significance	
		One-Sided *p*	Two-Sided *p*
a. I understood the comments.	PF*—AIF**	.347	.694
b. The comments were detailed	PF*—AIF**	.001	.002
c. I will use/have used the comments to improve subsequent work.	PF*—AIF**	.408	.816
d. The comments were personalised to me.	PF*—AIF**	.411	.823
e. The comments included statements about my specific assignment.	PF*—AIF**	.329	.658

2

Balancing Innovation and Integrity: Integration and Implications of Generative Artificial Intelligence in Legal Education

Anne Pickering, Kunle Ola, and Khorsed Zaman

2.1 Introduction

The meteoric rise of artificial intelligence (AI), specifically Generative AI (GenAI) [1], has sparked increased interest in its impact on the future trajectory of tertiary teaching and learning. An industry report suggests that GenAI could raise Australia's economy by AUD$115 billion a year by 2030 through enhancing existing industries and facilitating the development of new products and services [2]. A recent survey of top tech leaders identifies AI as the defining technology trend in Australia in 2024 [3]. Globally, AI was earmarked to contribute up to USD$15.7 trillion to the economy by 2023 [4]. Given these projections and the growing adoption of GenAI across various sectors, it is equally important to consider how GenAI impacts the education sector, particularly legal education. Recent developments in AI technology have the potential to drastically change traditional teaching methods, enhance student engagement, and, most importantly, personalise the learning experience. It is thus imperative to thoroughly investigate GenAI's role in teaching and learning practices, including the opportunities and challenges it presents. This is an important juncture in legal education. Law schools are expected to train job-ready graduates, and universities must therefore navigate the integration of GenAI into curricula, teaching methods, and legal practice skills [5]. Integrating AI brings opportunities and threats, especially regarding academic integrity and ethical practices. To remain competitive and relevant, it is imperative that universities prioritise striking a balance between integrating AI technology and establishing clear guidelines for its use with attention to academic integrity and legal ethics.

This chapter focuses on the implications of GenAI on legal education and how universities are responding to its challenges. First, the chapter explores the rapid changes in university education driven by GenAI, particularly

DOI: 10.1201/9781032632483-2

following the release of improved versions of ChatGPT, a conversation-oriented large language model (LLM) initially introduced by OpenAI in November 2022. Second, the chapter examines the recent evolution of university teaching and the impact of teaching and learning on law students, as well as the future of AI on the legal profession: whether an AI-led profession is possible, the legal profession's response, and potential ethical implications. Third, the focus is on the response of law schools to the challenges presented by GenAI. The conclusion provides suggestions on how to integrate GenAI into legal education and practice while preserving and maintaining the integrity of both.

2.1.1 Human Intelligence, Artificial Intelligence, and Generative Artificial Intelligence

It is important to understand the fundamental distinction between human and artificial intelligence—a topic extensively researched that could warrant separate chapters, which is not within the focus of this chapter [6]. While acknowledging that one of the key questions would be whether machines can replicate or even surpass human cognitive abilities and development—an issue that continues to be relevant to any discussion on AI and higher education—this chapter limits its scope to considering current implementations of GenAI and their impact [7]. Technology-driven learning is not a recent phenomenon, as various tools have been used in teaching and learning for some time. Nevertheless, adapting to virtual learning during the COVID-19 pandemic requires attention when considering the key objective of the chapter.

Simply explained, human intelligence is the ability to comprehend, reason, learn and, importantly, to form the link between events and objects [8], which requires the skills of solving problems in a variety of daily contexts. Artificial intelligence has been described as "the science and engineering of making intelligent machines" [9]—the capacity of computers or other machines to mimic the cognitive functions of humans [10]. GenAI leverages generative modeling, a form of machine learning that learns patterns and structures from training data, to synthesise new content [11]. This allows for the development of GenAI tools such as chatbots, which are trained to interface with human instructions and provide content such as text, images, and audio—ChatGPT, for instance, is built around an LLM, a form of generative modeling, and is capable of producing content when prompted by a keyword or a query [12]. Given its broad training dataset, which includes books, journal articles, websites, blogs, and social media, it is capable of carrying out various tasks such as writing essays, conceptualising stories, summarising texts, and answering questions. Other prominent GenAI tools that are influencing university education include Google's chatbot Gemini, Anthropic's Claude, and Microsoft's Copilot, to name a few [13]. Naturally, the capabilities of these tools have the potential to impact virtually every aspect of human lives that is already driven by technological tools. One of the most important questions is what are the transformative effects of GenAI on legal education?

2.1.2 Understanding the Broader Response and the Challenges Presented by Generative AI

GenAI has shown enormous potential in reshaping industries, with the world outside of universities appearing to embrace GenAI at a faster pace than universities. It is being rapidly integrated into industries such as healthcare, advertising, marketing, finance, and technology to enhance medical images, simplify patient notes and information, create new products, develop product descriptions, design marketing text and images for customers, enhance financial operations, integrate software into existing systems, and more. One example is the first drug designed and discovered by GenAI, developed by the biotech company *Insilico* Medicine, for the treatment of lung scarring [14]. A multitude of companies and multinational businesses such as Morgan Stanley, Master Card, Golden Sachman, Microsoft, Amazon, and Shopify have already integrated GenAI into their commercial activities. In contrast, universities have been slower in adopting GenAI-induced changes to curricula.

Those who are interested in engaging with GenAI face the challenge of a lack of understanding of how to use and evaluate recent technologies, which hinders their ability to effectively integrate AI into teaching and learning systems. As a result, there is a lack of published evidence of the use of GenAI by academics and students. This is confirmed by Universities Australia (UA) in a submission to the House Standing Committee on Employment, Education and Training's inquiry [15]. In December 2023, one of the authors of this chapter conducted a survey of undergraduate law students and academics from three states of the same university in Australia (the survey) to understand the use of AI tools to assist with this particular law school's future planning. The survey captured feedback from 77 students and 17 academics. The project used a mixed-method approach. A qualitative survey method was employed to gather information for the project by way of an anonymous online survey. According to the feedback of the students who completed the survey, 54 students (70.1%) said that they had never used ChatGPT to complete an assignment in a law unit while 21 (27.3%) indicated that they used ChatGPT for activities other than to complete assessments. Based on the responses, 40% of student respondents was not comfortable with the idea of receiving assistance from AI systems while studying law. Students indicated that AI tools can be effectively integrated, but they were equally of the view that the use of AI tools like ChatGPT in legal education should be restricted to specific tasks such as research assistance or drafting documents. Four of the survey questions captured students' views on integrating AI tools into the learning process, particularly its importance in training law students to be lawyers of the future. A total of 304 comments were submitted by student respondents in response to the four questions. Four themes emerged from the analysis of these comments on the question regarding the role of the law school in incorporating AI to enhance the learning and teaching process. These four themes were—that GenAi can provide enhanced and personalised learning; the need for training on how to interact effectively with AI-generated content; that there is a need to be up-to-date with technology trends; and that AI threatens the cognitive abilities required of law students. The need for training highlighted in the survey feedback resonates with UA's submission to the government, and the findings of a national survey undertaken to understand the extent and nature of AI adoption by Australian universities. While this study found that almost 30% of university staff had never used GenAI for work, the majority of the participants of the survey recognised the potential of AI to enhance productivity [16]. The authors concluded that institutional support is needed through clear policies, focused training and strategic investment in AI technologies tailored to specific roles and disciplines.

Universities traditionally work within slow-moving frameworks involving processes and lines of approvals. A challenge for universities is how to keep up with the fast-moving AI developments. The slower pace of curriculum redesign contributes to the slower integration of AI into curricula, which prevents universities from adapting to technological developments. From the perspective of a law school, the slower integration reflects the broader struggle to balance the development of analytical skills and ethical standards required of future lawyers. In a vicious cycle, the slower integration into curricula leads to fewer opportunities to be familiar with AI tools. Moreover, slower integration questions the competitiveness of law schools where some schools are likely to be ahead of others purely by integrating AI tools into teaching and learning. For example, in 2023, Torrens University commenced streamlining its digital learning environment using Microsoft's Azure OpenAI service to improve and standardise all course curriculums on one intuitive platform [17]. According to Torrens University, in doing so, the university achieved improved accessibility with all course materials accessible from any mobile device, thereby saving approximately AU$2.4 million [18]. As AI tools are increasingly embraced as evidenced by Torrens University, other universities face growing pressure to ensure that their programs remain relevant. Students who pay high education fees are likely to demand programs that ensure their job readiness [18]. Thus universities must act swiftly to align their courses with technological development in order to demonstrate the value of their programs [19]. However, UA highlights that AI experts currently disagree on the expected pace of AI adoption due to a lack of full understanding of its threats [20].

2.2 Recent Evolution of University Teaching and Learning and the Use of Generative AI

In the recent past, teaching and learning in higher education has been significantly transformed by the increased use of digital technology and tools, demonstrating a precedent for potential future AI-driven transformations. The most significant change in the landscape of higher education took place during the COVID-19 pandemic when universities transitioned to a fully online mode of delivery [21]. There is no doubt that the changes to teaching and learning during this time have caused a fundamental shift in the way courses will be offered in the future, particularly regarding the modes of delivery [22]. While many universities, particularly law schools, accustomed to traditional content delivery methods, were new to fully delivering online courses during the pandemic, distance education providers had long been using educational technologies for online teaching and assessment [22]. The rapid speed with which universities modified established methods is a testament to the human ability of both teachers and students to quickly adopt and adapt new technology in all aspects of learning, creating online classrooms, content delivery methods, and assessment tasks; this shift is evidenced by post-pandemic reflections on the transition to online teaching and indicates that a well-executed integration plan for AI may also yield a positive response [23].

Web-based technology and tools now play a pivotal role in students' learning experiences, changing the traditional education paradigms of teacher-led instruction and classroom-based teaching. The established university teaching methods can be best described as teaching staff imparting knowledge by way of face-to-face, online, or blended methods of teaching, and guiding students through the learning process, organised and managed on learning management systems (LMSs) [24]. Over the years, LMSs have become a necessary web-based technology to plan, implement, and assess the learning processes of specific courses. LMSs have started to integrate AI-powered tools to facilitate personalised learning experiences, allowing teachers to tailor teaching activities to suit the needs of students. For instance, Canvas, a web-based management system, provides various built-in course creation and management tools that can be customised for each course [25] to gather information on engagement and performance, helping academics to make informed decisions to support students. Thus when COVID-19 forced a shift in course delivery and assessments, universities already had established web-based systems in place to facilitate virtual teaching and learning. Although these changes did not always align with the best pedagogical practices, they highlight that teaching and learning has the capacity to adapt to new technologies [26].

Data analytics within LMSs have enabled universities to gather information, particularly by using tools to detect plagiarism. A key tool integrated into Canvas is Turnitin, which is a web-based text-matching software that provides academics with the ability to generate similarity reports to determine the originality of work submitted by students to detect plagiarism. Over the past 18 months, Turnitin has extended its offering to incorporate technology to detect AI-generated content [27]. The AI writing detection reports are aimed at detecting students' use of GenAI to complete their assessments. The drawback is unlike Turnitin similarity reports; its AI writing detection indicator merely highlights the AI-generated text in the submission indicating the percentage of AI use, but it cannot provide links connecting the highlighted text to relevant sources. From an academic integrity stance, academics follow their universities' policies and procedures, and in most cases, students are reported for academic misconduct if these reports indicate that students completed the assessment using GenAI tools. These considerations highlight how the pedagogy of teaching is ever-changing in the face of the new challenges introduced by the use of GenAI.

2.2.1 Implications of Unauthorised Use of Generative AI on Law Students and Their Future Profession

Many Australian law schools have seen a rise in the unauthorised use of GenAI tools, particularly ChatGPT, to complete assessments, initially resulting in many students being reported for academic misconduct. While this initial approach has been effective, academics report that students continue to submit AI-generated assessments. The question is whether the similarity and AI reports are reliable. As teaching staff and academic integrity officers have found out, a key concern of relying on AI detection tools is the accuracy and the reliability of the content flagged as AI-generated, particularly where false positives may lead to students being penalised unfairly [28]. The collective experience of academics concerning AI detection tools [28] is that students are increasingly contesting referral to academic integrity teams on the basis that software like Grammarly that they use for checking spelling and grammar incorporates some GenAI capabilities that have been wrongly identified as intentionally using GenAI to complete assessment tasks. While students may have been unfairly penalised in the first six months of ChatGPT, in recent times, in response to false positives and other issues of the first versions of the Turnitin AI detection tool, Turnitin has updated its AI detection tool. Until recently, the Turnitin AI detection tool captured a percentage score of 1% to 100%, leading to false positives of the use of GenAI. In the early days of introducing its AI detection feature, the chief product officer of Turnitin encouraged universities to consider false positives within Turnitin's AI writing detection capabilities [29]. However, as of July 2024,

Turnitin-generated AI reports will no longer display highlights or scores below 20% of the submission, which appears to introduce a margin of error. Instead, the Turnitin-generated AI reports will now display the AI-generated text that has been paraphrased using an AI-paraphrasing tool or AI word spinner such as QuillBot [30]. Regarding the accuracy and reliability of the Turnitin reports, an independent study evaluating 16 publicly available AI text detectors found that Turnitin has a very high accuracy rate [31].

Equally important is that false negatives may allow AI-generated content to go undetected. To make the issue worse, there are now YouTube channels [32] and other resources dedicated to showing students how to bypass AI detection, thus encouraging students to engage in academic dishonesty. Academic dishonesty undermines the integrity of law students' training and their futures as lawyers, therefore jeopardising their credibility and the prospect of obtaining a practicing certificate to work as lawyers. If caught, academic dishonesty can lead to academic misconduct. For law students, even if the matter is merely investigated without a penalty imposed for academic misconduct, this is sufficient grounds for refusal of admission as a lawyer due to strict rules concerning suitability for admission as lawyers in Australia [33]. The underlying matter is that academic dishonesty compromises the learning process and assessment results, giving an unfair advantage to some students. Most importantly, it hinders the development of essential skills and ethical standards that are the hallmark of the legal profession and professionals.

What distinguishes lawyers from non-lawyers is the training, knowledge, and expertise in law that they gain in law schools. Clients depend on their knowledge and skills to represent them in legal matters and pay them for their expertise and skills. Even if lawyers produce AI-generated work, they must still be able to use their independent skills and expertise to assess the material before them. Otherwise, the court is bound to consider that lawyers "abandoned their responsibilities" as in the New York case of *Mata v. Avianca Inc*, [34] (*Mata* case), where the lawyer submitted an AI-hallucinated case brief generated by ChatGPT containing fake case citations and judicial opinions. The tendency for ChatGPT to produce false information as fact is referred to as "artificial hallucination."[35] The lawyers in that case, being unaware that ChatGPT can sometimes hallucinate, submitted a brief without checking the cases leading to the court dismissing their client's case and subsequent sanctions against the lawyers for acting in bad faith [35]. This case highlights the primary concern: whether students fully appreciate the importance of acquiring core knowledge and research skills during their legal education and training and whether they can effectively apply these competencies independently as practicing lawyers.

Despite the high-level performance of ChatGPT and similar GenAI chatbots, it is still not a complete replacement for human cognition and deductive reasoning. In fact, ChatGPT is prone to producing content that is false, as evidenced by the widely publicised *Mata* case. [36] While the *Mata* case is a clear example of the use of GenAI by a legal practitioner, it is also an example of how it is not meant to be used. Users must remember that it is not a replacement for human methods of critical thinking. Therefore, lawyers must not completely rely on chatbot tools like ChatGPT but must instead use their own expertise and knowledge to undertake tasks such as legal research and document preparation. The case is instructive for students who completely rely on it to research and write. Ultimately, the responsibility rests on lawyers in legal matters, and the same principle applies to law students who intend to join the legal profession. Their future profession requires that they have the necessary skills to be able to identify the law. In light of this need, it is entirely appropriate to question whether students should be permitted to use GenAI tools before being able to fully appreciate the essential skills required to function effectively as lawyers. The answer to this question remains a work in progress.

2.2.2 An AI-Led Legal Profession—Is It Possible?

The idea of an AI-led legal profession is as complex as much as it is a possibility. It is more than likely now than it was in 1984 when John Searle famously distinguished between syntax and semantics to point out that "no computer program can ever be a mind" [37]. Searle's suggestion of a limitation in the capacity of computers is a thing of the past now with the progress of AI technology able to clone a voice [38]. The impact of AI extends to various aspects of legal practice, including legal research and document preparation, delivery of legal services, and the management of legal practice. Recently LexisNexis introduced Lexis+ AI Insider program, a legal GenAI solution providing drafting, research assistance, legal summaries, and conversational responses to requests and refining answers [39]. The Lexis+ AI Insider program is available for all legal professionals and supports the legal industry with GenAI education [40]. However, despite law firms like Clayton Utz, Gilbert + Tobin, and Holding Redlich adopting Lexis+ AI and the impressive innovative approach to using AI in the legal industry, the Allens AI Australian Law Benchmark (Allens Benchmark) cautions against using LLMs such as GPT-4, Perplexity, LLaMa2, Claude 2, and Gemini 1 for providing legal advice on Australian law without expert human supervision [41]. These observations are based on the assessment conducted by Allens in February 2024, before Lexis+ AI was introduced [41] and became resonate elsewhere in the world where the European Union recently passed the first Act dealing with artificial intelligence in June 2024 [42]. The key principle upon which the Act is developed is that the approach to AI must be human-centric.

In Australia, the caution on absolute reliance on GenAI tools is reflected in the Allens Benchmark, and it is further supported by a survey conducted by ANZ Bank and LexisNexis in 2023 and 2024 (ANZ Survey 2023–2024).

The primary factors influencing this lack of confidence include ethical concerns, information reliability and traceability, information accuracy, the inability to trace source information for answers generated, and the completeness of information generated [43]. From the perspective of an AI-led profession, the crux of the issue that underlines these concerns is applicability of AI in human-based roles, which deserves attention. When considered from this angle, first, it is important to ask whether GenAI tools used for legal reasoning can replicate the complex reasoning, analysis, and cognitive ability of humans. These tools are based on computational reasoning that is not inherently human-interpretable and instead mimics human reasoning to assess cases, apply logic, and define legal concepts [44]. The answer for now is that AI is evolving, and GenAI models have become more capable of mimicking certain aspects of human cognitive processes. For example, how GenAI is used by Lexis+ AI to produce research documents using its database of cases and other resources is a demonstration of legal research and deductive reasoning [45]. Yet GenAI lacks the subjective experience to understand the complexity and context of social, cultural, and personal contexts, which is necessary when applying law. As the former Chief Justice of the Federal Court of Australia explains, the human element of public institutions like courts is assigned a special kind of power—judicial power, which involves human reasoning and emotion that are subject to abstraction and deconstruction—where complex human qualities, values, and institutions are organised into abstract definitional terms [46]. The exercise of judicial power requires both substantive and apparent impartiality, and the fair and accurate determination of questions of fact and law [46]. All of these are the human elements necessary for the functioning of courts and show the interposition of courts, law, and human elements.

A central part of the practice of law is the importance of explanations—for example, in a court case, the parties have a right to an explanation of the case decision to ensure that the decision was based on sound reasoning in order to be able to understand the basis of an appeal and for the public interest [47]. Thus when applying the law, consideration of social objectives and social effects is important. Can computational models be trained to respond to emotional cues, and, if so, would their emotional intelligence reflect the knowledge, information, social, political, and racial biases of their developer? Can computational models be influenced by the subjective experience of someone who may not necessarily understand the law or holds biases? These are risks that must be considered, and in the context of universities, the risk of systematic biases and discrimination have been pointed out in the UA's submission [48]. Nevertheless, Collenette et al., who undertook a significant research project to design, implement, and evaluate explainable decision support tools for deciding human rights cases in the European Court of Human Rights (ECHR), state that their tool had an accuracy rate of 97% [49].

Despite its success rate, the tool was used within an experimental setting focusing on human rights cases. The same results may not be achieved in complex human rights or other cases that require a nuanced understanding and decision-making based on fairness and compassion—the human element. For instance, a human rights case involving leaving a country for fear of personal safety is significantly different from a person escaping actual physical torture. In such a case, empathy and compassion are required, but the concern is whether GenAI tools can accurately evaluate the personal factors and emotions involved.

Furthermore, Collenette did not explain the accountability of AI decision-making. If an AI decision led to an unexpected outcome due to a technical error, it may be difficult to determine who is responsible and how to navigate the appeal process. From a social justice perspective, it is important to consider the deeper implications of such a judgment on a person's health and well-being. As noted, while AI is rapidly evolving and new developments are on the horizon, law schools and the legal profession must address the ethical implications of GenAI advancements.

2.2.3 Legal Profession's Response and Ethical Implications

As machines grow more capable through training on large language models (LLMs), their evolution presents both challenges and opportunities. On the one hand, as evidenced by Lexis+ AI, [50] GenAI is capable of performing some of the basic functions, thereby allowing lawyers to focus on the more complex cases. On the other hand, the rapid development of GenAI raises significant ethical concerns for the legal profession and its impact on legal ethics. The LexisNexis GenAI tool leverages LexisNexis's legal database to provide a means of reviewing documents, undertaking legal research, and producing predictive analytics [51]. As these technologies evolve, the legal industry must proactively establish guidelines and best practices to ensure responsible use.

According to Kirby, who had the foresight to consider the possibility of the use of AI in legal practice over 30 years ago, the "special strength" of the profession is that practitioners are "repositories and disseminators of special knowledge" [52]. Any time this knowledge is being integrated as is being done with GenAI, the issue of the future of the profession arises, which is why it is important to find out the response of the profession. The peak representative bodies for the legal profession in Australia continue to develop frameworks and guidance notes for the responsible and ethical use of artificial intelligence in legal practice. For example, the Queensland Law Society introduced a guidance statement for legal practitioners while the New South Wales Law Society announced that a task force of legal and tech experts will convene to explore how best to harness what AI has to offer the legal profession [53].

Against this backdrop, Australian law schools face significant obstacles in embracing GenAI, as the difficulty strikes at the very core of the legal profession, challenging the foundational concepts that underpin it. A profession is a group of individuals who conform to ethical standards, who are seen by the wider community as having specialised knowledge and skills acquired through education and training, and who apply this expertise in the interest of others [54]. In the context of the legal profession, this definition refers to legal professionals who, having undergone legal training, uphold these ethical standards. This definition naturally includes a code of ethics that governs the activities of each profession that require a high standard of behaviour beyond the personal moral obligations of a person [55]. Ethical codes are enforced by the profession and accepted by the community, who set high expectations of conduct regarding the services and dealings with the public and professional colleagues [55]. The structure and rules of professional conduct for barristers and solicitors align with the definition. Their conduct is governed by ethics and professional rules by a range of regulatory structures and bodies. For example, the *Legal Profession Act 2007* (Qld) governs the professional conduct of lawyers in Queensland, Australia. Similarly, other states and territories have established comparable statutory frameworks on lawyers' professional conduct.

In Australia, practicing law requires admission as a legal practitioner and holding a current practicing certificate as either a barrister or a solicitor [56]. When admitted to the legal profession, lawyers take an oath as officers of the court, and they owe a paramount duty to the courts, which includes the duties of being frank, honest, and candid in dealing with the court [57]. Lawyers serve this paramount duty when they serve in the best interest of their clients. A certain level of competency is required of lawyers that encompasses the skill of communication and advocacy aimed at helping their clients navigate legal matters. Thus lawyers have a special responsibility towards the courts, their clients, and the legal profession. The first issue is the question of how a lawyer who uses GenAI acts in the best interest of a client. The second issue is whether the lawyer is competent or merely reliant on technology. Cases from the US highlight how these matters were treated in that jurisdiction. In a Colorado Supreme Court case in the US in *People v. Crabill* [58], a client hired a lawyer to prepare a motion to set aside a judgment and the lawyer drafted a motion using AI, and included a case generated by Chat-GPT in the motion. Unlike in the *Mata* case, here the lawyer initially blamed a legal intern for the accuracy of the cases used when the matter was heard but later admitted in an affidavit that he had drafted the motion himself [58]. The lawyer was suspended for misconduct for violating several ethical rules, including not competently representing the clients, acting without reasonable diligence and promptness when representing a client, knowingly making a false statement of material fact or law to a tribunal, and engaging in conduct involving dishonesty, fraud, deceit, or misrepresentation [59]. This example highlights that, despite using GenAI, the lawyer is responsible for the accuracy of documents, and that responsibility is still very much connected with the competency to act as a lawyer.

Ethical implications are not limited to lawyers' responsibilities. Fairness and the affordability of legal services are also important considerations. Top-tier law firms can invest in costly GenAI systems to manage basic tasks, while smaller firms may struggle to afford such technology. This sparks up the "haves and have-nots" conflict and could widen the gap between wealthy firms and struggling ones, potentially leading to the elimination of smaller law firms [60]. There are also ongoing issues concerning plagiarism, privacy, and data protection that GenAI tools do not appear to address. For Lexis-Nexis, this is not an issue because its Lexis+ AI prepares research documents using resources that are already available in its database, which already complies with copyright and privacy standards. Although the LexisNexis tool offers positive benefits, affordability remains a concern for firms seeking access to it.

2.3 How Must Universities Navigate the Challenges Presented by AI?

There is a need for universities to consider how technological advances affect teaching and learning. Lack of consensus on the use of AI in law schools can create a barrier between students who are exposed to GenAI in their learning journey to becoming lawyers and those who have not had this opportunity. Universities are responsible for preparing future graduates, but if some students do not have the opportunity, they will be unfairly disadvantaged in the job market. Law schools have a compelling reason to lead an innovative approach to this issue rather than completely disregarding GenAI. By collaborating with the private sector, industry, community, and students to revise curricula that are fit for purpose, law schools can effectively address the issue and, more importantly, prepare students for future employment opportunities. Such a collaborative approach will enable law schools to align with the skills needed by future lawyers while ensuring their graduates are well-prepared for the future.

2.3.1 Striking a Balance Between Adapting to AI and Retaining the Integrity of the Training of Future Lawyers

Striking a balance will require academics' asking the right questions. Currently, the questions are about how to avoid academic misconduct and maintain academic integrity instead of questions about how to integrate GenAI into the curriculum, assessment, and learning outcomes. It should therefore not come as a surprise that there has been a sharp increase in academic misconduct cases in many universities. This is connected to the fact that, when GenAI is viewed as a threat rather than a learning opportunity, we risk criminalising a widely accepted technology. As American legal scholar Lawrence Lessig opined, when a system criminalises practices that have become entrenched and established, we must ask the question, who is the villain? [61] The primary focus should be on harmonising academic integrity with the integration of AI into the educational curriculum. To achieve this, it is pertinent to ask constructive questions about how GenAi can be effectively used as a learning tool rather than simply questioning its potential for cheating. By asking the right questions, we can ensure that AI is used constructively as a tool for academic advancement, not as a means to undermine it.

Some of the questions currently being considered within a university setting include whether GenAI can automate routine tasks, and, if so, what are the implications? For instance, does that free up time for other teaching activities? Does it enhance efficiency? How does it impact the critical thinking skills and problem-solving skills required of law students? Can GenAI effectively challenge and assist students in developing these skills? How reliable is the feedback it provides? These are the questions that need to be addressed by academics or universities that are in the process of integrating or have to some extent integrated GenAI into their curricula and assessment regimes. Most universities have not yet reached that stage, making it crucial to explore potential strategies, and that must be done by considering how law schools want to approach GenAI. Two options include completely ignoring GenAI and refusing integration, fully integrating GenAI (which is impractical due to the reasons examined in this chapter) or taking the middle path by fostering ethical lawyering by integrating the use of GenAI into units that can benefit from integration.

The third option could involve incorporating GenAI into the legal curriculum. One means of achieving this could be to offer one or more units (subjects) in the law degree to cover the fundamentals, capabilities, limitations, and ethical considerations of AI in a legal context for law students. These units could also address broader ethical considerations—such as social, political, and racial biases, data, and privacy concerns. Emphasis would be placed on the importance of critical thinking, integrity, academic conduct, and ethics in using GenAI, as well as course content, could explore the analysis and evaluation of work generated by GenAI tools. Another valuable strategy for mitigating the overreliance of students on GenAI tools across all legal units is to explore the balance between supervised assessments—invigilated exams, oral presentations, and tutorials—and unsupervised assessments—assignments, online quizzes, and problem sets—so that students are monitored and assessed for their performance in both. By thoroughly considering the role of GenAI in curricula design, universities can ensure that students develop not only the necessary critical thinking skills to fulfil the requirements of their studies but also a strong understanding of the capabilities and ethical considerations of GenAI within a legal context. To this end, recently, the three authors of this chapter received a teaching and development grant to undertake a project in 2025 to review three units in order to consider whether GenAI can be integrated. From a teaching and learning perspective, the project is based on two imperatives. First, education must be student-centred and aligned with industry needs to incorporate recent technologies, including AI to enhance content to promote ethical, efficient and future-ready graduates. To achieve this, the authors will collaborate with students and an industry partner in the curriculum development process. The second imperative of the project is evaluation. The aim is to assess whether our AI-integrated curricula are achieving the intended learning outcomes. This evaluation will allow us to identify areas for improvement and ensure that our curriculum remains aligned with both academic goals and industry expectations.

2.4 Conclusion

This chapter has considered the transformative potential of GenAI in legal education, highlighting its significant impact on both teaching and learning within law schools. While GenAI offers exciting opportunities to enhance the educational experience, it also presents significant challenges for law students, educational institutions, and the legal profession, which is deeply rooted in high ethical and professional standards. As law schools navigate these challenges, it is crucial to strike a balance between human expertise and artificial intelligence. By integrating GenAI thoughtfully into legal education, law schools can enrich the learning process while upholding the ethical principles essential to the legal profession. Adapting to the evolving nature of the legal field requires a proactive approach—one that not only embraces GenAI but also rigorously examines its implications.

The most effective strategy for achieving this balance is to incorporate GenAI into the legal curriculum through one or multiple specialised units dedicated to educating students on GenAI fundamentals, its capabilities, limitations, and ethical considerations. By doing so, law schools can equip future lawyers with the knowledge and critical thinking skills necessary to use GenAI responsibly, ensuring that they are prepared for the challenges and opportunities of a rapidly changing legal landscape.

Acknowledgements

A note of acknowledgement of comments and feedback by Mr. Samuel Pickering, The University of Queensland, on the draft of this chapter, which greatly contributed to its development.

References

[1] For a comprehensive overview of generative AI, see generally, Stuart Russell, *Human-Like Machine Intelligence*, ed Stephen Muggleton and Nick Charter (Oxford University Press, 2021); Richard J Wallace, *Artificial Intelligence/Human Intelligence: An Indissoluble Nexus* (World Scientific, 2021).

[2] *Generative AI Could Contribute $115 Billion Annually to Australia's Economy 2030* (Tech Council of Australia, 19 July 2023). https://techcouncil.com.au/news room/generative-ai-could-contribute-115-billion-annually-to-australias-economy-by-2030/.

[3] Tech Council Australia and Datacom, *Australian Tech Leaders Survey 2024* (Report, 19 April 2024). https://techcouncil.com.au/wp-content/uploads/2023/07/230 714-Australias-Gen-AI-Opportunity-Final-report-vF4.pdf.

[4] Price Water Cooper, *Sizing the Prize: What's the Real Value of AI for Your Business and How Can You Capitalise?* (Report, 2017) 1.

[5] Caroline Hart and Aaron Timoshanko, 'Ready for a Reboot: Law Schools Need to Reboot and Upgrade the Law Curriculum now to Better Meet the Impact of Technology' (2022) 15 *Journal of the Australasian Law Academics Association* 31–48, 31.

[6] For a comprehensive overview, see generally, Stuart Russell, *Human-Like Machine Intelligence*, eds. Stephen Muggleton and Nick Charter (Oxford University Press, 2021); Richard J Wallace, *Artificial Intelligence/Human Intelligence: An Indissoluble Nexus* (World Scientific, 2021); and Christian Lexcellent, *Artificial Intelligence versus Husman Intelligence: Are Humans Going to Be Hacked?* (ebook, Springer Link, 2019).

[7] For an analysis of the rise of educational technology, see John Biggs, Catherine Tang, and Gregor Kennedy, *Teaching for Quality Learning at University 5e* (Open University Press, 5th ed, 2022) 1–25.

[8] Oxford Reference Dictionary, "intelligence".

[9] John McCarthy, *What is Artificial Intelligence?* (Stanford University, 2007) (online). For the beginnings of AI and machine learning, see Alan Turing, 'Computing Machinery and Intelligence' (1950) 59 *Mind* 433.

[10] Oxford English Dictionary (online, 15 July 2024), "artificial intelligence".

[11] Zhihan Lv, 'Generative artificial intelligence in the metaverse era' (2023) 3 *Cognitive Robotics* 208.

[12] Sissie Hsiao and Eli Collins, *Try Bard and Share Your Feedback* (Google blog, 21 March 2023). https://blog.google/technology/ai/try-bard/; 'GPT-4 OpenAI's most advanced system, producing safer and more useful responses', *OpenAI* (Web Page). https://openai.com/index/gpt-4/.

[13] 'Top 20 generative AI tools & applications in 2024', *EWeek* (Web Page, online, 20 February 2024). https://www.eweek.com/artificial-intelligence/generative-ai-apps-tools/.

[14] 'New milestone in AI drug discovery: First generative AI drug begins phase II trials with patients', *Insilico Medicine* (Web Page, 14 July 2024). https://insilico.com/blog/first_phase2. See also, McKinsey & Company, *Generative AI in the Pharmaceutical Industry: Moving from Hype to Reality* (Report, 9 January 2024).

[15] Universities Australia, *Submission to the Senate Inquiry on Adopting Artificial Intelligence*, Parliament of Australia (23 July 2023) 1–7. https://universitiesaustralia.edu.au/submission/submission-to-the-inquiry-into-the-use-of-generative-artificial-intelligence-in-the-australian-education-system/.

[16] Paula McDonald, Stephen Hay, Abby Cathcart, and Alicia Feldman, *Apostles, Agnostics and Atheists: Engagement with Generative AI by Australian University Staff* (Report, September 2024) 8, 79–80.

[17] 'Torrens University leverages generative AI to uplift its online learning experience, saving 20,000 hours and $2.4 million in time and resources', *Microsoft* (Web Page, 23 July 2024). https://news.microsoft.com/en-au/features/torrens-university-leverages-generative-ai-to-uplift-its-online-learning-experience-saving-20000-hours-and-2-4-million-in-time-and-resources/.

[18] Caroline Hart and Aaron Timoshanko, 'Ready for a Reboot: Law Schools Need to Reboot and Upgrade the Law Curriculum now to Better Meet the Impact of Technology' (2022) 15 *Journal of The Australasian Law Academics Association* 31–48, 31.

[19] John Biggs, Catherine Tang, Gregor Kennedy, *Teaching for Quality Learning at University 5e* (Open University Press, 5th ed, 2022) 4.

[20] University Australia, *Submission to the House of Representatives Inquiry Highlighted into the Digital Transformation of Workplaces*, Parliament of Australia (June 2024) 3. https://universitiesaustralia.edu.au/wp-content/uploads/2024/07/UAS-SUBMISSION-TO-THE-HOUSE-OF-REPRESENTATIVES-INQUIRY-INTO-THE-DIGITAL-TRANSFORMATION-OF-WORKPLACES.pdf.

[21] Read generally, John Biggs, Catherine Tang, Gregor Kennedy, *Teaching for Quality Learning at University 5e* (Open University Press, 5th ed, 2022) 3.

[22] Jason Lodge et al, *Final Report: Modes of Delivery in Higher Education. The Australian Government Department of Education and the Higher Education Standards Panel* (Report, The University of Queensland, 31 August 2022) 8, 4–10.

[23] Raoul Mulder, Elisa Bone, Sarah French, and Farley Connelly, *Navigating the Transition to Online Teaching at the University of Melbourne during COVID-19: Approaches, Reflections and Insights* (Occasional Paper, Melbourne Centre for the Study of Higher Education, 2023) 1–32.

[24] 'What is Canvas?', *Canvas* (Web Page, 15 July 2024). https://community.canvaslms.com/t5/Canvas-Basics-Guide/What-is-Canvas/ta-p/45.

[25] 'Turnitin's AI writing detection capabilities FAQ', *Turnitin* (Web Page, 18 July 2024). https://www.turnitin.com/products/features/ai-writing-detection/.

[26] Raoul Mulder, Elisa Bone, Sarah French, and Farley Connelly, *Navigating the Transition to Online Teaching at the University of Melbourne during COVID-19: Approaches, Reflections and Insights* (Occasional Paper, Melbourne Centre for the Study of Higher Education, 2023) 25.

[27] 'Turnitin's AI writing detection capabilities FAQ', *Turnitin* (Web Page, 18 July 2024). https://www.turnitin.com/products/features/ai-writing-detection/.

[28] See especially, Robert Topinka, 'The software says my student cheated using AI. They say they are innocent. Who do I believe?', *The Guardian* (online, Tuesday 13 February 2024).

[29] Annie Chechitelli, *Understanding False Positives within our AI Writing Detection Capabilities* (Blog, 6 March 2023). https://www.turnitin.com/blog/understanding-false-positives-within-our-ai-writing-detection-capabilities.

[30] 'Turnitin's AI writing detection model', *Turnitin* (Web Page, 9 July 2024). https://guides.turnitin.com/hc/en-us/articles/28294949544717-AI-writing-detection-model.

[31] William H Walters, 'The Effectiveness of Software Designed to Detect AI-Generated Writing: A Comparison of 16 AI Text Detectors' (2023) 7(1) *Journal of Open Information Science* 20220158. https://doi.org/10.1515/opis-2022–0158.

[32] For example, Jason West, *Bypass ALL AI Detectors* (YouTube, 14 March 2024) garnered 545,166 views in four months since its creation on 14 March 2024.

[33] *Legal Profession Act* 2007 (Qld) s 31–32; and *Legal Profession Uniform Admission Rules* 2015 (Qld) r 10. See also, *Re OG (a Lawyer)* (2007) 18 VR 164 where the Victorian Court of Appeal revoked the admission of a lawyer for deliberately misrepresenting to the Board of Examiners the circumstances of which the lawyer was awarded a zero mark for an assignment while a student.

[34] *Mata V Avianca Inc,* 1 2022cv01461 (United States District Court Southern District Court of New York, 2023).

[35] Hussam Alkaissi and Samy I McFarlane, 'Artificial Intelligence in ChatGPT: Implications in Scientific Writing' (2023) 15(2) *Cureus*. https://doi.org/10.7759/cureus.35179.

[36] *Mata V Avianca Inc,* 1 2022cv01461 (United States District Court Southern District Court of New York, 2023). Affidavit by Steven A Schwartz admitting that he used OpenAI's chatbot (Online, 21 July 2024). https://s3.documentcloud.org/documents/23826751/mata-v-avianca-airlines-affidavit-in-opposition-to-motion.pdf.

[37] John R Searle, 'Can Computers Think? Brain, Minds and Science' (1986) *Harvard University Press* 28–41.

[38] 'Navigating the challenges and opportunities of synthetic voices', *OpenAI* (Web Page, 15 August 2024). https://openai.com/index/navigating-the-challenges-and-opportunities-of-synthetic-voices/.

[39] 'AI search that interacts', *LexisNexis* (Web Page, 15 August 2024). https://www.lexisnexis.com.au/en/products-and-services/lexis-plus-ai.

[40] 'LexisNexis Australia launches Lexis+ AI, a Generative AI solution that is set to change the game for Australian legal practitioners', *LexisNexis* (Web Page, 3 June 2024). https://www.lexisnexis.com.au/en/insights-and-analysis/media-release/2024/lexis-plus-ai-launches-in-australia#:~:text=This%20follows%20a%20successful%20trial,practitioners%20across%20the%20entire%20industry.

[41] Allens, *The Allens AI Australian Law Benchmark: Introduction* (Report, 9 June 2024). https://www.allens.com.au/insights-news/explore/2024/the-allens-ai-australian-law-benchmark/introduction/.

[42] European Parliament, *Artificial Intelligence Act 2024*. https://www.europarl.europa.eu/thinktank/en/document/EPRS_BRI(2021)698792.

[43] LexisNexis, *Generative AI and the Future of the Legal Profession: LexisNexis 2023–2024 ANZ AI Sentiment Survey Findings* (Report, 2024, LexisNexis Australia) 10.

[44] Joe Collenette, Katie Atkinson, and Trevor Bench-Capon, 'Explainable AI Tools for Legal Reasoning About Cases: A Study on the European Court of Human

Rights' (2023) 317 *Artificial Intelligence* 2. See also, Xin Zhao, 'Construction of Artificial Intelligence Model of Legal Reasoning Based on Judicial Precedents' (2023) 2(2) *Science of Law Journal Canada* 23–31.

[45] 'LexisNexis Australia launches Lexis+ AI, a Generative AI solution that is set to change the game for Australian legal practitioners', *LexisNexis* (Web Page, 3 June 2024). https://www.lexisnexis.com.au/en/insights-and-analysis/media-release/2024/lexis-plus-ai-launches-in-australia#:~:text=This%20follows%20a%20successful%20trial,practitioners%20across%20the%20entire%20industry.

[46] The Honourable Justice Allsop AO, "Technology and the future of the courts," in *Handbook for Judicial Officers* (Online, Judicial Commission of New South Wales, 2022). https://www.judcom.nsw.gov.au/publications/benchbks/judicial_officers/technology_and_future_of_courts.html.

[47] Joe Collenette, Katie Atkinson, and Trevor Bench-Capon, 'Explainable AI Tools for Legal Reasoning About Cases: A Study on the European Court of Human Rights' (2023) 317 *Artificial Intelligence* 2. See also, Xin Zhao, 'Construction of Artificial Intelligence Model of Legal Reasoning Based on Judicial Precedents' (2023) 2(2) *Science of Law Journal Canada* 23–31.

[48] Universities Australia, *Submission to the Senate Inquiry on Adopting Artificial Intelligence* (23 July 2023). https://universitiesaustralia.edu.au/submission/submission-to-the-inquiry-into-the-use-of-generative-artificial-intelligence-in-the-australian-education-system/.

[49] Joe Collenette, Katie Atkinson, and Trevor Bench-Capon, 'Explainable AI Tools for Legal Reasoning About Cases: A Study on the European Court of Human Rights' (2023) 317 *Artificial Intelligence* 2.

[50] 'LexisNexis Australia launches Lexis+ AI, a Generative AI solution that is set to change the game for Australian legal practitioners', *LexisNexis* (Web Page, 3 June 2024). https://www.lexisnexis.com.au/en/insights-and-analysis/media-release/2024/lexis-plus-ai-launches-in-australia#:~:text=This%20follows%20a%20successful%20trial,practitioners%20across%20the%20entire%20industry.

[51] 'LexisNexis Australia launches Lexis+ AI, a Generative AI solution that is set to change the game for Australian legal practitioners', *LexisNexis* (Web Page, 3 June 2024). https://www.lexisnexis.com.au/en/insights-and-analysis/media-release/2024/lexis-plus-ai-launches-in-australia#:~:text=This%20follows%20a%20successful%20trial,practitioners%20across%20the%20entire%20industry.

[52] The Hon Michael Kirby CMG, "Legal and Ethical Issues in Artificial Intelligence" (1987) *International Computer Law Adviser* 6.

[53] The Law Society of New South Wales, *Expert Taskforce to Guide the Legal Profession Through the Challenges of AI* (News & Media Release, 2024). https://www.lawsociety.com.au/publications-and-resources/news-media-releases/expert-taskforce-guide-legal-profession-through#:~:text=%E2%80%9CThe%20goal%20for%20the%20AI,%2C%20academia%2C%20and%20government.%E2%80%9D.

[54] 'What is a profession?', *Australian Council of Professions* (Web Page, 2023). https://professions.org.au/what-is-a-professional/#:~:text=A%20Profession%20is%20a%20disciplined,and%20who%20are%20prepared%20to.

[55] 'What is a profession?', *Australian Council of Professions* (Web Page, 2023). https://professions.org.au/what-is-a-professional/#:~:text=A%20Profession%20is%20a%20disciplined,and%20who%20are%20prepared%20to.

[56] *Legal Profession Act 2007* (Qld) s 24. Exclusion to this provision is stated in ss 23(1), 24(2)(d),(e). See also, *Supreme Court (Admission) Rules 2004* (Qld).

[57] In Queensland, *Australian Solicitors' Conduct Rules* 2012 (Qld) ('ASCR'); *Barristers' Conduct Rule 2011* as amended. In Victoria and New South Wales, *Legal Profession Uniform Conduct (Barristers) Rules* 2015; *Legal Profession Uniform Law Australian Solicitors' Conduct Rules* 2015; *Legal Profession Uniform Law Application Act 2014.*

[58] *People v. Crabill,* 23-PDJ067 (Colorado Supreme Court Office of the Presiding Disciplinary Judge, Nov 22, 2023).

[59] See, Colorado Rules of Professional Conduct ('CRPC') as adopted by the Colorado Supreme Court on May 7, 1992 as amended through Rule Change 2022(13), effective September 8, 2022. The rules violated are CRPC 1.1 a lawyer must competently represent a client); Colo. RPC 1.3 (a lawyer must act with reasonable diligence and promptness when representing a client); Colo. RPC 3.3(a)(1) (a lawyer must not knowingly make a false statement of material fact or law to a tribunal); and Colo. RPC 8.4(c) (it is professional misconduct for a lawyer to engage in conduct involving dishonesty, fraud, deceit, or misrepresentation).

[60] Read generally, The Hon Michael Kirby CMG, "Legal and Ethical Issues in Artificial Intelligence" (1987) *International Computer Law Adviser* 7.

[61] Lawrence Lessig, *Free Culture: How Big Media Uses Technology and the Law to Lock Down Culture and Control Creativity* (Penguin Press, 2004) 199. "Overregulation stifles creativity. It smothers innovation. . . The war that is being waged today is a war of prohibition . . . it is targeted against the behaviour of a very large number of citizens. According to The New York Times, 43 million Americans downloaded music in May 2002. According to the RIAA, the behaviour of those 43 million Americans is a felony". See also, Jonathon W Penny, 'Privacy and the New Virtualism' (2008) 10 *Yale Journal of Law and Technology* 196–198.

3

Three Technical Routes of AI

**Weisi Chen, Francesco Cauteruccio, Yuan Li,
Jiaxin Zheng, and Wulong Liu**

3.1 Introduction

In recent years, the development of artificial intelligence (AI) has stunned the world and gradually become an integral part of modern technology, transforming industries and shaping the future of human–computer interaction. There are multiple technical routes of AI, each with unique methodologies and applications. Among these, three primary pathways have emerged in the last decade: knowledge-based expert systems, data-driven machine learning, and intelligent optimization. This chapter will focus on these three routes, explaining concepts, relevant techniques, application scenarios, and case studies. Understanding these pathways provides a clear and comprehensive overview of the AI world and how AI systems can be designed, implemented, utilized, and integrated to solve complex problems across diverse domains.

Knowledge-based expert systems (ESs) (Shu-Hsien, 2005) represent one of the earliest forms of AI, developed to emulate the decision-making abilities of human experts. These systems rely on a rich knowledge base, consisting of domain-specific rules and facts, and an inference engine to derive conclusions or solutions. ESs are particularly effective in fields where human expertise is paramount, such as medical diagnosis, financial analysis, and legal reasoning. By codifying expert knowledge, these systems can provide consistent and reliable advice, supporting or even replacing human experts in specific tasks.

Data-driven machine learning (ML) (Sarker, 2021) has surged to the forefront of AI research and application in recent decades. Unlike ES, which depends on explicit structured knowledge like rules and knowledge graphs, ML systems learn patterns and relationships directly from data. This approach is powered by algorithms that can improve their performance over time as they are exposed to more data. Machine learning encompasses a wide range of techniques, including supervised learning, unsupervised learning, and reinforcement learning. It has been successfully applied in various fields, such as

DOI: 10.1201/9781032632483-3

image and speech recognition, natural language processing, and predictive analytics, driving significant advancements in these areas.

Intelligent optimization (IO) (Mohammadi & Sheikholeslam, 2023) involves finding and optimizing the best solutions to complex problems, often under constraints. This pathway leverages methods such as genetic algorithms (Sohail, 2023) and particle swarm optimization (Nayak et al., 2023) to navigate large search spaces and identify optimal or near-optimal solutions. Intelligent optimization is crucial in scenarios where traditional methods may fall short due to the scale or complexity of the problem. Applications of intelligent optimization are widespread, including logistics, resource allocation, and engineering design, where finding the most efficient solution can lead to substantial cost savings and performance improvements.

The rest of this chapter will explore these three technical routes of AI in turn, ES (Section 2), ML (Section 3), and IO (Section 4), delving into their foundational principles, methodologies, and real-world applications. Section 5 will explore how these routes can be integrated with practical hints.

3.2 Knowledge-Based Expert Systems

Knowledge-based expert systems (ES) are a branch of artificial intelligence designed to emulate the decision-making abilities of human experts in specific domains. These systems are built around a robust knowledge base and an inference engine. The knowledge base contains domain-specific information, often in the form of rules, facts, or knowledge graphs, while the inference engine applies logical rules to the knowledge base to derive conclusions or solutions. ESs are particularly valuable in areas where decision-making relies heavily on specialized knowledge and expertise.

3.2.1 Knowledge Inference Framework

ES is based on the assumption that intelligence consists of knowledge and inference capability:

$$Intelligence = Knowledge + Inference$$

Thus an ES generally works by coupling at least a knowledge base, which stores various types of knowledge, and an inference engine, which interprets and evaluates facts against the knowledge stored in the knowledge base to generate results (see Figure 3.1).

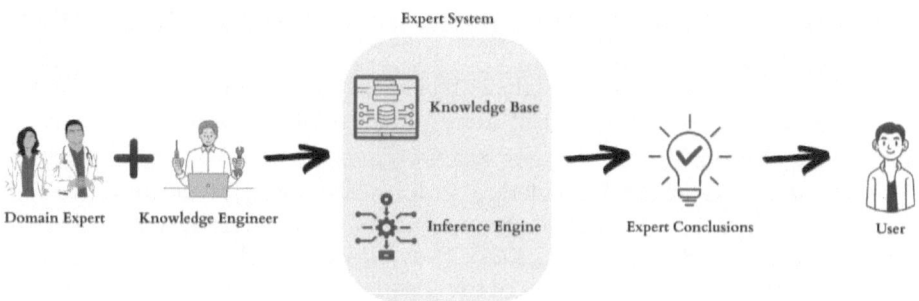

FIGURE 3.1
General architecture of knowledge-based expert systems.

3.2.1.1 Knowledge Base and Knowledge Representation

The knowledge base can be in various forms of representation, which define how knowledge is structured within the system. Effective knowledge representation in the knowledge base enables the system to process and infer information efficiently. There are several types of knowledge representations, each suited to different types of knowledge and reasoning processes.

Logic-Based Representations: Logic-based representations use formal logic to represent knowledge (Calegari et al., 2020). Propositional logic and first-order logic are common examples. These representations are powerful for expressing complex relationships and enabling formal reasoning, but they require sophisticated inference mechanisms.

Production Rules: Generally, these are if-then rules that represent knowledge in the form of condition–action pairs (Hanson & Widom, 1993). Production rules are widely used in rule-based expert systems to model decision-making processes. They are easy to understand and implement but can become complex to manage as the number of rules increases.

Frames: Frames are data structures for representing stereotyped situations (Nazaruks & Osis, 2021). They consist of slots (attributes) and values (data or pointers to other frames). Frames are particularly useful for representing objects, their properties, and their relationships in a structured way.

Ontologies: Ontologies provide a formal representation of a set of concepts within a domain and the relationships between those concepts (Mora et al., 2022). They are used to model domain knowledge in a structured and reusable way. Ontologies are essential for interoperability between different systems and for supporting complex queries.

Semantic Networks: These are graphical representations of knowledge where nodes represent concepts and edges represent relationships between them (Pereira et al., 2022). Semantic networks are intuitive and useful for representing hierarchical relationships and associations among concepts.

Knowledge Graphs: Knowledge graphs are more structured than semantic networks and focus on entities, their attributes, and their interrelationships (Ji et al., 2021). They allow for richer and more precise queries and integration of diverse data sources, often using standardized schemas and ontologies.

Equations/Formulas: These consist of mathematical representations of knowledge. Useful for domains requiring precise and quantitative reasoning, such as physics or engineering. Such precision often requires ad hoc solutions to infer new knowledge from data.

Natural Language: Using human language to represent knowledge. Natural language processing (NLP) techniques enable the system to understand and generate human language, facilitating interaction, and information extraction. Natural language has historically been overlooked for knowledge representation due to its inherent complexity, but in recent years, several approaches have focused on this challenge, thanks to the advent of models such as Transformers (Lin et al., 2022) and large language models (LLMs) (Chang et al., 2024).

Each type of knowledge representation has its strengths and is chosen based on the specific requirements of the expert system and the nature of the knowledge it needs to handle. Combining multiple types of representations can enhance the system's capability to model complex domains and support robust decision-making processes.

3.2.1.2 Inference Engine

Several techniques are fundamental to the development and operation of ES:

Rule-Based Reasoning: This is the most common technique, where the knowledge base generally consists of if-then rules (Kierner et al., 2023). The inference engine applies these rules to known facts to infer new facts. Two main types of rule-based reasoning are forward chaining and backward chaining. Forward chaining starts with known facts and applies rules to infer new facts. It is data-driven, meaning the inference engine starts from the available data and works its way forward to deduce conclusions. On the contrary, backward chaining starts with a goal and works backward to determine whether the known facts support the goal. It is goal-driven, meaning the inference engine begins with a hypothesis and searches for data that supports or refutes it.

Knowledge Graph Reasoning: Knowledge graphs structure information in nodes (entities) and edges (relationships), allowing the inference engine to traverse these connections to infer new relationships or validate existing ones. This method supports more complex queries and integration of diverse data sources, often leveraging ontologies to enhance reasoning capabilities. Nodes represent entities (e.g., objects, concepts), and edges represent relationships between these entities. For example, in a medical knowledge graph, nodes might represent diseases and symptoms, while edges represent the relationships (e.g., "causes" or "symptoms of"). Ontologies could be used to provide a formal representation of a set of concepts and their relationships within a domain. They enrich knowledge graphs by defining classes, properties, and rules that govern the relationships between nodes. This integration enhances the graph's semantic understanding and enables more accurate reasoning. The inference engine can use graph traversal algorithms to explore paths between nodes, enabling it to infer new relationships or validate existing ones. For instance, if a knowledge graph contains nodes for "Fever" and "Infection," and an edge indicating that fever is a symptom of infection, the system can infer a potential diagnosis based on observed symptoms. Knowledge graph reasoning often employs techniques like SPARQL (a query language for RDF databases) (Ali et al., 2022) to perform complex queries and retrieve relevant information. These queries can be used to find direct and indirect relationships, detect patterns, and generate insights from the interconnected data.

Uncertainty Management: Techniques like Bayesian networks (Kitson et al., 2023), fuzzy logic (Serrano-Guerrero et al., 2021), and certainty factors (Yu et al., 2023) are used to handle uncertainty in ES. Bayesian networks are probabilistic graphical models that represent variables and their conditional dependencies via directed acyclic graphs. They are used to compute the probability of different outcomes given certain evidence, thus managing uncertainty effectively. Fuzzy logic handles reasoning that is approximate rather than fixed and exact. In ES, it is used to deal with uncertainty by applying degrees of truth rather than the usual true or false (1 or 0) Boolean logic. Certainty factors are a simpler approach, wherein each piece of information is assigned a confidence level (Sembiring et al., 2019). The inference engine adjusts these levels as the inference progresses, allowing for decisions to be made even when complete certainty is not possible.

3.2.1.3 Representative Applications

Medical Diagnosis Systems: A prominent application of ES is in the field of medical diagnostics. One notable example is a generic knowledge-based system designed for diagnosing diseases based on symptoms (Saibene et al., 2021). This system uses backward chaining to verify hypotheses about possible diagnoses and incorporates a user-friendly GUI to visualize decision-making processes. Such systems can significantly assist healthcare professionals by providing diagnostic support, especially in regions with limited access to expert medical practitioners.

Civil Engineering Applications: ES has been employed in civil engineering for tasks such as planning, analysis, design, and construction management. These systems integrate domain-specific knowledge to support engineers in decision-making processes, from designing structures to managing construction projects. The ability to simulate various scenarios and to predict outcomes based on expert knowledge is particularly valuable in this field (Akram et al., 2014).

Overall, ES plays a crucial role in various domains by leveraging specialized knowledge to support decision-making processes. The combination of robust knowledge representation, effective reasoning techniques, and user-friendly interfaces makes these systems invaluable tools in addressing complex problems. Through case studies, we can see their practical applications and the significant impact they have in fields such as medicine, engineering, and service management.

3.3 Case Study: Financial ES for Data Preprocessing

Traditionally, data collection and preprocessing were conducted manually by finance domain experts for financial data analytics, which is a crucial task in obtaining the measures to be used and ensure the quality and reliability of financial data analysis results. This case study presents our previous work proposing an ES that features a rule-based knowledge base and an inference engine matching the rules and processing historical data downloaded from Refinitiv tick data provided by Datascope (Chen et al., 2023; Chen & Rabhi, 2016). The rules define event patterns to be detected and the relevant actions to be taken if the condition is met. The ES handles these complex event processing rules for financial studies, and, in this case study, we demonstrate six rules, each necessitating incremental modifications to the business logic rules, for one preprocessing task, i.e. calculating the price/earnings (P/E) ratios of different companies.

The P/E ratio, which is the market value per share divided by earnings per share, is crucial for investors to assess a company's potential for future earnings growth. To calculate the P/E ratio, both price data (providing market value per share) and corporate action data (providing earnings per share) are required. The task involves determining the correct value of earnings per share from the earning data for each trading day (End Of Day event). The six rules involved in calculating the P/E ratio are shown in Table 3.1.

The ES architecture is shown in Figure 3.2. It comprises three main components: a user interface that allows the user to define and execute rules, a rule component that manages the rules, and an inference engine that processes the rules in the rule base and executes reasoning. A prototype was developed using EventSwarm as the chosen inference engine, and the rules were managed in a relational database. To ensure rapid and convenient development, event pattern definition constructs are provided as Ruby wrappers around the core Java library of EventSwarm. Event pattern types are specified in Ruby as directed acyclic graphs with nodes representing events and edges

TABLE 3.1

Sample of Six Rules for Financial Data Preprocessing (P/E Ratio Calculation)

Rule ID	Condition	Action
1	An event with type "Earning" (E) happens before an event with type "End Of Day" (EOD).	Calculate the earnings of the EOD event using the following formula: $EOD.earnings = E.epsAmount * 10^{EPS\_scaling\_factor}$
2	Two events $E_{6(1)}$ and $E_{6(2)}$ with type "Earning" ($E_{6(2)}$ before $E_{6(1)}$) happen before an event with type "End Of Day" (EOD)	Calculate the earnings of the EOD event using the following formula: $EOD.earnings = (E_{6(1)}.epsAmount + E_{6(2)}.epsAmount) * 10^{EPS\_scaling\_factor}$
3	Three events with type "Earning" ($E_{3(2)}$ before $E_{3(1)}$ before E_6) happen before an event with type "End Of Day" (EOD)	Calculate the earnings of the EOD event using the following formula: $EOD.earnings = (E_6.epsAmount + E_{3(1)}.epsAmount + E_{3(2)}.epsAmount) * 10^{EPS\_scaling\_factor}$
4	One 3-month earning and one 9-month earning before End Of Day	Calculate the earnings of the EOD event using the following formula: $EOD.earnings = E_9.epsAmount + E_3.epsAmount$
5	Four 3-month earnings before End Of Day	Calculate the earnings of the EOD event using the following formula: $EOD.earnings = (E_{3(1)}.epsAmount + E_{3(2)}.epsAmount + E_{3(3)}.epsAmount + E_{3(4)}.epsAmount) * 10^{EPS\_scaling\_factor}$
6	One 9-month earning and one 3-month earning before End Of Day	Calculate the earnings of the EOD event using the following formula: $EOD.earnings = (E_3.epsAmount + E_9.epsAmount) * 10^{EPS\_scaling\_factor}$

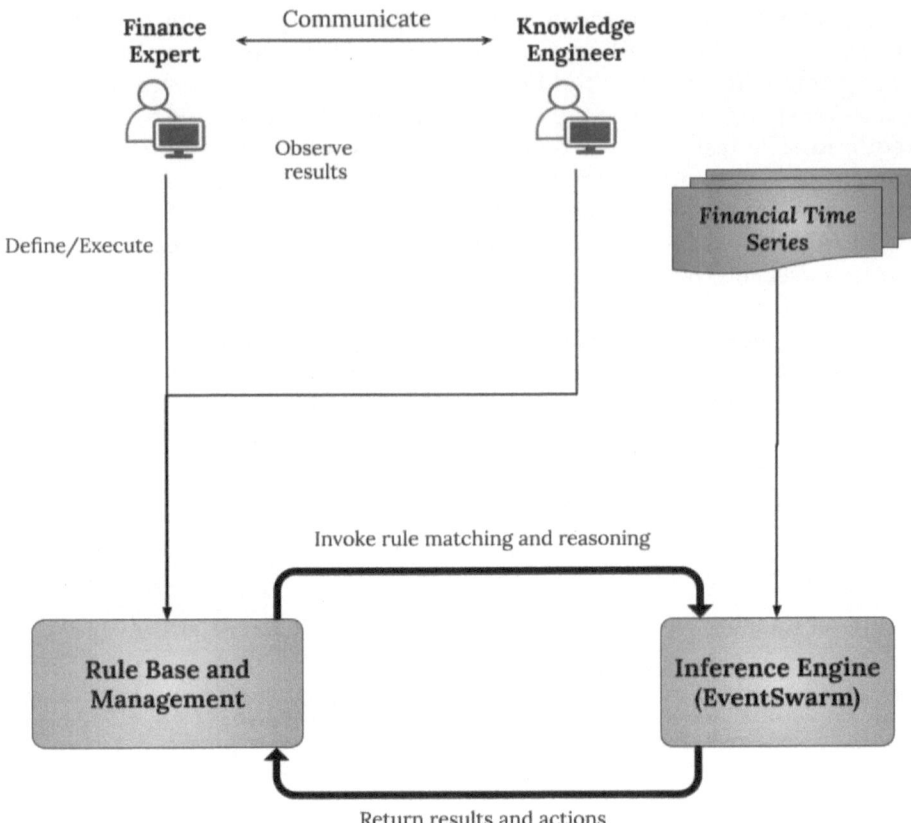

FIGURE 3.2
Rule-based expert system for financial data preprocessing.

representing relationships and functions such as sliding windows, filters, and abstractions. Detected event pattern occurrences are then sent back to the rule component for subsequent calculations, actions, or alerts.

The event patterns defined in the rules were described in natural language by a financial expert and communicated to the system developer, i.e., the knowledge engineer, who then coded the event pattern types in the CEP component. The finance expert used the rule component to define the six rules and selected the data to be processed. The inference engine then matches the rules to be executed, via an HTTP GET request to a configurable URL. Detected event pattern occurrences were returned in JSON format and sent back to the rule component for further processing, allowing the finance expert to download and review the results. The experimental results demonstrated the application's advantages, including a user-friendly API that facilitates easy integration of EventSwarm into various applications; efficient inference with an average processing rate of over 10,000 events per second on the financial market data, comparable to the performance of a locally deployed specialized program; and well-structured output in JSON format, which is convenient for downstream analysis.

3.4 Data-Driven Machine Learning

3.4.1 Concept of Machine Learning

Data-driven machine learning (ML) involves creating models and algorithms that learn patterns and make decisions based on large volumes of data. Unlike traditional programming, where explicit instructions are provided, machine learning models improve their performance through exposure to more data over time. This approach is particularly effective in situations where deriving rules manually would be impractical due to the complexity and volume of data involved.

3.4.1.1 Definition

The core concept of data-driven machine learning is to utilize algorithms that can process data, recognize patterns, and make predictions or decisions without human intervention. This involves various types of learning, including supervised learning, unsupervised learning, and reinforcement learning. Supervised learning uses labelled data to train models, unsupervised learning finds hidden patterns in unlabelled data, and reinforcement learning involves learning optimal actions through trial and error. Ultimately, ML aims to train a model that can be considered as a formula, $Y = f(X)$ that takes data X as input and generates the output Y. Note that the formula can be as simple as a linear one containing just a few parameters or as complicated as an artificial-neural-network-based large model like GPT containing billions of parameters that one can hardly write down on paper. As shown in Figure 3.3, the representative products of OpenAI (Roumeliotis & Tselikas, 2023) are essentially such large models, GPT (X = text, Y = text), Dall E (X = text, Y = image), Sora (X = text, Y = video), and these can be combined into multimodal models (Wang et al., 2023). Another example is Yolo (Jiang et al., 2022), which is a model for image classification and object detection where X could be an image and Y is the corresponding classification.

3.4.1.2 Taxonomy of Machine Learning

Supervised Learning: This technique involves training a model on a labelled dataset, which means that each training example is

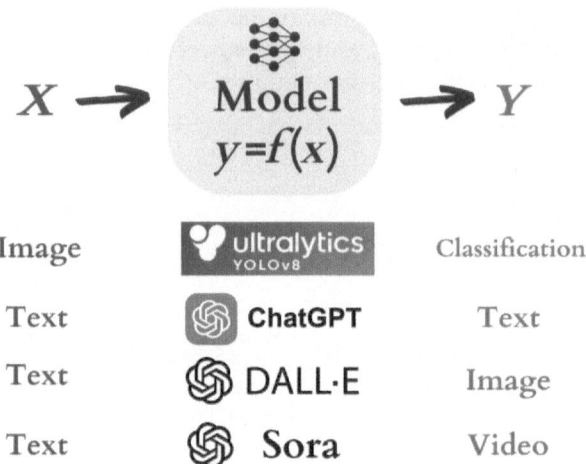

FIGURE 3.3
Concept of machine learning and representative example models.

paired with an output label. Algorithms such as decision trees, support vector machines (SVM), and neural networks are commonly used. These models are trained to predict outcomes based on input data by minimizing the error between the predicted and actual outputs.

Unsupervised Learning: This approach is used when the data is not labelled. The goal is to uncover hidden patterns or intrinsic structures in the input data. Clustering algorithms like *k*-means (Ahmed et al., 2020), hierarchical clustering (Murtagh & Contreras, 2017), and latent dirichlet allocation (LDA) (Al Qudah et al., 2022; Chen et al., 2023), as well as association algorithms like Apriori (Wang & Gao, 2021), are typical examples.

Reinforcement Learning: This involves training agents to make a sequence of decisions by rewarding them for correct actions and penalizing them for incorrect ones. Techniques such as Q-learning (Wang & Gao, 2021) and deep reinforcement learning (Ladosz et al., 2022) are used to develop models that can handle complex decision-making processes.

Deep Learning: A subset of machine learning, deep learning uses neural networks with many layers (deep networks) to model complex patterns in large datasets. Techniques like convolutional neural networks (CNNs) for image processing and recurrent neural networks (RNNs) for time-series data are prevalent in this field (Chen, Hussain, et al., 2024).

The most important fields of ML applications include computer vision (such as image classification and object detection) and natural language processing (such as topic modeling, sentiment analysis (Chen et al., 2022), named-entity recognition (Chen, Qiu, et al., 2024), etc.).

3.4.1.3 Representative Applications

ML has been applied in almost all fields. Here are some representative examples.

Healthcare Diagnostics: Data-driven machine learning models have revolutionized medical diagnostics. Many studies have attempted to develop machine learning and deep learning models to diagnose diseases from various datasets including medical records of symptoms, histories, test results, and relevant images, enhancing the accuracy and speed of diagnosis compared to traditional methods (Azad et al., 2021).

Cybersecurity: ML is crucial in identifying and mitigating cybersecurity threats. Techniques such as anomaly detection and classification algorithms are used to analyze network traffic and detect potential security breaches. A recent review highlighted the use of deep learning in cybersecurity (Mahdavifar & Ghorbani, 2019).

Environmental Engineering: ML models have been applied to environmental engineering problems, such as predicting the nutrient removal efficiency in sewage treatment plants using LSTM (Yaqub et al., 2020). Such models help optimize the treatment processes, ensuring compliance with environmental regulations and improving operational efficiency.

In summary, ML leverages vast amounts of data to train models that can make accurate predictions and decisions across various domains. The techniques involved range from supervised and unsupervised learning to deep learning and reinforcement learning, each suited to different types of problems and data structures.

3.4.2 Case Study: Depression Detection in Speech Using Deep Learning

The case study presents our recent work using ML to address the challenge of detecting depression in speech within low-resource environments by employing transfer learning with the wav2vec 2.0 model (Zhang et al., 2024). The primary goal is to develop an effective ML model that could leverage limited annotated data to accurately identify depression-related features in speech. Two main datasets were involved in this study: (1) the DAIC-WOZ dataset, comprising 189 clinical interviews designed for diagnosing psychological distress conditions such as anxiety, depression, and PTSD. The dataset includes audio recordings of interviews, which are divided into training, development, and test subsets. (The average length of each interview is approximately 15 minutes.) (2) The second is the CMDC dataset, a Chinese multimodal depression corpus consisting of 78 samples, including 26 cases of severe depression and 52 healthy individuals. The dataset includes semi-structured interviews with fixed questions and is smaller in scale compared to the DAIC-WOZ dataset.

The study proposed a novel model framework that integrates several advanced techniques:

Audio Preprocessing: The audio data was segmented into fixed-duration intervals of 7 seconds, eliminating non-subject segments such as interviewer speech, silence, and background noise.

Feature Extraction: The wav2vec 2.0 model was fine-tuned to extract robust frame-level features from the segmented speech data. This model employs self-supervised learning techniques to generate meaningful speech representations.

Segment-Level Feature Encoding: A 1D-CNN combined with attention pooling was used to encode frame-level features into segment-level representations, capturing temporal relationships within the audio frames.

Depression Classification: The model used a combination of long short-term memory (LSTM) networks and self-attention mechanisms to predict depression based on the learned segment-level features. The LSTM network captured temporal dependencies, while the self-attention mechanism emphasized important segments related to depression.

The proposed method demonstrated significant improvements in depression detection performance compared to existing approaches. For the DAIC-WOZ dataset, the model achieved an F1 score of 79.00%, outperforming other

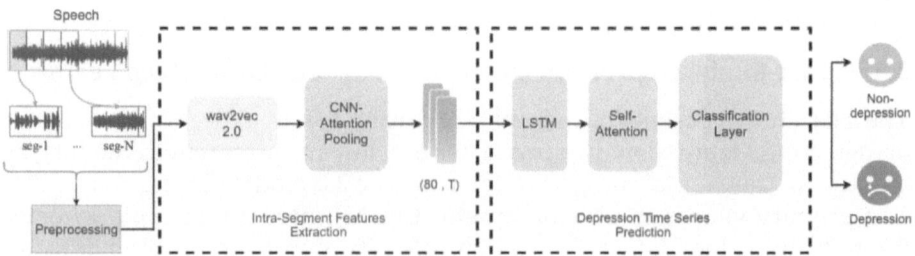

FIGURE 3.4
Deep learning model for depression detection in speech (Zhang et al., 2024).

methods that relied on features like spectrograms and MFCC. The use of wav2vec 2.0 features and the incorporation of self-attention mechanisms were key factors in this improved performance. For the CMDC dataset: The model achieved an F1 score of 90.53%, highlighting its effectiveness even in datasets with limited samples. This performance was superior to previous methods, demonstrating the model's ability to generalize well across different languages and recording conditions.

3.5 Intelligent Optimization

3.5.1 Concept of Intelligent Optimization

Intelligent optimization involves the use of advanced algorithms to find the best solutions to complex problems, often under constraints. These techniques are inspired by natural and artificial processes and are designed to efficiently navigate large search spaces to identify optimal or near-optimal solutions. Intelligent optimization encompasses a range of methodologies including evolutionary algorithms, swarm intelligence, and other heuristic-based approaches. The goal is to improve decision-making processes in various applications by leveraging computational power and innovative algorithmic strategies.

3.5.1.1 Intelligent Optimization Algorithms

Some prevalent algorithms are illustrated as follows. Note that this is a non-exhaustive list as many algorithms are available.

First, the A* Algorithm is widely used in pathfinding and graph traversal. It employs a best-first search approach and uses heuristics to efficiently find the shortest path to the goal. While it is better known as a graph traversal and pathfinding algorithm, it is extensively used in many subfields of computer science, thanks to its different properties such as completeness and optimality (Russell & Norvig, 2016).

Second, evolutionary algorithms are inspired by the process of natural selection. They involve mechanisms such as mutation, crossover, and selection to evolve a population of solutions toward better fitness. Genetic algorithms (GA) are a prime example, where potential solutions are encoded as chromosomes and iteratively improved based on a fitness function.

Third, swarm intelligence comprises a group of algorithms inspired by the collective behavior of decentralized, self-organized systems. Examples include particle swarm optimization (PSO) (Shami et al., 2022) and ant colony optimization (ACO) (Skinderowicz, 2022). PSO, for instance, models the social behavior of birds flocking or fish schooling to find optimal regions in a search space by adjusting the trajectories of individual particles based on their own and their neighbors' experiences.

Last but not least, simulated annealing is a probabilistic technique that searches for an optimal solution by mimicking the annealing process of metals. It allows for occasional uphill moves to escape local optima, gradually reducing the frequency of these moves as the "temperature" decreases.

3.5.1.2 Representative Applications

Fluid Machinery Optimization: An intelligent CFD-based optimization system was developed to enhance the performance of automotive electronic pumps (Si et al., 2020). This system integrates computational fluid dynamics (CFD) with multi-objective optimization methods, including the use of a multi-island genetic algorithm (MIGA). The optimization process significantly improved the pump's efficiency by redesigning the impeller geometries based on detailed fluid dynamic analyses and experimental validations.

Industrial Process Optimization: Data-driven intelligent optimization algorithms have been increasingly applied in industrial processes to enhance efficiency, reliability, and adaptability. Techniques such as hybrid modeling, which combines fuzzy logic with the genetic algorithm, have been used to optimize parameters in complex systems, leading to improved performance and sustainability in various industrial applications (Mariajayaprakash et al., 2015).

Traffic Congestion Management: An intelligent transportation system application has adopted ACO to optimize decreasing congestion in smart cities (Khoza et al., 2020).

Advanced Sequences Comparison: Sequence comparison is a valuable task for identifying similarities and differences between various sequences, such as DNA, proteins, or text strings, enabling researchers to infer evolutionary relationships, detect mutations, and understand functional similarities. This technique is essential in fields like bioinformatics, for comparing genetic material, and in computer science, for applications such as text analysis, data deduplication, and plagiarism detection. Lately, advanced algorithms have been presented exploiting intelligent optimization algorithms, such as hill climbing, evolution strategies, and more (Cauteruccio et al., 2020).

3.5.2 Case Study

In this case study, we demonstrate a prototype that we have developed and that leverages the genetic algorithm to optimize the formation of exam questions. The system can generate a set of exam questions that meet specific criteria. These criteria include coverage of various topics, varying difficulty levels, and ensuring a balanced assessment. The process includes encoding potential solutions, evaluating their fitness, and applying genetic operations to evolve better solutions over successive generations.

First, by design, each chromosome represents a potential set of exam questions. A chromosome is encoded as a list of question IDs or a binary vector where each bit indicates whether a particular question is included in the exam. An initial population of chromosomes is generated randomly at the start of the execution.

The fitness function evaluates how well a set of questions meets the desired criteria, including the following key points:

Topic Coverage: Ensure all key topics are covered.

Difficulty Levels: Maintain a balance of easy, medium, and hard questions.

Question Quality: Include questions that are well-formulated and relevant.

Total Marks: Ensure the total marks of the questions match the exam's requirements.

$$\text{Fitness} = w1 \cdot \text{Topic Coverage} + w2 \cdot \text{Difficulty Balance} + w3 \cdot \text{Question Quality} + w4 \cdot \text{Total Marks}$$

where w1, w2, w3, and w4 are weights assigned to each criterion based on its importance.

The core functions of the genetic algorithm include selection, crossover, and mutation. For selection, roulette wheel selection has been adopted, with the chromosome that has the highest fitness score kept in each iteration without selection. The crossover operators are applied to pairs of selected parents to produce offspring. We have adopted single-point crossover to combine parent chromosomes. The mutation operator has been adopted to introduce variability and avoid premature convergence by flipping a bit in the binary representation or replacing a question ID with another in the list representation. The algorithm runs until a stopping criterion is met, including a maximum number of generations or a satisfactory fitness level. The best chromosome (set of exam questions) is chosen as the final solution. Now we will demonstrate an example scenario. Suppose we have a pool of 100 questions categorized by topic and difficulty. The goal is to create an exam with ten questions covering five topics, with a balanced difficulty distribution, ensuring the total marks are 100. Each chromosome is a vector of ten-question IDs. The fitness function evaluates topic coverage, difficulty balance, question quality, and total marks. The initial population is generated randomly with 50 sets of ten questions. The program runs for 100 generations of selection, crossover, and mutation or until a high fitness score is achieved.

3.6 When These Routes Meet

The convergence of ES, ML, and IO creates powerful hybrid approaches that leverage the strengths of each method to enhance AI applications. In short, ES is advantageous when there is sufficient established knowledge and there is no need to train a new model. ML's benefits include finding out new "knowledge" from a large amount of data, which is previously unknown. IO is capable of searching, optimizing, and automatically finding out the best solution for a given problem. This integration can lead to more robust, efficient, and accurate AI systems capable of tackling complex real-world problems.

First, combining ES with ML allows the incorporation of expert knowledge into data-driven models (Kierner et al., 2023). For instance, a knowledge-based system can provide initial rules and constraints, which are then fine-tuned using machine learning algorithms to improve accuracy and adaptability. This approach is particularly useful in domains like medical diagnosis and predictive maintenance, where domain expertise and large datasets are both crucial. Also, it is often one of the most reliable ways to infer knowledge in an explainable way; that is, it is possible to explain, to a certain extent, the nature of the results given by the model. As another example, in recent years, researchers have focused on studying the evolution of diseases by exploiting the inferred knowledge of an ES along with ML. For instance, in (Calimeri et al., 2021), the authors coupled logic programming and machine learning to define an ES capable of analyzing the evolution of neurological disorders.

Second, IO techniques, such as genetic algorithms and PSO, can be used to optimize the parameters and structures of machine learning models (Guo et al., 2020). This enhances model performance by finding optimal configurations that might not be achievable through traditional training methods alone. For example, optimizing the architecture and hyperparameters of neural networks using evolutionary algorithms can lead to more efficient and effective models.

Third, integrating theoretical models with machine learning helps in creating models that are not only data-driven but also consistent with known physical laws and expert knowledge. This synergy ensures that the predictions are both accurate and interpretable. An example is using physical laws as constraints in a machine learning model for better predictive performance in engineering applications.

3.7 Conclusion

In this chapter, we have explored three major technical routes of artificial intelligence (AI): knowledge-based expert systems, data-driven machine learning, and intelligent optimization. Each of these pathways offers unique methodologies and applications, contributing significantly to the advancement and versatility of AI.

Knowledge-based expert systems (ESs) leverage structured knowledge bases and inference engines to emulate human decision-making. These systems are particularly effective in domains requiring specialized knowledge and expertise, such as medical diagnosis, financial analysis, and legal reasoning. By formalizing and codifying expert knowledge, ES provides reliable and consistent solutions, supporting or even replacing human experts in specific tasks.

Data-driven machine learning (ML), powered by algorithms that learn from data, has become the cornerstone of modern AI applications. ML techniques, including supervised, unsupervised, and reinforcement learning, enable systems to identify patterns, make predictions, and improve over time. This approach has led to groundbreaking advancements in fields like image and speech recognition, natural language processing, and predictive analytics. The ability to derive insights from vast amounts of data has transformed industries, driving innovation and efficiency.

Intelligent optimization (IO) encompasses a range of techniques designed to find optimal solutions to complex problems. Methods such as genetic algorithms, particle swarm optimization, and simulated annealing navigate large search spaces to identify the best possible outcomes under given constraints. IO is crucial in applications where traditional methods fall short, such as logistics, resource allocation, and engineering design. By optimizing processes and solutions, IO contributes to significant cost savings and performance improvements.

The integration of these AI routes can lead to more robust and efficient systems. Hybrid approaches that combine ES with ML allow for the incorporation of expert knowledge into data-driven models, enhancing accuracy and adaptability. Similarly, IO techniques can optimize the parameters and structures of ML models, leading to more effective solutions. This synergy between different AI methodologies opens new avenues for innovation and application, addressing complex real-world problems with greater precision and effectiveness.

As we look to the future, the continuous evolution and integration of these AI techniques promise to further enhance the capabilities and impact of artificial intelligence across various domains. By leveraging the strengths of knowledge-based systems, machine learning, and intelligent optimization, we can develop AI solutions that are not only more intelligent and adaptable but also more aligned with human needs and societal goals. This convergence of AI methodologies marks a significant step toward creating more comprehensive and powerful AI systems that can address the challenges of tomorrow.

References

Ahmed, M., Seraj, R., & Islam, S. M. S. (2020). The k-means algorithm: A comprehensive survey and performance evaluation. *Electronics*, 9(8), 1295.

Akram, M., Rahman, I. A., & Memon, I. (2014). A review on expert system and its applications in civil engineering. *International Journal of Civil Engineering and Built Environment*, 1(1), 24–29.

Al Qudah, I., Hashem, I., Soufyane, A., Chen, W., & Merabtene, T. (2022). Applying Latent Dirichlet Allocation Technique to Classify Topics on Sustainability Using Arabic Text. In K. Arai (Ed.), *Intelligent Computing*. Cham.

Ali, W., Saleem, M., Yao, B., Hogan, A., & Ngomo, A.-C. N. (2022). A survey of RDF stores & SPARQL engines for querying knowledge graphs. *The VLDB Journal*, 1–26.

Azad, M. M., Ganapathy, A., Vadlamudi, S., & Paruchuri, H. (2021). Medical diagnosis using deep learning techniques: A research survey. *Annals of the Romanian Society for Cell Biology*, 25(6), 5591–5600.

Calegari, R., Ciatto, G., Denti, E., & Omicini, A. (2020). Logic-based technologies for intelligent systems: State of the art and perspectives. *Information*, 11(3), 167.

Calimeri, F., Cauteruccio, F., Cinelli, L., Marzullo, A., Stamile, C., Terracina, G., Durand-Dubief, F., & Sappey-Marinier, D. (2021). A logic-based framework leveraging neural networks for studying the evolution of neurological disorders. *Theory and Practice of Logic Programming*, 21(1), 80–124. https://doi.org/10.1017/S1471068419000449

Cauteruccio, F., Terracina, G., & Ursino, D. (2020). Generalizing identity-based string comparison metrics: Framework and techniques. *Knowledge-Based Systems*, 187, 104820. https://doi.org/https://doi.org/10.1016/j.knosys.2019.06.028

Chang, Y., Wang, X., Wang, J., Wu, Y., Yang, L., Zhu, K., Chen, H., Yi, X., Wang, C., & Wang, Y. (2024). A survey on evaluation of large language models. *ACM Transactions on Intelligent Systems and Technology*, 15(3), 1–45.

Chen, W., Hussain, W., Cauteruccio, F., & Zhang, X. (2024). Deep learning for financial time series prediction: A state-of-the-art review of standalone and hybrid models. *Computer Modeling in Engineering & Sciences*, 139(1), 187–224. http://www.techscience.com/CMES/v139n1/55114

Chen, W., Liu, B., Zhang, X., & Al-Qudah, I. (2022, 6–8 Jan 2022). An Event-Based Framework for Facilitating Real-Time Sentiment Analysis in Educational Contexts. *2022 11th International Conference on Educational and Information Technology (ICEIT)*.

Chen, W., Milosevic, Z., Rabhi, F. A., & Berry, A. (2023a). Real-time analytics: Concepts, architectures, and ML/AI considerations. *IEEE Access*, 11, 71634–71657. https://doi.org/10.1109/ACCESS.2023.3295694

Chen, W., Qiu, P., & Cauteruccio, F. (2024). MedNER: A service-oriented framework for Chinese medical named-entity recognition with real-world application. *Big Data and Cognitive Computing*, 8(8), 86. https://www.mdpi.com/2504–2289/8/8/86

Chen, W., Rabhi, F., Liao, W., & Al-Qudah, I. (2023b). Leveraging state-of-the-art topic modeling for news impact analysis on financial markets: A comparative study. *Electronics*, 12(12), 2605. https://www.mdpi.com/2079–9292/12/12/2605

Chen, W., & Rabhi, F. A. (2016). Enabling user-driven rule management in event data analysis. *Information Systems Frontiers, 18*(3), 511–528. https://doi.org/10.1007/s10796-016-9633-2

Guo, Y., Li, J.-Y., & Zhan, Z.-H. (2020). Efficient hyperparameter optimization for convolution neural networks in deep learning: A distributed particle swarm optimization approach. *Cybernetics and Systems, 52*(1), 36–57.

Hanson, E. N., & Widom, J. (1993). An overview of production rules in database systems. *The Knowledge Engineering Review, 8*(2), 121–143.

Ji, S., Pan, S., Cambria, E., Marttinen, P., & Philip, S. Y. (2021). A survey on knowledge graphs: Representation, acquisition, and applications. *IEEE Transactions on Neural Networks and Learning Systems, 33*(2), 494–514.

Jiang, P., Ergu, D., Liu, F., Cai, Y., & Ma, B. (2022). A Review of Yolo algorithm developments. *Procedia Computer Science, 199*, 1066–1073.

Khoza, E., Tu, C., & Owolawi, P. A. (2020). Decreasing traffic congestion in VANETs using an improved hybrid ant colony optimization algorithm. *Journal of Communications, 15*(9), 676–686.

Kierner, S., Kucharski, J., & Kierner, Z. (2023). Taxonomy of hybrid architectures involving rule-based reasoning and machine learning in clinical decision systems: A scoping review. *Journal of Biomedical Informatics, 144*, 104428.

Kitson, N. K., Constantinou, A. C., Guo, Z., Liu, Y., & Chobtham, K. (2023). A survey of Bayesian Network structure learning. *Artificial Intelligence Review, 56*(8), 8721–8814.

Ladosz, P., Weng, L., Kim, M., & Oh, H. (2022). Exploration in deep reinforcement learning: A survey. *Information Fusion, 85*, 1–22.

Lin, T., Wang, Y., Liu, X., & Qiu, X. (2022). A survey of transformers. *AI Open, 3*, 111–132.

Mahdavifar, S., & Ghorbani, A. A. (2019). Application of deep learning to cybersecurity: A survey. *Neurocomputing, 347*, 149–176.

Mariajayaprakash, A., Senthilvelan, T., & Gnanadass, R. (2015). Optimization of process parameters through fuzzy logic and genetic algorithm—a case study in a process industry. *Applied Soft Computing, 30*, 94–103.

Mohammadi, A., & Sheikholeslam, F. (2023). Intelligent optimization: Literature review and state-of-the-art algorithms (1965–2022). *Engineering Applications of Artificial Intelligence, 126*, 106959. https://doi.org/https://doi.org/10.1016/j.engappai.2023.106959

Mora, M., Wang, F., Gómez, J. M., & Phillips-Wren, G. (2022). Development methodologies for ontology-based knowledge management systems: A review. *Expert Systems, 39*(2), e12851.

Murtagh, F., & Contreras, P. (2017). Algorithms for hierarchical clustering: An overview, II. *Wiley Interdisciplinary Reviews: Data Mining and Knowledge Discovery, 7*(6), e1219.

Nayak, J., Swapnarekha, H., Naik, B., Dhiman, G., & Vimal, S. (2023). 25 Years of particle swarm optimization: Flourishing voyage of two decades. *Archives of Computational Methods in Engineering, 30*(3), 1663-1725. https://doi.org/10.1007/s11831-022-09849-x

Nazaruks, V., & Osis, J. (2021). An Overview of Knowledge Representation with Frames. In Y. Rhazali (Ed.), *Advancements in Model-Driven Architecture in Software Engineering* (pp. 46–63). IGI Global. https://doi.org/10.4018/978-1-7998-3661-2.ch003

Pereira, H. B. d. B., Grilo, M., Fadigas, I. d. S., Souza Junior, C. T. d., Cunha, M. d. V., Barreto, R. S. F. D., Andrade, J. C., & Henrique, T. (2022). Systematic review of the "semantic network" definitions. *Expert Systems with Applications, 210,* 118455. https://doi.org/https://doi.org/10.1016/j.eswa.2022.118455

Roumeliotis, K. I., & Tselikas, N. D. (2023). ChatGPT and open-ai models: A preliminary review. *Future Internet, 15*(6), 192.

Russell, S. J., & Norvig, P. (2016). *Artificial intelligence: a modern approach.* Pearson.

Saibene, A., Assale, M., & Giltri, M. (2021). Expert systems: Definitions, advantages and issues in medical field applications. *Expert Systems with Applications, 177,* 114900. https://doi.org/https://doi.org/10.1016/j.eswa.2021.114900

Sarker, I. H. (2021). Machine learning: Algorithms, real-world applications and research directions. *SN Computer Science, 2*(3), 160. https://doi.org/10.1007/s42979-021-00592-x

Sembiring, A. S., Manahan, O., Napitupulu, M. H., Hasugian, P. S., Riandari, F., Simanjorang, R. M., Simangunsong, A., Utami, Y., & Sihotang, H. T. (2019). Implementation of certainty factor method for expert system. *Journal of Physics: Conference Series, 1255,* 012065.

Serrano-Guerrero, J., Romero, F. P., & Olivas, J. A. (2021). Fuzzy logic applied to opinion mining: A review. *Knowledge-Based Systems, 222,* 107018.

Shami, T. M., El-Saleh, A. A., Alswaitti, M., Al-Tashi, Q., Summakieh, M. A., & Mirjalili, S. (2022). Particle swarm optimization: A comprehensive survey. *IEEE Access, 10,* 10031–10061.

Shu-Hsien, L. (2005). Expert system methodologies and applications—a decade review from 1995 to 2004. *Expert Systems with Applications, 28*(1), 93–103. https://doi.org/https://doi.org/10.1016/j.eswa.2004.08.003

Si, Q., Lu, R., Shen, C., Xia, S., Sheng, G., & Yuan, J. (2020). An intelligent CFD-based optimization system for fluid machinery: Automotive electronic pump case application. *Applied Sciences, 10*(1), 366.

Skinderowicz, R. (2022). Improving Ant Colony Optimization efficiency for solving large TSP instances. *Applied Soft Computing, 120,* 108653.

Sohail, A. (2023). Genetic algorithms in the fields of artificial intelligence and data sciences. *Annals of Data Science, 10*(4), 1007–1018. https://doi.org/10.1007/s40745-021-00354-9

Wang, H.-B., & Gao, Y.-J. (2021). Research on parallelization of Apriori algorithm in association rule mining. *Procedia Computer Science, 183,* 641–647.

Wang, X., Chen, G., Qian, G., Gao, P., Wei, X.-Y., Wang, Y., Tian, Y., & Gao, W. (2023). Large-scale multi-modal pre-trained models: A comprehensive survey. *Machine Intelligence Research, 20*(4), 447–482.

Yaqub, M., Asif, H., Kim, S., & Lee, W. (2020). Modeling of a full-scale sewage treatment plant to predict the nutrient removal efficiency using a long short-term memory (LSTM) neural network. *Journal of Water Process Engineering, 37,* 101388.

Yu, Y.-X., Gong, H.-P., Liu, H.-C., & Mou, X. (2023). Knowledge representation and reasoning using fuzzy Petri nets: a literature review and bibliometric analysis. *Artificial Intelligence Review, 56*(7), 6241–6265.

Zhang, X., Zhang, X., Chen, W., Li, C., & Yu, C. (2024). Improving speech depression detection using transfer learning with wav2vec 2.0 in low-resource environments. *Scientific Reports, 14*(1), 9543. https://doi.org/10.1038/s41598-024-60278-1

4

Multi-Criteria Decision-Making for Operating ATM Systems

Reetika Singh, Shivani Kalyan, and LN Das

4.1 Introduction

Multiple-criteria decision-making (MCDM) deals with cases of conflicting goals among decision-makers. Before explaining this in more detail, it is important to understand what we mean by the terms used in MCDM. Therefore, the criteria in decision-making define the degree of the judgment of the course of action as more desirable than the other. Considering the different options that conflict on a large scale becomes a problem of MCDM.

MCDM is generally characterized by the presence of complex, contradictory information that reflects different perspectives and changes over time. The MCDM's approach aims to assist decision-makers by organizing information in a certain way, considering possible conditions, and reducing the likelihood of remorse after the decision. It leads to a feeling of satisfaction and confidence about deciding which way is best. The best can be obtained by analyzing the different range of terms and conditional weights and choosing the most appropriate ones. By systematically weighing and relating trade between terms, the MCDM results in clear and consistent decisions.

In this sense, multi-criteria decision analysis (MCDA) describes a set of legal mechanisms that explicitly consider multiple conditions in guiding individuals or groups to make critical decisions. It has also seen an amazing amount of use in the last few decades. Its role in the various areas of application has increased significantly, especially as new methods and older methods develop.

There are some myths about the MCDA, one of which is that it will provide a "correct" answer, provide an "objective" analysis that will relieve decision-makers of the burden of making difficult decisions, and ease the pain of decision-making.

Despite the model used, we must understand that there is no such thing as a "correct answer." Because the concept of optimality does not relate to a multiple-criteria framework, MCDA cannot be excused from within the

DOI: 10.1201/9781032632483-4

development approach commonly adopted by ordinary performance research or management science. By using the MCDA, compliance can be clarified and regulated by mixing objective measurement and value judgment. As such, this is not an invalid submission; the MCDA merely attempts to be more transparent in its subjective judgments and to be explicit in its needs. While this is not always an easy process—for instance, trading is difficult—it cannot be avoided entirely. Through the MCDA, decision-makers will be able to identify these situations and assist in thinking of creative ways to overcome the need for complex trade, perhaps by promoting the development of new options. It can also maintain a level of equality by allowing inaccurate judgments, but it cannot eliminate the whole need for harsh judgments.

Overall, the MCDM aims to reduce the incidence and impact of bias from decision-makers relying on their "gut feeling," as well as the team's decision-making failure, which inevitably hampers decision-making. We believe the purpose of MCDA should be to evaluate the main benefits in order to help decision-makers learn about the problems they are facing, including priorities, organizations, values, and goals, and to evaluate these in context. The problem is in guiding them in identifying the preferred course of action.

Automated teller machines (ATMs) are essential for consumers to access their bank accounts, yet the cash withdrawal process involves a series of intricate validation steps designed to ensure both security and operational efficiency.

The MCDM framework relates to ATM systems because it provides a framework for prioritizing multiple conflicting factors that influence decision-making. We will discuss how they are interconnected in the following points.

Criteria Assessment: At each stage of ATM operation, multiple criteria are evaluated, such as the validity of the card, the accuracy of the PIN, the account balance, and the withdrawal limit. The MCDM automates the assessment and prioritization of these criteria to ensure that transactions are as secure and efficient as possible.

Decision-Making: At every stage of an ATM's operation, conflicts between competing criteria must be balanced, such as whether to dispense cash or block a card. Through MCDM techniques, ATMs are set up within defined parameters of security and service by analyzing potential trade-offs.

User Preferences: ATM operations are customized according to user preferences and behaviors using MCDM. As an example, it can enhance user experience by speeding up transactions, making them easier to use and providing security.

Performance Evaluation: The MCDM assists in evaluating ATM performance by analyzing various operational metrics, such as transaction success rates, downtime, and user satisfaction. It is possible to improve ATM functionality and design based on the results of this analysis.

Resource Management: As MCDM manages cash availability and maintenance schedules, resource allocation can be optimized. In addition to determining the best locations for servicing ATMs based on usage patterns and operational criteria, it also helps determine the best schedule for servicing ATMs.

This chapter presents a detailed examination of the multiple selection criteria evaluated by ATMs during cash withdrawals, outlining the various stages involved in the transaction process. When a user initiates a transaction, the ATM evaluates various criteria at each stage to ensure security and functionality. Initially, it checks the card's authenticity, including the hologram and magnetic stripe. If valid, the system verifies the PIN, followed by criteria related to the withdrawal amount, such as account balance and cash availability. Each of these checks is crucial for a successful transaction and helps prevent errors and fraud. We developed an abstract transition model of the operating ATM system using multi-criteria decision-making (MCDM), which we define as a non-deterministic Turing machine referred to as DATAMST. We structure it as a seven-tuple $(S, C, \Sigma, b, F, \delta, \gamma)$, where S represents the set of valid states in the ATM system compassing 14 distinct operational states. C denotes the multiple criteria applicable at each state, while Σ includes binary events (0 or 1). The symbol b represents a blank state. The set F identifies the final state. The transition function, δ, defines how the ATM moves between states. In our model, we compute all the possible decisions that the ATM processor can make at each state with the help of the transition state table.

This paper is organized as follows: Section 2 provides a detailed literature review. Section 3 focuses on classification techniques for addressing the MCDM (multi-criteria decision-making) problem, specifically exploring multi-objective and multi-attribute decision-making approaches. In Section 4, we examine the ATM operating system, covering the fundamental components of the ATM, its functionality, and key features. Section 5 delves into the theory of computation, with an emphasis on languages, grammars, finite automata, and a thorough exploration of deterministic and non-deterministic finite automata, culminating in a discussion of the Turing machine. Section 6 presents our proposed methodology, outlining the various selection criteria at each operational stage of the ATM. Section 7 highlights the challenges encountered in ATM systems following the discussion of the proposed model. Finally, Section 8 offers the conclusion of our work.

4.2 Literature Survey

The first official example of the MCDM approach is seen in Benjamin Franklin's "moral or intellectual algebra" from 1772, in which he discussed how to determine important issues on a simple paper [1]. Write down the positive arguments for the decision on one side and write down the arguments against it on another side. Next, eliminate all issues on each side of the paper that are related and equally significant. In the absence of all disputes on one side, the side with the remaining arguments must be supported. Franklin used this method when making critical decisions.

Bernard et al. formed ELECTRE, a family of Europe's multi-criteria decision-making techniques [2]. They aim to create a targeted network of preferences. By putting these methods into practice, you create superior decisions or decisions that are the best. Then the EURO Working Group called Multiple Criteria Decision Aiding was founded by Roy [3]. Ralph et al. [4] published their final book, *Decisions with Multiple Objectives: Preferences and Value Trade-Offs*. This book was instrumental in establishing the refined methods for choosing between more than just two alternatives, and it involves many decision-makers who gave birth to a multi-qualification theory as a discipline that has become a common indicator and text for many generations of decision-making research and the MCDM.

Surprised by the multicriteria crisis, Stanley Zionts met Jyrki Wallenius at the European Institute for Advanced Studies in Management in Brussels. Collectively, they have worked on methods and systems to support problem-solving decisions for many interactive multiple-objective mathematical programming systems. In 1979, the Zionists helped develop the MCDM summary with his management article: "MCDM—If Not Roman numerals, Then What?" [5]. Daniel et al. made significant contributions to the ethics of behavioral decision theory, and Kahneman went on to win the Nobel Prize in Economics in 2002 for his contributions to this field [5]. It is widely believed that if Tversky had lived, he would have shared the Nobel Prize with Kahneman.

MCDM is widely applicable across various fields, including economics, engineering, healthcare, and environmental management, where decision-makers must assess numerous alternatives based on diverse criteria. Over the years, MCDM has evolved, with new methods and advancements emerging to improve decision-making accuracy, robustness, and computational efficiency. This review outlines recent developments in MCDM techniques, focusing on hybrid models, applications of machine learning (ML) and artificial intelligence (AI), fuzzy logic, and sustainability assessments. Kahraman et al. [6] provided a comprehensive literature review on the applications of fuzzy logic in MCDM, highlighting its flexibility in handling uncertainty. Petrovic et al. developed a hybridized IT2FS-DEMATEL-AHP-TOPSIS multi-criteria decision-making approach to study the selection and evaluation of criteria for the determination of air traffic control radar position [7]. Additionally, Yazdani et al. incorporated machine learning techniques into hybrid MCDM models to enhance their predictive capabilities [8].

The use of MCDM has also expanded into new domains. Mardani et al. examined the integration of sustainability criteria into MCDM frameworks, reflecting the growing importance of environmental and social factors [9]. Stojčić et al. explored the application of MCDM methods for risk assessment, demonstrating the versatility of these techniques in decision-making under uncertainty [10]. Building upon these developments, Alamri et al. introduced a hybrid entropy-based MCDM framework to analyze the economic evaluation of hydrogen generation techniques [11].

In the context of automated teller machine (ATM) operations, multiple interrelated factors, such as security, efficiency, cost, and user satisfaction, must be managed simultaneously. MCDM techniques have been increasingly applied to optimize decision-making processes within ATM systems. Recent applications include Tseng et al. utilizing a hybrid DEMATEL-ANP method to assess security risks and the interdependencies between security measures and operational factors in ATM networks [12]. Luthra et al. employed hybrid MCDM models, such as AHP-TOPSIS, to optimize cash replenishment and reduce logistics costs [13]. Yildiz et al. propose an integrated methodology combining interval-valued intuitionistic fuzzy analytic hierarchy process (AHP) and technique for order of preference by similarity to ideal solution (TOPSIS) to determine the safest routes for cash-in-transit operations in Istanbul, addressing uncertainties in the decision-making process [14]. Tunç et al. propose a hybrid fuzzy AHP and arithmetic optimization algorithm to optimize cash management in ATMs, enhancing operational efficiency and cost-effectiveness [15].

4.3 Classification for Solving MCDM Problems

Multi-criteria decision-making is classified into the following categories.

4.3.1 Multi-Objective Decision-Making (MODM)

This stems from the idea that multi-objective decision-making is concerned with problems in which we have a continuous decision space, such as mathematical programming problems with multiple objective functions. The first reference to this problem, also known as the vector-maximum problem, was given by Kuhn and Tucker in 1951. [16]

4.3.2 Multi-Attribute Decision-Making (MADM)

Multi-attribute decision-making concentrates on those decision problems in which we have discrete decision spaces. In these problems, the set of alternatives has been predetermined. Even though its methods are wide-ranging, many of them share certain characteristics [17].

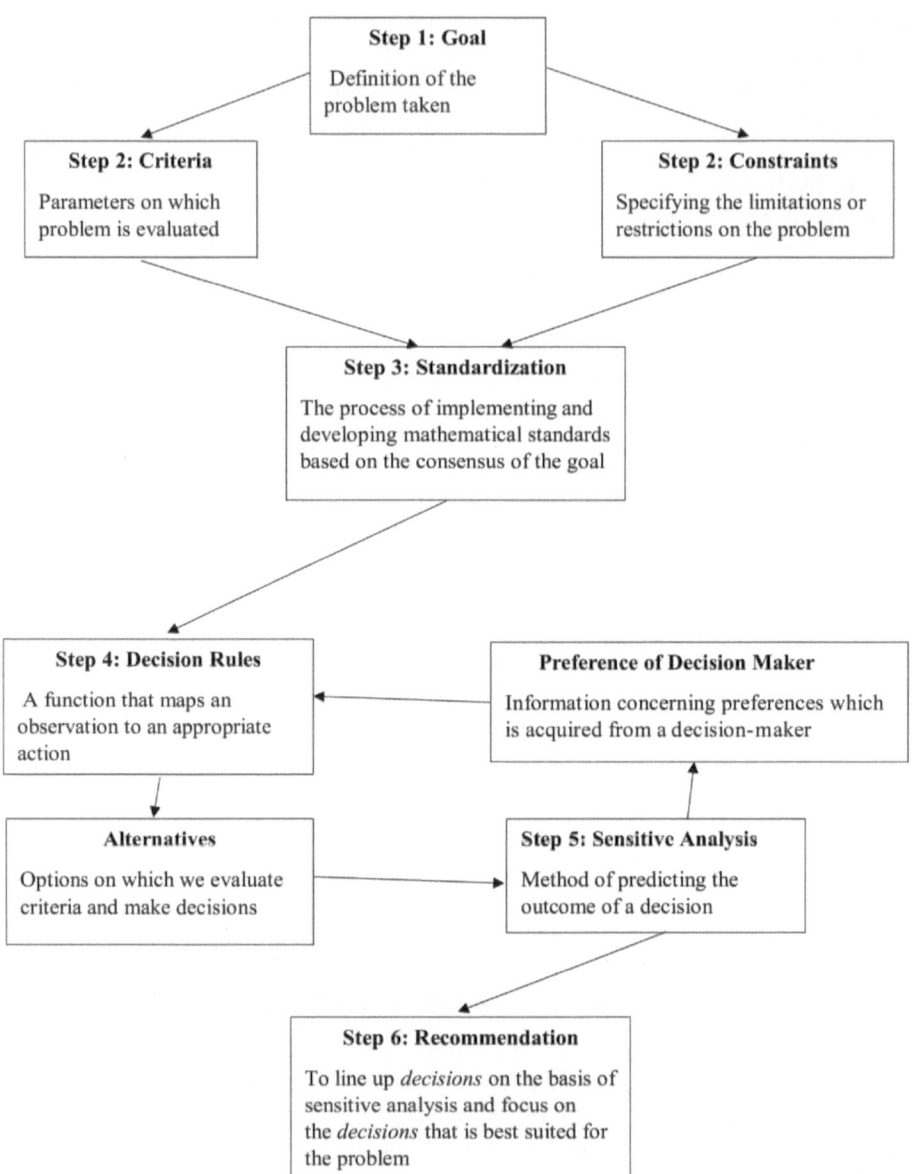

FIGURE 4.1
Approach for solving the MCDM problem.

Table 4.1 describes the key differences between these categories.

TABLE 4.1

Differences Between MODM and MADM

MODM	MADM
1. When there are several objectives to make a decision. These objectives are the constraints.	When several alternatives are carried out based on various attributes of the object to make a decision.
2. The objectives considered are functions: $f_1, f_2, f_3, \ldots$	We consider alternatives: $A_1, A_2, A_3, \ldots A_n$
3. The objectives or goals are explicitly defined as: Example: While buying some products, we need to maximize the quality as well as the savings.	The objectives are implicitly defined, i.e., we don't directly say we need to maximize the profit. Example: If we are selecting the candidates out of 50 applicants for our company.
4. Attributes are defined implicitly. Example: Maximize $f(x)$ Subject to $g(x) \leq 0$	Attributes are defined explicitly Example: To evaluate an applicant for a job, we need to evaluate his/her • Resume. • Experience. • Knowledge.
5. Alternatives are infinite in number. That is, we can have a very large number of feasible solutions.	Alternatives are finite in number. Example: While selecting a candidate we are taking not millions of alternatives but a small (finite) number of alternatives.
6. Alternatives are implicit.	Alternatives are explicit.
7. The modeling paradigm is process-oriented.	The modeling paradigm is outcome-oriented.

4.4 ATM Operating System

The automated teller machine, also known as an ATM, is money transmission equipment that is one of the best developments in the banking sector. Using an ATM, customers can perform several quick self-help functions, including withdrawals, deposits, and transfers.

There were some groups around the world in the 1960s, working independently to devise a way to withdraw money from the bank by committing no crime. In 1959, an American named Luther George Simjian founded the Bankograph, which allowed customers to place cash and checks on it [18]. The first ATM was established in June 1967 on the road in Enfield, London, at the Barclays bank branch [18]. The British founder John Shepherd-Barron is said to have been founded. Customers have been able to withdraw up to the GBP10 limit within a set period.

Almost all countries now use ATMs. Over the past 50 years, ATMs have become ubiquitous. ATMs have eliminated the need to visit a bank branch for simple banking transactions, such as depositing cash or withdrawing cash. Gone are the days when customers primarily used bank branches during business hours.

ATMs fall into two categories:

1. Basic ATMs allow customers to withdraw cash and receive account balance information.

2. Another one is the more sophisticated deposit processing machine, which provides credit card payment services and reports account details.

4.4.1 Basic Parts of ATM

Card Reader: Every ATM has a card slot. An ATM card's magnetic stripe captures account information via the device's card reader when the card is swiped or pressed against the reader [19].

The host processor uses this information to deliver the transaction to the cardholder's bank.

Key Pad: A keypad is given in all ATMs where you can insert numbers to enter the PIN or the amount to be withdrawn. The keypad also allows the cardholder to tell the bank what type of work will be required such as withdrawals, balance checks, etc. These keypads can either be physical buttons at an ATM or virtual keypad on the touch screen.

Speaker: There is a speaker in most of the ATMs where the auditory instructions for accessing the machine and doing transactions are given.

Display Screen: In addition to being a guide to the operator at every stage of the transaction, the display screen shows information to the cardholder. Leased-line ATMs usually use a monochrome or CRT color (cathode ray tube) display while dial-up ATMs usually use a monochrome or color LCD [20].

Receipt Printer: It records all the details of the transaction, like the type of transaction, amounts withdrawn, date and time, and the remaining balance of your account in the receipt. On request, the printer prints out a worksheet receipt for the cardholder [21].

Cash Dispenser: It is called the heart of an ATM. From this, you can collect cash after withdrawing a certain amount. The entire lower part of ATMs is a cash-containing filter. The cash dispenser calculates each bill and provides the required amount. Money is stored securely in the automated teller machine by bank officials.

All of these actions are performed by sensors of high accuracy. The ATM maintains a complete record of all transactions with the aid of the RTC.

4.4.2 How Does the ATM Work?

First Step: You need to swipe your ATM card. A card reader is installed inside the machine. The card reader reads the magnetic stripe of the card and stores the amount recorded on it (which shouldn't be scratched) [22].

Second Step: A message is displayed on the screen i.e., "ENTER PIN." First, the bank assigns each account holder a PIN, which is then changed by that account holder. As soon as the user enters the PIN, the machine encodes the PIN, and it is sent to the host processor, which then connects it to the bank terminal. To verify the accuracy of the PIN, the processor compares it to the recorded information.

Third Step: ATM sends the request i.e., "Request Amount." Input from the ATM is sent to the host processor, which then forwards it to the networks for approval, such as Visa, Master Card, etc.

Fourth Step: As soon as the network requests the withdrawal, the bank checks to see whether that amount is available on the customer's account.

Fifth Step: By saying YES, the bank makes an electronic transfer to the account of the host processor. The host will forward the authorization code to the bank.

Sixth Step: Bills in the cash cartridges under or at the back of the computer screen are calculated by the electronic eye and pushed out of the cash slot.

4.4.3 Features of ATM

1. **Versatility of ATM:** ATM is not bound to only dispense cash, but also you can get certain facilities such as:
   - Depositing the cash,
   - Transferring funds between connected bank accounts,
   - Paying bills,
   - Finding the account balance,
   - Printing a list of recent activities,
   - Generating mini-statements.

2. **User-Friendly:** It is designed in such a way that anyone can use it. Even illiterate individuals and especially abled people. With the introduction of biometric identification scanners and speakers, it has become easier for users.

3. **Less Language Barrier:** In a country like India where many languages are spoken, ATMs need to be multilingual to operate properly. You can use the ATM of your comfort language. You can also perform a range of features in your foreign language as well.

4.5 Theory of Computation

In the course of our research, we will explore the working of ATMs in the domain of theory of computation, which is defined in three fundamental ideas: languages, grammars, and automata. First, we discuss the definition of these parameters in formal languages and then illustrate the process of the Turing machine.

4.5.1 Language

According to the definition provided in the dictionary, language involves the use of symbols and ambiguous rules to convey ideas, facts, or concepts. This definition allows us to grasp the concept of language intuitively; however, it isn't enough to define the meaning of the language used in formal languages. Language in a formal language is a subdivision of set Σ that's defined for a finite and non-empty set of symbols known as the alphabet. Here set is denoted by this Σ [23]. From each symbol, we form strings, which are a finite sequence of symbols from the alphabet.

4.5.2 Grammar

Since we know that our daily language is vague and inaccurate, informal definitions in English are often inadequate. So we learn a common and powerful concept, namely grammar. In the English language, well-formed sentences are indicated by grammar. The same idea is expressed in formal languages.

In natural languages, Grammar indicates a finite set of syntactical rules for establishing meaningful conversations. Chomsky provided the mathematical model of grammar in 1956 who is very good at writing computer languages. Grammar plays a key role in defining ways to learn natural languages mathematically [24].

Definition: A grammar G is defined as a quadruple $G = (V, T, S, P)$ where

V is a finite set of objects called variables,

T is a finite set of objects called terminal symbols,

S belongs to V, a special symbol called the start variable,

P is a finite set of productions [25]. By defining the production rules, grammar is defined as a process of transforming one string into another, and, by doing so, the language associated with that grammar is defined.

Here we also assume that the sets *V* and *T* are non-empty and disjoint. So, by applying the production rules in a different order, grammar can generate a variety of strings. All of these terminal strings are collectively referred to as grammar's language, which is the language defined by the grammar.
Definition: Let $G = \{V, T, S, P\}$ be a grammar. Then the set

$$L(G) = \{w \in T : S \Rightarrow w\}$$

is the language generated by the grammar G [25].
Here if $w \in L(G)$ then the sequence $S \Rightarrow w_1 \Rightarrow w_2 \Rightarrow w_3 \Rightarrow \ldots \ldots \Rightarrow w_n \Rightarrow w$ is derived from the sentence w, the strings $S, w_1, w_2, w_3, \ldots w_n$, which contain variables as well as terminals, are called sentential forms of derivation.
4.5.3 Automata An automaton is an abstract digital computer model. It has an input reader. A series of characters, i.e., strings are assumed to be the input written on an input file, which is read by the automaton but not changed by it.
Figure 4.2 shows a schematic representation of a general automaton.
In this, each **input file** is divided into cells, and each input file can hold one symbol [26]. The input mechanism reads the input file one symbol at a time, left to right. It is also possible to sense the end of an input string via the end-of-file condition in the input mechanism. The automaton produces the **output** of some form, which may have a temporary **storage** device, consisting of an unlimited number of cells, each capable of holding a single symbol from an alphabet that is not necessarily the same one as the input alphabet [26]. Automatons can read and change the content of storage cells.

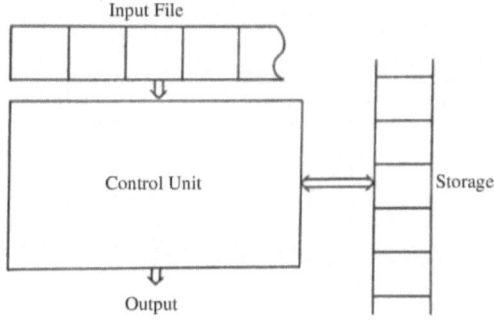

FIGURE 4.2
Schematic representation of a general automaton.

Last but not least, the automaton has a **control unit** that can be in one of a few limited internal states and can change its state in a defined manner.

It is assumed that the automaton operates in a distinct time frame. A control unit is in a particular state at any given time, and the input method scans a certain symbol on the input file. The next state or transition function establishes the **internal state** of the control unit at the next time step.

This **transition function** provides the following state depending on the current state, the current input symbol, and the information currently in temporary storage. The output may be generated or the temporary storage may be updated during the transition from one period to another. The term **configuration** is used whenever we refer to a specific state of a control unit, input file, and temporary storage [26]. Furthermore, the act of moving an automaton from one configuration to another is called a **move**.

4.5.3 Finite Automata

Finite automata, or finite state machines, are the simplest abstract machines that can recognize patterns. They have five elements or tuples. The input symbol determines the tool's state and rules for moving from one state to another. In essence, it functions as an abstract digital machine model. Figure 4.3 describes some of the key components of general automation.

There are two types of automata:

1. Deterministic automata
2. Non-deterministic automata

4.5.3.1 Deterministic Finite Automata (DFA)

As the name suggests, deterministic automata determine their movements separately by the current configuration. Knowing the internal state, inputs,

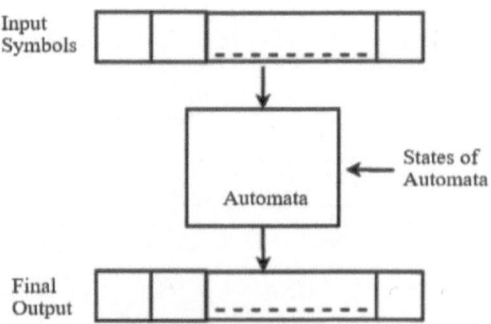

FIGURE 4.3
Key components of finite automata.

and contents of temporary storage will provide us with an exact prediction of how the future automaton will behave.

Acceptors are automatons that respond with only a "yes" or "no" when asked. When presented with an input string, an accepter either accepts or rejects the string. There is a more general automaton known as a transducer that can produce strings of symbols as output. By deterministic, we mean that when the input symbols are read, the automaton changes its current state to another state or may remain in the same state.

Definition: A deterministic finite automaton (DFA) is defined by a quintuple that consists of five-tuples $\{S, \delta, s, F, \Sigma\}$ where

S is a set of all states,

Σ is a set of input symbols that the machine takes as input,

s: is the initial state of a machine,

F: is a set of the final state,

δ: is the transition function, defined as $\delta: S \times \Sigma \to S$ [27].

The DFA machine stays in only one state at a time for particular character input. Every state has its transition function. Null (or $\in$) moves are also forbidden in DFA; i.e., DFA cannot change state without input.

4.5.3.2 Non-Deterministic Finite Automata

On the other hand, a non-deterministic automaton may have a wide range of possible moves at any given point, so we can only anticipate a handful of possibilities. A non-deterministic finite automata is a state machine that consists of states and transitions capable of either accepting or rejecting a finite string.

Symbols in non-deterministic finite automata can undergo several transitions from the same state. It is similar to deterministic finite automata, except for the following additional features:

It is allowed to perform a null (or ε) move, which is to say it can proceed forward without reading symbols.

A particular input can be transmitted to any number of states.

An NFA consists of a quintuple (or five-tuple) such that $M = (S, \Sigma, \delta, s, F)$, where

S is a finite set of all states,

Σ is a finite set of all symbols of the alphabet,

$\delta: S \times (\{\Sigma \cup \varepsilon\}) \to 2S$ is the transition function from state to state,

$s \in S$ is the start state, in which the start state must be in the set S,

$F \subseteq S$ is the set of accept states, in which the accept states must be in the set S. [28] Here, the order of the elements does matter.

The standard Turing machine shows deterministic behavior as one can either go in the left direction or the right direction for a particular input, whereas, in the case of a non-deterministic Turing machine, one can go in both directions.

4.5.4 Turing Machine

A Turing machine is an imaginary machine that reads an infinite tape through which it interacts with the outside world. A tape is divided into cells with symbols (one symbol at a time) or blank spaces, and, as the reading progresses, the output is recorded on that tape as well. A "head" is placed on a specific cell of the tape that moves left (L) or right (R) one cell at a time as it performs reads and writes. We may say, therefore, that the computation in the Turing machine is done with the help of a transition function, which directs the machine on how to react to the symbols on the tape.

The Turing machine was first proposed by Alan Turing in 1936 [29]. Unlike physical machines, Turing machines are mathematical machine objects. Turing proposed that it is not necessary to discuss how the machine actually does its work. It is enough to believe that it can accomplish the actions as specified and to believe that those actions can be uniquely described.

Alternatively, Turing machines can be called general-purpose computers having infinite tapes.

It consists of the control unit that helps to read the current tape symbol, writes a symbol on the tape, moves one place to the left or right, switches to the following state, which is read as, "If the machine is in the current state, i.e., $State_{current}$, and the cell being scanned contains Symbol, then move into the next state, i.e., $State_{next \text{ taking action.}}$"

A Turing machine can therefore mark a symbol on the tape in the current cell or move the head cell left or right while acting. However, if it reaches a point where it cannot make a particular/unique transition, it is said to halt.

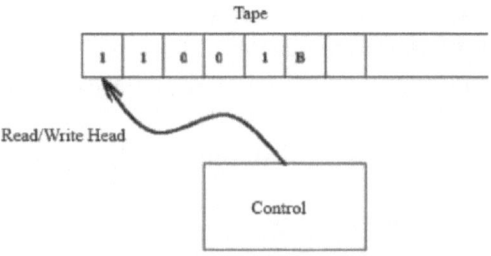

FIGURE 4.4
Turing machine where each transition of the machine is a four-tuple, which can be represented as ($State_{current}$, Symbol, $State_{next}$, Action).

Moreover, one could consider a Turing machine as a finite-state machine that resides in a horizontal form stretched across an infinitely long tape containing symbols from a finite alphabet Σ. Based on the symbol it's currently reading and its current state, the Turing machine writes a new symbol "0" or "1" in that location, moves left or right, or stays in place, and then enters a new state. The numbers "0" and "1" denote blanks and symbols, respectively.

The transition function on the machine gives instructions on how to perform various tasks, such as overwriting a symbol, moving left or right, entering a new state, optionally stopping, and outputting an answer given the current state and symbol that the machine is reading.

Definition

Turing machines are composed of seven-tuples $(S, s_0, \Gamma, b, \Sigma, F, \sigma)$, where:

S is a finite set of states with one of them $s_0 \in S$ being a designated starting state, which is defined as a state the machine starts its operation in,

Γ is a finite set of symbols with one of them $b \in \Gamma$ being a designated starting state, $\Sigma \subset \Gamma$ is a subset of input symbols,

$P \subset S$ is a subset of accepting states that finalizes the computation that is when the machine reaches F, the computation's final state,

$\sigma: S \times \Gamma \rightarrow S \times \Gamma \times \{L, R\}$ is a partial transition function [30].

If the machine reaches a state and inputs that are not defined for σ, the machine will halt. Here, in this transition function, $s_0 \in S$ represents the start state, $s_{accept} \in S$ represents the accepted state, and $s_{reject} \in S$ represents the reject state, where $s_{accept} \neq s_{reject}$.

The transition function σ is referred to as the heart of Turing machines because it describes how the machine moves between different configurations.

Since the transition function σ tells us how the machine gets from one configuration to another, it is also known as the heart of a Turing machine. In Turing machines, one's current state, tape content, and head location describe its configuration.

The machine at state $s \in S$ reads the current symbol $\gamma \in \Gamma$ on the tape loading to

$$\sigma(s, \gamma) = (s^1, \gamma^1, d)$$

where:
s^1 is the next state,
γ^1 is the output symbol written by the head on the tape,
$d \in \{L, R\}$ is the movement of the head (left or right) on the infinite tape [30].

Example
The following examples can be modeled as a Turing machine.

Text Editor as a Turing Machine: A text editor can be effectively modeled as a Turing machine to formally represent its core functionality and behavior. In this conceptual framework, the different states (S) of the Turing machine correspond to the various modes or states of the text editor software, such as insert mode, delete mode, copy/paste mode, and so on. The set of tape symbols (Γ) represents the repertoire of characters that can be entered into the document, including letters, numbers, special characters, and punctuation.

The transition function (σ) of the Turing machine then describes how the text editor transitions between these different states based on the user's interactions—such as pressing a key, clicking a button, or invoking a command. As the user makes edits, the Turing machine updates the contents of the tape, which represents the evolving text document being edited, as well as the position of the tape head, which corresponds to the cursor location. Starting from an initial state (s_0) when the document is opened, the Turing machine follows a sequence of state transitions, modifying the tape contents and tape head position until it reaches a final state representing the completed, edited document. This formal model provides a rigorous, step-by-step account of how a text editor operates at a fundamental computational level.

Traffic Light Control System as a Turing Machine: Similarly, a traffic light control system can be mapped to a Turing machine representation to capture its core algorithmic logic and functionality [31]. In this case, the states (S) of the Turing machine correspond to the different phases of the traffic light cycle, such as red, green, yellow, and all-red. The tape symbols (Γ) represent the inputs received from vehicle and pedestrian sensors, as well as any user-initiated requests like pedestrian crossing buttons.

The transition function (σ) of the Turing machine then specifies how the traffic light control system transitions between these various states based on the sensor data and user inputs it receives, as well as the current state of the traffic lights. As vehicles and pedestrians interact with the intersection, the Turing machine updates the tape, which serves as a record of the changing traffic patterns. Through this sequence of state transitions controlled by the transition function, the Turing machine model governs the dynamic adjustment of traffic signal timing and sequencing to optimize traffic flow, enhance safety, and minimize congestion at the intersection. This formal representation provides a rigorous framework for analyzing and reasoning about the core algorithmic principles underlying traffic light control systems.

In both the text editor and traffic light control system examples, the Turing machine model offers a precise, step-by-step computational account of how these systems operate and respond to user/environmental inputs. By mapping the core components of state, tape symbols, and transition functions, the Turing machine framework enables a formal, algorithmic understanding of these real-world software and control systems.

4.6 Multiple Selection Criteria at Each Working Stage of ATM

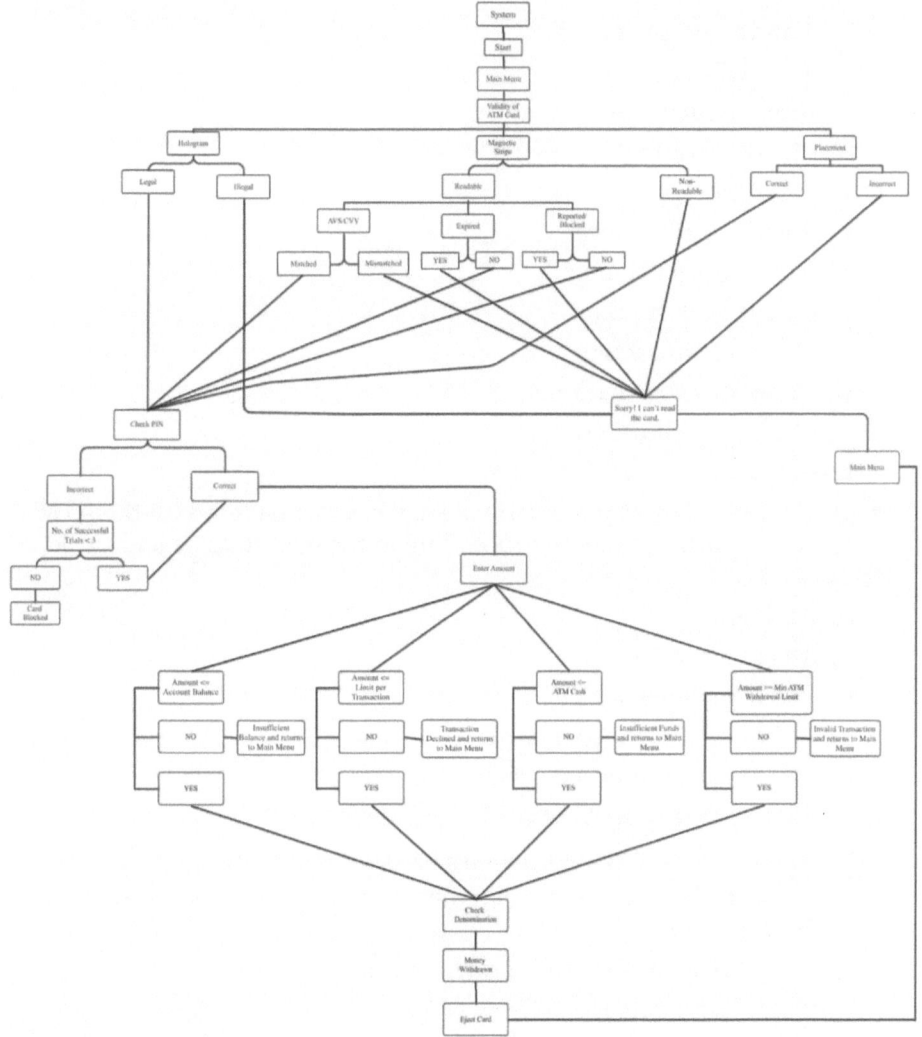

FIGURE 4.5
Transition model of multiple selection criteria at each stage of ATM.

4.6.1 Notations/Terminologies for Determination of Transition Table and Graph

The formal model of an operating ATM system using MCDM is defined as a non-deterministic Turing machine DATAMST.

DATAMST | | $(S, C, \Sigma, s, b, \delta, F)$ represents seven-tuple relationships where:

- S is the set of valid states that represents the domain of the working of the ATM system; in $S = \{s_0, s_1, s_2, \ldots, s_{13}\}$ here the states are:

  s_0 –System

  s_1 –Main menu

  s_2 –Validity of ATM card

  s_3 –Check PIN.

  s_4 – Sorry! Can't read the card.

  s_5 – Enter amount.

  s_6 –Card blocked

  s_7 –Insufficient balance

  s_8 –Transaction declined

  s_9 –Insufficient funds

  s_{10} –Invalid transaction

  s_{11} –Check denomination

  s_{12} –Money withdrawn

  s_{13} –Eject card.

- C is the set of multiple criteria at each state considered by the ATM to make a decision before proceeding to the next state, where $C = \{c_1, c_2, \ldots, c_8\}$:

  c_1 –Hologram

  c_2 –Magnetic stripe

  c_{21} –CVV matches with AVS or not.

  c_{22} –ATM card is expired or not.

  c_{23} –ATM card is blocked/reported or not.

  c_3 –Placement of the ATM card

  c_4 –When the number of unsuccessful trials is greater than 3

  c_5 –Account balance is greater than the amount to be withdrawn or not.

  c_6 – Limit per transaction is crossed or not.

  c_7 – Cash availability at ATM

  c_8 – Minimum ATM withdrawal limit is crossed or not.

- Σ is the set of events that the ATM may accept and process, $\Sigma = \{0,1\}$.

- s is the start state of the ATM, $s = s_1$ (main menu).
- b is the blank symbol; this happens when we insert a card but do not perform any action.
- F is the set of ending set, $F = \{s13\}$ (eject card).
- δ is the transition function of the ATM that determines the next state of the Turing machine, s_{i+1}, based on the current state s_i and a specific incoming event $\{0,1\}$, i.e.,

$$s_{i+1} + 1 = \delta(s_t, \{0,1\}), \text{ where}, \delta = f : (S,C) \times \Sigma \rightarrow S.$$

4.6.2 State Transition Table

Table 4.2 shows the state transition table.

TABLE 4.2

State Transition Table

States	Σ	Next State
(s_0)	b	$\{s_0\}$
(s_0)	0	$\{s_0\}$
(s_0)	1	$\{s_1\}$
(s_1)	0	$\{s_1\}$
(s_1)	1	$\{s_2\}$
(s_2, c_1)	0	$\{s_4\}$
(s_2, c_1)	1	$\{s_4, s_3\}$
(s_2, c_2)	0	$\{s_4\}$
(s_2, c_2)	1	$\{s_4, s_3\}$
(s_2, c_3)	0	$\{s_4\}$
(s_2, c_3)	1	$\{s_4, s_3\}$
(s_3)	1	$\{s_5\}$
(s_3, c_4)	0	$\{s_5\}$
(s_3, c_4)	1	$\{s_6\}$
(s_4)	1	$\{s_1\}$
(s_5, c_5)	0	$\{s_7\}$
(s_5, c_5)	1	$\{s_{11}\}$
(s_5, c_6)	0	$\{s_8\}$
(s_5, c_6)	1	$\{s_{11}\}$
(s_5, c_7)	0	$\{s_9\}$
(s_5, c_7)	1	$\{s_{11}\}$
(s_5, c_8)	0	$\{s_{10}\}$
(s_5, c_8)	1	$\{s_{11}\}$
(s_{11})	1	$\{s_{12}\}$
(s_{12})	1	$\{s_{13}\}$

TABLE 4.3

Transition Behavior of State s_2

c_1	c_2	c_3	F
0	0	0	$\{s_4, s_{13}\}$
0	0	1	
0	1	0	
0	1	1	
1	0	0	
1	0	1	
1	1	0	
1	1	1	$\{s_3\}$

Using all of the possible decisions based on the following criteria, Table 4.3 illustrates the transition behavior of state s_2.

Here we can observe from this table that the transition behavior of state s_2 is determined by three criteria that are c_1, c_2, and c_3. Therefore, the total number of possible decisions made from this criterion will be $2^3 = 8$. This signifies that ATM can face eight possible scenarios on the state s_2, out of which only one decision will lead to that next state s_3 i.e. (1,1,1) case, and the rest will lead to the states $\{s_4, s_{13}\}$.

Similarly, we can define the transition behavior for states s_3 and s_5. We can observe from Figure 4.6 that the transition behavior of state s_3 is determined from a single criterion c_4, and state s_5 is determined by four criteria. Therefore, ATMs can face $2^1 = 2$, $2^4 = 16$ scenarios on state s_3 and s_5, respectively.

4.6.3 Explanation of Multiple Selection Criteria at Each Stage of the ATM System

In this section, we have described the multiple selection criteria evaluated by ATMs during cash withdrawal at each working stage. This is a multi-attribute decision-making problem as it deals with multiple attributes and has a single objective, which is to withdraw money.

4.6.3.1 State 1: Main Menu

This is the first stage of ATM where it shows the main ATM functions. When withdrawing money from an ATM, a user selects the withdrawal option from the menu and inserts the respective ATM card.

4.6.3.2 State 2: Validity of ATM Card

When the user places the ATM Card inside the machine, the ATM first checks the validity of the card by considering the following criteria.

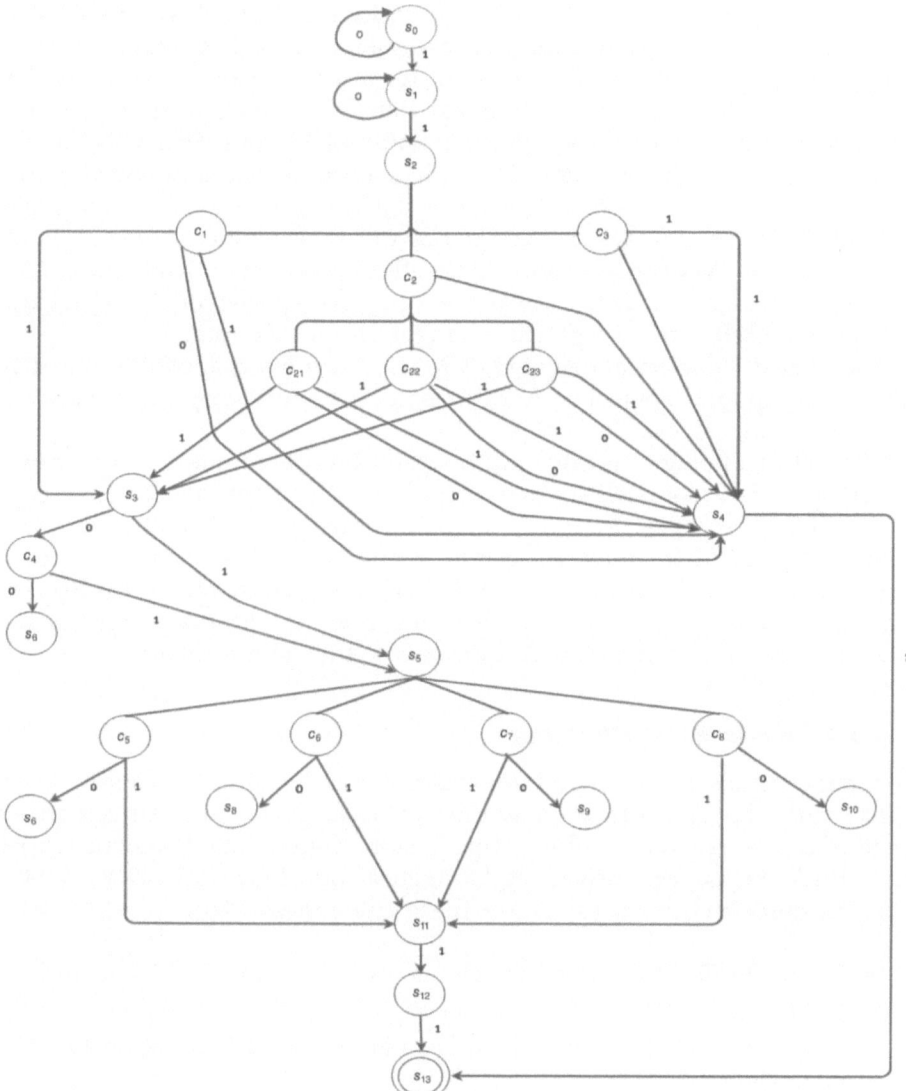

FIGURE 4.6
Abstract transition model of multiple selection criteria at each stage of ATM.

4.6.3.3 Criteria 1-Hologram

Payments can be processed more securely when using debit/ATM card holograms. If someone pays you with a card, it is crucial that you look at the hologram to confirm it is real. It indicates a valid card and is a valid identification. In the absence of a hologram, an issue may exist with the card or the card may be forged by the person using it.

A card reader is installed in ATMs to perform this function. The ATM is designed with a hologram code reading system that utilizes reconstruction light from a light source to illuminate the recorded areas of the hologram that contain codified data recorded as image data, and a code reading sensor is positioned at the reconstruction position within the reconstruction image created by the reconstruction light. The code reading sensor is provided with a control means to obtain codified data from the hologram reconstruction image.

Multiple layers of images are stacked on top of each other to create a hologram on the ATM card. This adds to the illusion of motion when the card is moved even slightly. Due to the way the image is displayed on the ATM card, it appears raised above the plastic, giving it a sense of depth.

The security hologram, invented by MasterCard International in the early 1980s, now appears not just on ATMs, credit cards, and passports, but also on electronic gadgets and banknotes.

The fact that holograms are multi-imaged prevents counterfeiting because the images of a hologram cannot be captured with an optical scanner or copied with a photocopier. Moreover, holograms are generally embedded with images that can be instantly verified to ensure immediate security.

In this way, ATMs verify whether the card inserted by the user is legal or not. In the case of a legal card, it will move forward with the process; otherwise, it rejects the card and directs the user to the main menu.

4.6.3.4 Criteria 2-Magnetic Stripe

Magnetic stripes are an imperative criterion for checking the validity of an ATM card. This stripe appears on the back of an ATM card. A magnetized pattern can be recorded on this stripe to store digital data. Magnetic stripes have three tracks, each measuring 110 inches wide. In accordance with ISO/IEC standard 7811, the bank follows these guidelines:

- There are 79 read-only characters on track one with 210 bits per inch (bpi).
- Track two is 75 bits per inch and can hold 40 four-bit plus parity bit characters.
- There are 107 four-bit plus parity bit characters on track three at 210 bps.

The ATM card utilizes only the first two tracks. The third track consists of the country code, units of currency, PIN protected by cryptography, and the authorized amount. However, its use is not standardized among banks.

There are two formats of track one information, A, which is reserved for the card issuer, and B, which includes the start sentinel of 1 character with format code="B". The primary account number varies by up to 19 characters: separator; 1 character, country code: 3 characters, name; 2 to 26 characters, separator; a single character, the expiration date or separator, which may differ from 1 character to 4 characters, discretionary data: 79 characters in total which is enough to fill out the maximum record length; end sentinel of 1 character, and longitudinal redundancy check (LRC); a computed check character, a single character [32].

Track two follows a format developed by the banking industry, with a start sentinel of 1 character, primary account number of up to 19 characters, a separator of 1 character, country code of 2 characters, expiration date or separator of up to 4 characters, discretionary data of 40 characters in total, which is sufficient to fulfill the maximum record length, and LRC of 1 character.

At an ATM, the validity of an ATM card is determined by electronic data capture (EDC) [33]. By inserting the ATM card through the card reader, the EDC software calls an acquirer by dialing a number stored in a modem. Acquirers are the computers that process ATM authentication requests and provide a transaction guarantee from the bank to the ATM.

As soon as the acquirer receives the card authentication request, it checks the transaction for validity and reads the record on the magnetic stripe. This record contains the valid card number, expiration date, ATM card limit, and usage.

It is probably either one of the following that is preventing the ATM from reading the card:

- The magnetic stripe is dirty or scratched.
- Magnetic stripes can be erased due to exposure to magnets and a store's electronic article surveillance tag demagnetizer.

4.6.3.5 Mismatch in AVS and CVV (c_{21})

An AVS or CVV error can also result in a transaction being declined. Card verification value (CVV) is a three-digit number on the back of your ATM card that acts as a security code. Banks develop the address verification system (AVS) to detect suspicious transactions.

There is a possibility of suspicious transactions when too many PINs are being fed at once at an ATM or observing spending patterns that differ from your usual habits. Many banks now have a whole upgraded system of security in place which can be way too safe and block your card.

Consequently, when you insert your ATM card at an ATM and these two security systems are mismatched with the data stored at the bank, your transaction will not be processed.

4.6.3.6 Expiry Date of ATM Card (c_{22})

There is an expiration date on every ATM card. There is an expiration date on the back of the card, written as XX/XX (month and year). A card can be used until the last day of the month in which it expires. For example: a card ending in 11/25 is valid until 30 November 2025. In such a case, your account will remain active but not your card.

Before proceeding with any transaction, the ATM checks whether the ATM card has passed its expiration date. Your old card will likely be declined if you try to use it after its expiration date, or the ATM will swallow it.

4.6.3.7 Blocked/Reported ATM Card (c_{23})

ATM also checks whether the user is using a blocked or reported card. Using such a card for the transaction will prevent the ATM from returning it and processing the transaction.

4.6.3.8 Criteria 3-Placement

When we swipe our ATM card into the card reader, a green light above the card reader will blink to indicate that the card has been properly inserted and access has been granted. A red light will blink, and the access will be rejected if the card is not positioned correctly.

Inserting an ATM card the right way requires the magnetic stripe to be at the bottom and the chip of the card must be facing up at the front.

You may be asked to return your card after your transaction has been completed by some ATMs, while others will simply ask for it back after reading the information stored on your card.

In most cases, the ATM will proceed with its process if the card is placed correctly; otherwise, it will prompt you to place it correctly.

4.6.3.9 State 3: Check PIN

If all the conditions of validity of the ATM card are met, then the processor will check whether the PIN is correct or incorrect.

So how do ATMs check your pin? It basically needs three things:-

- An algorithm that encompasses a complex formula embedded in the ATM software;
- A 16-digit number that encrypts your ATM card data;
- And the hash key, which is your PIN, which is not stored anywhere.

The bank gives you an account by combining these three items into an exponential logical operation and then making junk of useless code that's stored on the server via the internet. A junk code is created from the algorithm which is performed again with the PIN and card number that you input into the software when you need money. This junk code is pulled from the bank's server and compared with the new one that has been generated, and if they match, you receive your money.

Interestingly enough, your PIN does not go anywhere beyond the ATM. Your card number, however, does go to the bank server to confirm that you have an account and to prepare for the operation. Unless the bank is provided with the PIN code, they have nothing more than this blob of encrypted information pertaining to our passwords.

After an operation, only junk code is compared. With only a one-bit output, the algorithm says 1 if the PIN was correct to indicate that the requested amount was discharged and says 0 to indicate that the password was incorrect.

An ATM card is simply a piece of plastic with a 16-digit number on the black magnetic strip. It can be cloned by anyone in less than 2 minutes using the right hardware. When you lose your card, any person can use it to make purchases, which is a big loophole because the bank doesn't use authentication. Nevertheless, a lost card cannot be used at an ATM without a pin. Using a brute force method, it would take billions of years to crack a key of this size. This is due to (the speed at which the computer cracks the code in flops) × 2the number of bits of encryption, usually 256.

Simply put, the bank has no idea what anyone's PIN is, and they therefore ask you to reset it rather than remind you or show the original PIN to you if you forget it. You are the only one who knows your PIN as well as the people with whom you shared it.

4.6.3.10 Correct PIN

If the PIN you entered is correct, then the ATM will proceed to the next step.

4.6.3.11 Incorrect PIN

An ATM card PIN is a crucial piece of information when withdrawing cash from an ATM. At the ATM, it is ok to put in the wrong PIN twice, but when you do it thrice, it becomes an issue.

In accordance with RBI guidelines, only three attempts should be made to enter an ATM card PIN when withdrawing cash from an ATM. Once you exceed three attempts, your card will be blocked automatically. In addition, the RBI advises customers not to write their PIN on their cards, not to share their PIN with anyone, and not to let anyone see their PIN while carrying out transactions. The RBI also recommends not keeping an easy PIN that combines elements like birth date, age, etc. While this may make it hard for most cardholders to remember their password, it is a preventative measure to protect against fraud.

Hence you can be blocked if you have entered your ATM card PIN incorrectly thrice at an ATM.

4.6.3.12 State 5: Enter Amount

When the user enters the amount, before proceeding to the next step, the ATM checks the following criteria.

4.6.3.13 Criteria 5—Account Balance

When the amount to be withdrawn ≤ Account balance:
   This will successfully lead to the next step, and the machine will process the amount.
   Amount to be withdrawn > Account balance
   If the amount to be withdrawn from the ATM exceeds what is in your account, then the ATM can withdraw money, or it will decline the transaction, depending on the arrangement with your bank.

4.6.3.14 Case 1: When You Cannot Complete the Transaction

A link is established between the ATM and the bank's database that displays your account balance. Due to insufficient funds in the account, the ATM will not process withdrawals that exceed the balance in your account.
   There are jurisdictions where withdrawing excessive amounts of money requires you to sign an agreement. In some cases, the bank takes a snap decision while the transaction is ongoing.

4.6.3.15 Case 2: When You Can Complete the Transaction

Banks may allow you to withdraw more than your account balance, but that will be enough to place your account in negative territory, depending on the terms of your **overdraft arrangement** (if any).
   To determine whether the withdrawal exceeded the available funds, or whether it exceeded the total funds, is crucial. Banks will reject transactions, even when there seem to be funds in a bank account, because account holders can only access or withdraw funds that they have in available funds. Here's how banks differentiate between these two types of funds:

An **available fund** is the amount a depositor can access at the time of withdrawal.

The **total fund** includes both available funds and funds that are not yet processed, such as uncleared checks or unpaid purchases/transactions.

There is a possibility of withdrawing funds beyond the account balance, but the withdrawals come with repercussions, bank terms, and fees. A withdrawal that exceeds the available funds is regarded as an overdraft and is subject to penalties. In this case, overdraft penalties will be paid from new deposits, while the remaining balance will be available to account holders.

Account holders need to understand how to protect themselves from overdrafts through **overdraft protection**.

The term "overdraft protection" refers to a service or program offered by financial institutions, i.e., account holders can opt in, which allows bank account holders to withdraw more than their account balance and be charged an overdraft fee. If you don't opt for some type of overdraft protection and withdraw funds over the amount in your account, the transaction will "fail" that is, the recipient of the check will not receive the funds.

4.6.3.16 Criteria 6-Limit per Transaction

"Limit per transaction" refers to the maximum accumulated daily limit permitted by the bank and communicated to the cardholder by the bank from time to time. This limit relates to each type of transaction to which the cardholder may have access.

The machine checks whether the amount entered by the user is less or greater than the limit per transaction.

Amount to be withdrawn ≤ Limit per transaction

This will successfully lead to the next step, and the machine will process the amount.

Amount to be withdrawn > Limit per transaction

The amount will not be processed in this case, as there is a daily spending limit, and if the amount is exceeded, the card will be declined.

For example: You can withdraw more money from an ATM using your savings account, but you cannot withdraw more than six times per month. This is a federal law, so it applies to all savings accounts at all banks. It is vital to know your debit card and bank financial transaction limits thoroughly.

The main reasons a bank restricts withdrawals are cash availability limits and security concerns:

Cash Availability Limits: When you deposit a paycheck into your checking account, the bank doesn't simply store it in a vault until you request it. Rather, banks use the money to lend to people and businesses, bundling it with other people's deposits.

It would be impossible for the bank to know which ATM to keep stocked with cash in order to meet your needs. This is even if it kept your cash on hand. Would you rather use the ATM at your local bank branch or the one at the corner store? Having withdrawal limits prevents customers from draining ATMs or causing the bank to run out of cash.

Security Concerns: In addition, banks limit ATM withdrawals out of concern for identity theft and unauthorized withdrawals. Often, it is difficult to get your money back if your rarely used credit card is stolen and you do not notice for a long time. By limiting withdrawals, a criminal is less likely to empty your account quickly.

4.6.3.17 Criteria 7—ATM Cash

The ATM evaluates this criterion as well before processing any transaction. It is the currency delivered to and maintained in each ATM before it is dispensed to the cardholder making a withdrawal transaction, to a person under an electronic check authorization transaction, or to a person under a credit card cash transaction.

Before processing any transaction, the ATM checks whether the amount entered by the user is less than the ATM cash.

Amount to be withdrawn ≤ Cash available in ATM

This will successfully lead to the next step, and the machine will process the amount.

Amount to be withdrawn > Cash available in ATM

This usually happens when an ATM runs out of cash. In such a scenario, an ATM can react in three ways:

1. You are notified that your selection cannot be completed by the ATM.
2. ATMs dispense less money than you entered. This occurs when the tray does not have all the available currency combinations.
3. The amount is deducted from the account, but the ATM is unable to disburse the cash.

4.6.3.18 Criteria 8—Minimum ATM Withdrawal Limit

Minimum ATM withdrawal limits are the amounts of cash that customers can withdraw from an ATM at a minimum. When processing transactions, ATMs evaluate this criterion. The machine determines whether the amount entered by the user is greater than the minimum ATM withdrawal limit.

Amount to be withdrawn ≥ ATM withdrawal limit

This will successfully lead to the next step, and the machine will process the amount.

Amount to be withdrawn < ATM withdrawal limit

Attempting to withdraw less than the minimum withdrawal limit will result in a "technical error" or "invalid transaction."

When all the four criteria, viz. once criteria $c5$, $c6$, $c7$, and $c8$ are satisfied together, the ATM will proceed to the next state. Here, the ATM will check the denomination of available cash from the cash tray.

4.6.3.19 State 11: Check Denomination

As we know, an ATM is an electromechanical device with a switch that knows how much and what denominations of cash are available. Upon entering your PIN and verifying that you have sufficient funds in your account, a switch instructs the ATM to withdraw the requested amount.

Isn't it curious how ATMs can decide which denominations and how many of each to give out?

Switches usually disburse the last note available in the ATM in the lowest denomination available at the time of withdrawal. For example, when withdrawing Rs 900 from an ATM, it will offer one Rs 500 note and four Rs 100 notes if the ATM has both Rs 500 and Rs 100 denominations. As an alternative to Rs 500 and Rs 100, it has Rs 200 and Rs 100, so the ATM will disburse four notes of Rs 200 and one note of Rs 100.

Within the ATM, currency notes are stacked inside "cassettes." Each cassette contains notes of one denomination. Some older ATMs may only have two cassettes, while most ATMs in the country have four. A cassette must be calibrated according to the length, width, and thickness of the notes it is supposed to hold for the ATM to recognize what denominations are available and on which cassettes. At the ATM factory or on the ATM site, trained technicians perform this process.

Staff from the bank or the bank's authorized agencies load currency notes into the cassettes in the ATM regularly. The banks must issue clean and crisp notes that are compatible with ATMs and ensure the notes are authentic. In security vans with armed escorts, cash is transported from the currency vaults of banks to ATMs.

ATMs are reloaded with cash depending on a vast array of factors, including the number of transactions made in the past, the value of withdrawals, the beginning of the month (salary period), festivals, long weekends, and the distance from the cash vault.

During an ATM withdrawal, you may hear a great deal of noise coming from within the machine. An ATM generates this noise when its dispenser arm pulls out the number of notes it needs from its cassette. From the cassette, notes are picked up one at a time and placed on dispenser belts, which then move and lead the notes up to the ATM outlet. Although ATMs accurately dispense cash, there may be occasions where there is an error and all notes cannot be disbursed to you.

Then ATM proceeds to the next state while dispensing the entered amount. Upon successful completion of a transaction, the user is prompted to eject the card.

4.7 Issues Faced by ATM

Your card can be compromised by scammers when your ATM does not dispense cash, despite a sufficient balance. What you can do is, get quick details of the ATM, time, and amount you were trying to withdraw. Visit your bank to notify them of the problem. They will immediately block your debit card and issue you a new one.

What's more frustrating is receiving an SMS telling you that the amount has been deducted from your account when the ATM declines your transaction. It is especially concerning if the amount is large.

Generally, this is due to two factors:

Technical Error: The ATM may be malfunctioning. This is due to poor internet connections, power outages, and too many transactions processing at once, among other factors. You can either wait a while and

TABLE 4.4

Technical Errors of ATM Components

S. No.	ATM Parts	Technical Errors
1	Card reader	• Card read failures (magnetic strip or chip not read) • Jammed cards • Card detection errors • Card skimming devices (fraudulent devices)
2	Keypad	• Unresponsive keys • Ghost inputs (multiple/no keypresses) • Damaged or stuck keys
3	Cash dispenser	• Cash jam • Incorrect cash dispensing • Out of service (low funds) • Cash stacking issues (misfeeds or jams)
4	Receipt printer	• Out of paper • Paper jams • Ink/toner issues (poor printing or no output) • Printer malfunction
5	Display screen	• Unresponsive screen • Display failures (flickering, no output) • Incorrectly displayed information
6	Network communication	• Offline mode (no connection to servers) • Slow response/timeout • Transaction errors (failed communication with bank servers)
7	Deposit module	• Deposit jams • Invalid deposit detection • Rejected deposits (invalid bills/checks) • Verification errors (miscounting deposit amount)
8	Cash storage and vault	• Vault locking mechanism failure • Low cash level alerts • Cash overflow (full storage prevents operation)
9	Power supply and battery	• Power failure (shutdowns or malfunctions) • Battery malfunction (backup power failure) • Surge protection failure (damage from electrical surges)
10	Security systems	• Camera malfunction (security footage issues) • Tamper detection failure (e.g., undetected card skimming devices) • Motion detection failure (no user detection)

try again or visit another ATM terminal. Otherwise, you can contact your bank about the problem. A bank's machines are normally checked periodically as normal procedure. All complaints received are resolved promptly. Therefore, your money should be credited to your account automatically in some time, and you will be notified of the same by the bank.

The following are the common errors faced by different ATM components that make it easier to identify potential problems in the ATM machine.

Fraud: Check the slot before inserting your card to avoid fraud. There have been cases where a skimmer was inserted into the slot and read all the information on the magnetic strip. Stolen information can be used to clone your card, allowing money to be withdrawn from your account.

4.8 Conclusion

Our paper presents multiple criteria that the ATM considers at each state before deciding whether to proceed to the next. The basis of this research was largely shaped by the concept of multi-criteria decision-making. It's a very vast and complex topic that helps to test many contradictory criteria and provide solid decisions in the most complex situations.

The concept of MCDM was first introduced, and then its origin and literature review were discussed. Having explained the approach to solve the MCDM problem through a flow chart, we have identified the differences between multi-attribute decision-making (MADM) and multi-objective decision-making (MODM) and have concluded that the problem considered is a multi-attribute decision-making (MADM) because, when operating ATM system multiple attributes are considered, here we have considered one objective, that is, to withdraw money.

An automated teller machine (ATM) is a money transmission equipment that is one of the best developments in the banking sector. We have briefly explained the workings of the ATM operating system followed by a discussion of the ATM's basic parts and the features involved. This chapter also shows the concept of the Turing machine and examines the working of ATM in the domain of theory of computation, which is defined by three key concepts: languages, grammar, and automata. We represented the transition model of multiple selection criteria at each stage of the ATM system, followed by the formal model of the same that is defined as a non-deterministic Turing machine. This is a seven-tuple relationship, i.e., $(S, C, \Sigma, s, b, \delta, F)$ where the transition function of the ATM is defined as:

$$s_{i+1} = \delta(s_i, \{0,1\}), \text{ where:}$$

$$\delta = f : (S,C) \times \Sigma \to S$$

Our model gives us a way to compute all the possible decisions that the ATM processor can make at each state with the help of the transition state table. Following this, we explained the whole process in detail as shown in the transition model of multiple selection criteria at each stage of ATM processing.

References

[1] Franklin, Benjamin. "Letter to Joseph Priestley, 19 Sept. 1772." *The Papers of Benjamin Franklin*, Vol. 19, pp. 299–300, edited by Leonard W. Labaree et al. Yale University Press, 1975.

[2] Roy, Bernard. "The outranking approach and the foundations of ELECTRE methods." *Theory and Decision* 31 (1991): 49–73. https://doi.org/10.1007/BF00134132.

[3] Roy, Bernard. "Founding of the EURO working group on multiple criteria decision aiding (MCDA)." *EURO Journal on Decision Processes* (1975). www.euro-online.org/web/ewg/22/multiple-criteria-decision-aiding.

[4] Keeney, Ralph L. *Decisions with multiple objectives: Preferences and value tradeoffs.* Cambridge University Press, 1993.

[5] International Society on Multi-Criteria Decision-Making. "The history of MCDM." *E-News: International Society on Multiple Criteria Decision-Making*, orbilu.uni.lu, Aug. 2009. https://orbilu.uni.lu/handle/10993/43141.

[6] Kahraman, Cengiz, Sezi Cevik Onar, and Basar Oztaysi. "Fuzzy multicriteria decision-making: a literature review." *International Journal of Computational Intelligence Systems* 8.4 (2015): 637–666.

[7] Petrovic, Ivan, and Milan Kankaras. "A hybridized IT2FS-DEMATEL-AHP-TOPSIS multicriteria decision-making approach: Case study of selection and evaluation of criteria for determination of air traffic control radar position." *Decision Making: Applications in Management and Engineering* 3.1 (2020): 146–164.

[8] Yazdani, Morteza, et al. "A grey combined compromise solution (CoCoSo-G) method for supplier selection in construction management." *Journal of Civil Engineering and Management* 25.8 (2019): 858–874.

[9] Mardani, Abbas, et al. "Multiple criteria decision-making techniques in transportation systems: A systematic review of the state of the art literature." *Transport* 31.3 (2016): 359–385.

[10] Stojčić, Mirko, et al. "Application of MCDM methods in sustainability engineering: A literature review 2008–2018." *Symmetry* 11.3 (2019): 350.

[11] Alamri, Faten S., Muhammad Haris Saeed, and Muhammad Saeed. "A hybrid entropy-based economic evaluation of hydrogen generation techniques using multi-criteria decision making." *International Journal of Hydrogen Energy* 49 (2024): 711–723.

[12] Tsai, Feng Ming, et al. "A causal municipal solid waste management model for sustainable cities in Vietnam under uncertainty: A comparison." *Resources, Conservation and Recycling* 154 (2020): 104599.

[13] Yan, Zhengchu, et al. "Catalytic ozonation for the degradation of polyvinyl alcohol in aqueous solution using catalyst based on copper and manganese." *Journal of Cleaner Production* 272 (2020): 122856.

[14] Yildiz, Aslihan, et al. "An integrated interval-valued intuitionistic fuzzy AHP-TOPSIS methodology to determine the safest route for cash in transit operations: A real case in Istanbul." *Neural Computing and Applications* 34.18 (2022): 15673–15688.

[15] Tunç, Ali, and SAkir TAŞdemir. "Optimization of cash management at ATMs using Fuzzy AHP weighted arithmetic optimization algorithm." *Journal of Multiple-Valued Logic & Soft Computing* 41 (2023).

[16] Kuhn, Harold W., and Albert W. Tucker. "Nonlinear programming." In *Traces and emergence of nonlinear programming*. Basel: Springer Basel, 2013. 247–258.

[17] Churchman, C. West, Russell L. Ackoff, and E. Leonard Arnoff. *Introduction to operations research*. John Wiley & Sons, 1957.

[18] Konheim, Alan G. "Automated teller machines: Their history and authentication protocols." *Journal of Cryptographic Engineering* 6.1 (2016): 1–29.

[19] Dutta, M., K. K. Psyche, T. Khatun, M. A. Islam, and M. A. Islam. "ATM card security using bio-metric and message authentication technology," *2018 IEEE International Conference on Computer and Communication Engineering Technology (CCET)*, Beijing, China, 2018, pp. 280–285. https://doi.org/10.1109/CCET.2018.8542227.

[20] Tyrrell, Stuart. *Using information and communication technology in healthcare*. No. 5. Radcliffe Publishing, 2002.

[21] Maizir, Ilham Frandinata, and Hartomo Soewardi. "Ergonomic concept design of the Automated Teller Machine for the physically disabled people." In *AIP Conference Proceedings*, Vol. 2860. No. 1. AIP Publishing, 2024.

[22] Lea, C.-T. "What should be the goal for ATM." *IEEE Network* 6.5 (1992): 60–66.

[23] Meduna, Alexander, Lukaš Vrabel, and Petr Zemek. "Mathematical foundations of formal language theory." Faculty of Information Technology, Brno University of Technology (2013).

[24] Chomsky, Noam. "Three models for the description of language." *IRE Transactions on Information Theory* 2.3 (1956): 113–124.

[25] Gurari, Eitan, and Eitan Gurari. *An introduction to the theory of computation*, Vol. 338. Rockville: Computer Science Press, 1989.

[26] Mishra, K. L. P., and N. Chandrasekaran. *Theory of computer science: automata, languages and computation*. PHI Learning Pvt. Ltd., 2006.

[27] Carroll, John, and Darrell Long. *Theory of finite automata: With an introduction to formal languages*. Prentice Hall, 1989.

[28] Salomaa, Arto. *Theory of automata*. Elsevier, 2014.

[29] Newman, Maxwell Herman Alexander. "Alan Mathison Turing, 1912–1954." *Biographical Memoirs of Fellows of the Royal Society* (1955): 253–263.

[30] Turing, Alan. "Turing machine." *Proceedings of the London Mathematical Society* 242 (1936): 230–265.

[31] Sehrawat, Rashmi, Honey Malviya, and Vanditaa Kaul. "Implementation of neural network with a variant of Turing machine for traffic flow control." *International Journal on Computer Science and Engineering* 5.05 (2013): 343–348.

[32] Masters, Gerry, and Philip Turner. "Forensic data recovery and examination of magnetic swipe card cloning devices." *Digital Investigation* 4 (2007): 16–22.

[33] Dutta, Mithun, et al. "ATM card security using bio-metric and message authentication technology." In *2018 IEEE International Conference on Computer and Communication Engineering Technology (CCET)*. IEEE, 2018.

5

FFP: Robust, Interpretable, and Lightweight Framework for Medical Image Diagnosis

Shancheng Jiang, Xing Zhang, Kun Xiang,
Jiawen Pan, Wenxiao Zheng, and Jiahao Xu

5.1 Introduction

Deep learning has achieved notable success in medical image diagnosis but remains vulnerable to adversarial attacks, posing risks in high-stakes healthcare applications. Adversarial training, particularly K-PGD, has shown promise in improving robustness, yet faces challenges like high computational demands and limited explainability. This paper presents a free and feature-preserving (FFP) framework that addresses adversarial robustness, model light weight, and interpretability. Using ResNet-50 and DeiT (data-efficient image transformers) backbones, we introduce a feature-preserving regularization term leveraging edge features from self-guided filters and propose an optimization framework that combines multiple distance metrics to handle worst-case uncertainty. Our approach also includes a robust pruning strategy, resulting in a compact, interpretable CAD system that enhances healthcare accessibility in resource-limited settings.

Deep learning has shown remarkable performance in medical image diagnosis, including the detection of Alzheimer's disease[1], diabetic retinopathy[2], COVID-19[3,4], etc. However, deep neural networks are often vulnerable to adversarial samples, which are carefully designed inputs with perturbations that are imperceptible to humans[5]. In medical domains, where security is of great importance, such vulnerability is dangerous. Statistics indicated that the healthcare industry suffers two to three times more cyberattacks than the average amount for other industries due to financial interests and that ransomware attacks on healthcare organizations were predicted to quadruple from 2017 to 2021 and 2022. Adversarial examples may present new opportunities for committing health insurance fraud against the AI system[6]. To make it worse, recent work has shown that small adversarial attacks on medical images can succeed with greater ease than those on natural images, since medical images are highly standardized and have complex biological

DOI: 10.1201/9781032632483-5

textures[7]. This has raised widespread safety concerns about the deployment of deep learning models in the medical images diagnosis system. Therefore, robustness against adversarial attacks has emerged as a critical factor when building trustworthy, reliable, and safe AI-based medical image classification systems.

To effectively defend the adversarial attacks, different strategies have been developed, including adversarial training[8], Bayesian method[9], TRADES[10], etc. Among these methods, K-PGD adversarial training[8], which can be formulated as a saddle point (min–max) optimization, are considered to be the most effective in withstanding strong attacks. In medical image domain, adversarial defense is more challenging. Compared to natural images, medical images are more difficult to analyze due to complex imaging parameters, interactions between different diseases, and subtle differences between images for different diagnostic decisions[11]. Recently some studies applied adversarial training and its variants on medical images and achieved good performance[12]. They found that the robustness of a medical DL model can be improved significantly via adversarial training[13]. In addition, Margeloiu et al.[14] found that adversarial training can improving the interpretability of medical image diagnostic models. They showed that adversarially trained models have sharper and more visually coherent gradient-based saliency maps, which can assist doctor in locating the lesion precisely. Adversarial training can help to build a robust interpretable computer-aided diagnostic (CAD) system for medical purposes, reducing the workloads for doctors.

Despite adversarial training proving to be effective, there remain problems in its implementation. First, K-PGD adversarial training is time-consuming. In fact, it takes 3–30 times longer to form a robust network with adversarial training than forming a non-robust equivalent[15]. On high-resolution medical image datasets, including CXR14[16], adversarial training is nearly intractable. The great computational demands of adversarial training can also render training of 3D medical models prohibitive[17]. Second, improving adversarial robustness has been shown to require even larger neural networks[8], but large model sizes have high computation and storage costs that represent significant challenges for deployment in resource-constrained applications. Thus robust model compression techniques for natural images, e.g., HYDRA[18], have gained significant traction. Unfortunately, in medical domains, a plethora of work lacks the joint consideration of the robustness of countermeasures and the light weight of models[19]. Finally, many adversarial algorithm studies lack interpretable analysis of the results. Due to the nested nonlinear structure of deep learning models, explicitly understanding why they produced particular predictions remains notoriously difficult[20]. In medical image diagnosis, it would be irresponsible to trust predictions of a black box system's lack of explainability. If a robust medical AI system is uninterpretable, we cannot consider it to have good generalizability.

In this chapter, we use Resnet-50 and DeiT as backbones and take the joint consideration of adversarial robustness, model lightweight, and explainability. We introduce a free and feature-preserving (FFP) framework for transparent and efficient adversarial training. In order to utilize the prior knowledge related to diagnosis, we generate a regularization term based on edge features extracted by a self-guided filter. Considering that a visual robust model should not rely on a single metric, we then propose an optimization framework with mixed distance metric. The framework uses different distance metrics in internal and external empirical risk calculations to correct the worst-case uncertainty. Finally, we lighten the robust pretraining model based on the optimization objective of FFP. We investigate the influence of adversarial training on the interpretability of convolutional neural networks. Results show that our method has good performance and good interpretability. We build a device-friendly and robust CAD system, which can mitigate the lack of medical resources in rural areas, improving the accessibility of trustworthy social healthcare. The main contributions of this chapter are summarized as follows:

- We design a feature-preserving regularization term based on self-guided filtering for medical images systems. The regularization introduces a soft constraint with interpretability, which injects the prior knowledge of organ contour and lesion texture into the networks.

- We apply a new robust training optimization mechanism for medical image classification, which improves the training efficiency and alleviates the trade-off problem. We update parameters and disturbances synchronously and use different distance measures in the min–max problem.

- We introduce a reliable robust pruning framework for medical image classification. we formulate pruning as an empirical risk minimization problem (ERM) with the proposed FFP robust optimization objective.

5.2 Related Work

The related work in this chapter discusses key advancements in adversarial training and model pruning to address vulnerabilities in medical image diagnosis systems. Adversarial training, formulated as a min–max optimization problem, is highlighted as one of the most effective defenses against adversarial attacks, despite its high computational cost. Methods like free adversarial training (FreeAT) offer faster solutions with minimal accuracy loss. Additionally, this chapter reviews pruning techniques to create lightweight robust models, essential for deployment in resource-constrained environments such as embedded systems. The chapter also explores various strategies to enhance the robustness of medical image analysis, emphasizing the need for efficient, interpretable, and clinically applicable solutions.

5.2.1 Adversarial Training

The existence of adversarial examples raises concerns from the public and motivates the proposals of defenses. Among various existing defense strategies, adversarial training[3,5] proves to be the most effective against adversarial attacks[8]. Mathematically, adversarial training is formulated as a min–max problem, searching for the best solution to the worst-case optimum[2]. However, the min–max problem is solved iteratively. which determines that adversarial training methods are time-consuming. Considering the high computational cost of adversarial training, Shafahi et al. proposed free adversarial training (FreeAT), in which model parameters and image perturbations are updated simultaneously[6,10]. Research on CIFAR-10/100 has shown that FreeAT can be 3–30 time faster that standard adversarial training without a significant accuracy drop[6].

5.2.2 Pruning of Robust Model

Adversarial robustness requires a significantly larger architectural capacity of the network than that for the natural training with only benign examples[9]. The required large network capacity by adversarial training may limit its use for security-critical scenarios especially in resource-constrained embedded and IoT systems. Therefore, weight pruning is becoming increasingly important for implementing robust DNNs. One such highly successful approach is a three-step compression pipeline[11], which involves pretraining, pruning, and fine-tuning. In the pruning step, the most straightforward way is to remove connections that have the lowest weight magnitude (LWM)[12]. Sehwag et al.[13] demonstrated early success of LWM pruning with adversarially robust networks, while Ye et al.[14] and Gui et al.[15] further improved its performance by integrating with the alternating direction method of multipliers (ADMM)–based optimization. While both LWM- and ADMM-based pruning techniques are successful with benign training[11,16], they performs poorly when integrated with robust training techniques, including adversarial training. Therefore, recent researches focus on the pruning of robust models. For example, Sehwag et al. formulated robust network pruning as an empirical risk minimization problem with a robust training objective[7].

5.2.3 Efficient and Robust Medical Image Diagnosis System

Many previous researches have analyzed the vulnerability of medical image analysis systems against attacks. Ma et al. have shown that complex biological textures in medical images lead to more high-gradient regions that are sensitive to small adversarial perturbations[1]. Thus researchers attempted to defend the networks by various methods. Xue et al.[17] improved the robustness of medical image classification systems by adding an auto-encoder on the CNN structure. However, embedding an auto-encoder into a CNN increases the complexity of the model. Vatian et al.[18] compared three different ways (adversarial training, Gaussian data augmentation, and bounded RELU [rectified linear unit]) of decreasing incorrectly recognized images in these networks where the most successful way is recognized to be adversarial training. In recent years, many studies applied adversarial training and its variants to improve the robustness of medical image analysis systems. For instance, Han et al.[19] improved both robustness and interpretation of model via adversarial training with dual batch normalization in datasets of X-rays, computed tomography, and magnetic resonance imaging scans. However, the acceleration of adversarial training has rarely been mentioned in the field of medical images.

Daza et al.[17] equip ROG (a novel lattice architecture for Robust Generic medical image segmentation, which is designed to segment organs and lesions on MRI and CT scans and can exploit increasingly larger receptive fields while preserving high – resolution features) with FreeAT. However, they did not comparatively explore whether there is a performance gap between the FreeAT and the standard AT for medical samples. To the best of our knowledge, current research has not jointly considered the light weight and interpretability of robust models, which are often key to clinical implementation.

5.3 Methodology

The methodology section introduces the free and feature-preserving (FFP) framework, designed to enhance adversarial robustness, efficiency, and interpretability for medical image analysis. First, it employs a self-guided filter to retain organ contours and lesion textures through feature-preserving regularization, integrating prior diagnostic knowledge. The section then details a hybrid distance metric to improve the empirical risk calculation in min–max optimization, and it proposes a synchronous update method to accelerate adversarial training by updating model parameters and perturbations simultaneously. Finally, it discusses model pruning based on robustness scores, focusing on retaining weights that enhance diagnostic accuracy, thereby achieving a compact, robust model suitable for clinical use.

5.3.1 Definition and Overview

Formally, for a given data point (x_1, y_1) sampled from the current C-class image dataset D_i (x_1, y_1), its augmentation is denoted as $(\tilde{x}i, \tilde{y}i)\sim D$, where $i \in \{1, L, N\}$ is the number of training examples. We represent f to be the discriminative model parameterized by θ. The input adversarial noise is denoted as δ, which is bounded by $\|\delta\|p \le \epsilon$.

In this section, we first employ a self-guided filter-based transformation for medical feature extraction. The prior information of organ contour and lesion texture is injected via a regularization term. Then we integrate hybrid distance metrics to formulate the empirical risk of min–max optimization. In order to accelerate the training process, we update the parameters and disturbances of the model at the same time. Finally, we automatically search for the position of robust weights through optimization based on robust scores to achieve a model's light weight. The diagram of our method is shown in Figure 5.1. We now discuss the technical details of our method.

5.3.2 Feature-Preserving Regularization

We first consider to leveraging strong prior knowledge acquired from practical diagnostic experience. In medical image diagnosis, organ contour and tissue texture are important information. Accordingly, we designed a feature-protected regularization mechanism to inject this prior information. Inspired

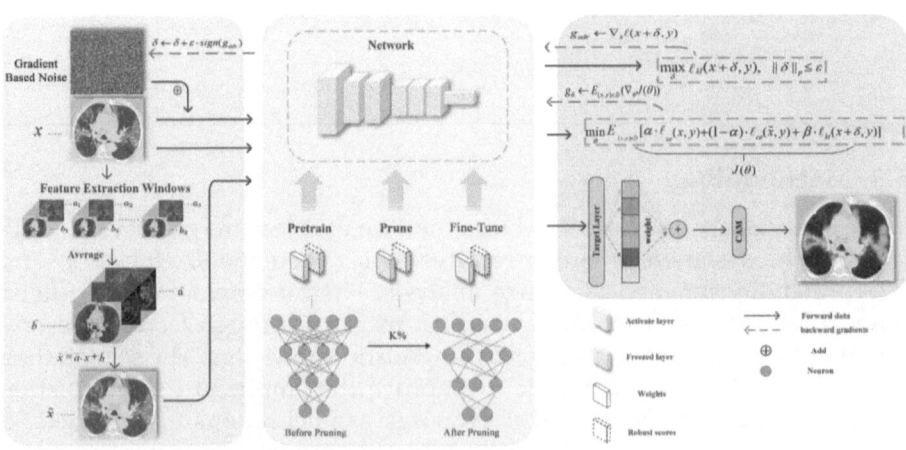

FIGURE 5.1
Overall framework of the proposed FFP.

by previous work, we adopt guided filter augmentation[2] to smooth artifacts and other interferences without losing texture edges details. We regard the image as a two-dimensional function that cannot be written analytically. Based on this, we assume that the output of the guided filter is linearly related to the input in a two-dimensional window. We assume the guidance image in pixel i is $I^{(i)}$, and the filtered output image is $\tilde{x}$ The transformation can be formulated as:

$$\tilde{x}i = \bar{a}k\, xi + \bar{b}k, \forall\in \omega i$$

where k is the position index of a local rectangle filter window E with size $\bar{a}_k$ and $\bar{b}_k$ are the average of linear coefficients a_k and b_k, respectively, which can be optimized by minimizing the difference between the output $\tilde{x}_i$ and the input pixel x_i. In order to avoid introducing deviations outside the current class, we assume the natural input image X as the self-guidance term I. The solution of this linear ridge regression is given as:

$$a_k = \frac{\frac{1}{|\omega|}\sum_{i\in\omega_k} x_i^2 - \mu_k \bar{x}_k}{\sigma_k^2 + t}, \bar{b}_k \tilde{x}_i = \tilde{x}_i - \bar{a}_k$$

Here, μ_k and σ_k are mean and variance of I in the window $k_{th}.\bar{x}_k$ is the average of X in $\acute{E}_k$, and we use a scaling temperature I to control the degree of smoothness. Since the filter is an edge-preserving function, the machine noise and ground glass in original scans will be dropped, leaving only a few trachea tissues and pulmonary nodules. The prediction error for filtered image is used as a regularization term to impose a more interpretable and robust constraint. Considering TRADES loss as the AT objective, the final training objective $\mathcal{L}_{TRADES}$ is as follows:

$$\mathcal{L}_{TRADES} = \alpha\cdot\mathcal{L}_1\big(f_\theta(x),y\big) + (1-\alpha)\cdot\mathcal{L}_2\big(f_\theta(\tilde{x}),y\big) + \beta\cdot\max_{\|\delta\|_p\le\epsilon} KL\big(f_\theta(x)\,f_\theta(x+\delta)\big)$$

Our regularization forces the medical image with prominent features to have similar prediction with the original instance. Compared with the frequency domain-based and interpolation-based methods, we highlight the semantic structures and global visual cues.

5.3.3 Synchronous Optimization Based on Hybrid Metrics

We improve the adversarial loss function with distance metric to substitute $\mathcal{L}_2$ in LTRADES. Considering a well-trained model that achieves high accuracy on both natural and adversarial data distributions, we believe that the input robustness should not completely depend on how the model measures a specific distribution shift in the adversarial training process. Starting from this point, we attempt to make some changes to the original adversarial framework with different distance metrics. In previous studies, cross entropy loss is often used as the natural loss function of adversarial training. However, When the input of cross entropy loss is a one-pot label, part of the information with the vector median value of 0 will be discarded. A metric satisfying the distance axioms, such as square loss, will retain the distance from the model output to the label outside the ground truth. In FFP framework, with the purpose of making full use of label information while maintaining invariance, we denote the class posterior probability as p $(xkxi)$ $p(y_k|x_i)$. Following Golik et al.[3], the square error can be written by:

$$\mathcal{L}_{se} = \Sigma \Sigma [p(y_k|x_i) - \psi(y_k, y_i)]^2$$

where $\psi(\cdot, \cdot)$ is the Kronecker function. Our final optimization objectives can be summarized as follows:

$$\mathcal{L}_{TRADES} = \alpha \cdot \mathcal{L}_{ce}(f_\theta(x), y) + (1-\alpha) \cdot \mathcal{L}_{se}(f_\theta(\tilde{x}), y) + \beta \cdot \max_{\|\delta\|_p \leq \epsilon} KL(f_\theta(x) f_\theta(x+\delta))$$

In the inner loop of the K-PGD adversarial training algorithm, the gradient $\nabla_x l(x_{adv}, y, \theta)$ for updating adversarial examples requires a forward–backward pass of the entire network, which has similar computation cost as calculating the gradient $\nabla_\theta l(x_{adv}, y, \theta)$ for updating network parameters. Inspired by previous work, FreeAT, our adversarial training algorithm computes the ascent step by reusing the backward pass needed for the descent step. Rather than using separate gradient computations for each update step, we update both the model parameters and image perturbations using one simultaneous backward pass. To update the network parameters, the current training minibatch is passed forward through the network. Then the gradient with respect to the network parameters is computed on the backward pass, while the gradient of the loss with respect to the input image is also computed on this same backward pass.

Algorithm 1 Free and Feature-Preserving Adversarial Training (FFP-m)

Require: Training samples x, perturbation bound $\grave{O}$, learning rate τ, hop steps m

```
1: Initial θ, δ ← 0
2: J(θ) = E_(x,y)∈D [α·ℓ_ce(x,y)+(1-α)·ℓ_se(x̃,y)+β·ℓ_kl(x+δ,y)]
3: forepoc = 1L N/m do
4: for minibatchB ∈ x do
5: for i = 1L N/m do
6: Update θ with stochastic gradient descent:
```

7: $g_\theta \leftarrow J(\theta)$

8: $g_{adv} \leftarrow \nabla_x l(x+\delta, y, \theta)$

9: $\theta \leftarrow \theta - \tau g_\theta$

10: Use gradients calculated for the minimization step to update δ.

11: $\delta \leftarrow \delta + \epsilon \cdot \text{sign}(g_{adv})$

12: $\delta \leftarrow \text{clip}(\delta, -\epsilon, \epsilon)$

13: end for

14: end for

15: end for

Unfortunately, this approach does not allow for multiple adversarial updates to be made to the same image without performing multiple backward passes. Thus we perform training on the same minibatch m times in a row for multiple adversarial updates. This strategy provides multiple adversarial updates to each training image, thus providing strong/iterative medical adversarial examples. Finally, when a new minibatch is formed, the perturbation generated on the previous minibatch is used to warm-start the perturbation for the new minibatch.

5.3.4 Model Light Weight Based on Robustness Score

Even if we accelerate adversarial training, it still requires a significant amount of computing resources to deploying robust models that are larger than regular models. To make the robust model compact, we consider pruning the pretraining network. However, simply inheriting the heuristic assumption that connections with the least magnitude are unimportant in the presence of robust training will incur a huge performance degradation with adversarial training. Inspired by previous work, HYDRA[1], we formulate pruning as an empirical risk minimization problem (ERM) with the FFP robust optimization objective.

Instead of random values, we initialize feature-preserving scores (FPS) proportional to pretrained network weights. With scaled initialization, we thus give more importance to large weights at the start and let the optimizer find a better set of pruned connections:

$$s_i^{(0)} \propto \frac{1}{max\left(\left|\theta_{pretrain,i}\right|\right)} \times \theta_{pretrain,i}$$

where $\theta_{pretrain,i}$ is the weight corresponding to ith layer in the pretrained network. We normalize each layer weight to map it to $[-1, 1]$ range. Given a pretrained network, we optimize FPS for each connection in the pruning step. Connections with the lowest FPS are pruned away:

$$\hat{m} = \underset{m \in \{0,1\}}{\text{argmin}} \ \underset{(x,y) \sim D}{E} \left[\mathcal{L}_{pruning} \left(\theta_{pretrain} \odot m, x, y \right) \right] \ \textit{s.t.} \ m_0 \leq n$$

$\theta \odot m$ refers to the element-wise multiplication of mask (m) with the weight parameters (θ). The predefined pruning ratio of the network can be written as $1 - \dfrac{n}{N}$, where n is the number of parameters we keep after pruning, and $N = \left| \theta_{pretrain} \right|$ is the total number of parameters in the pretrained network. It assigns an FPS (floating point) to each weight, indicating its robustness to the predictions on all input samples, and optimizes based on the score. While making a prediction, it only selects the top k weights with the highest magnitude of FPS. However, on the backward pass, it will update all scores with their gradients. As a result, we can introduce prior knowledge of medical image features into pruning, automatically removing weights that are not conducive to accurate diagnosis.

5.4 Experiments

The experiments section evaluates the proposed FFP framework on the SARS-COV-2 CT dataset, which includes 1252 COVID-19 and 1230 non-COVID-19 CT scans. Using ResNet-50 and DeiT-Tiny backbones, we compare FFP with baselines such as FGSM, FreeAT, and TRADES in terms of adversarial robustness and training efficiency. Results show that FFP achieves competitive robustness with reduced computational cost. The pruning effectiveness of FFP is further assessed, demonstrating a substantial reduction in model size while maintaining performance. Ablation studies validate the impact of key FFP components, including feature-preserving regularization and hybrid distance metrics. These findings suggest that FFP offers an efficient, robust, and lightweight solution for medical image diagnosis.

5.4.1 Dataset

In this chapter, we introduce a public COVID-19 CT databases for evaluation, i.e., SARS-COV-2[4]. The dataset is composed of 1252 CT scans of patients infected by the SARS-COV-2 virus and 1230 CT scans of patients who were non-infected by SARS-CoV-2 but who had other pulmonary diseases. Data was collected from hospitals of Sao Paulo, Brazil (2482 CT scans in total). Figure 5.2 illustrates some examples of the dataset.

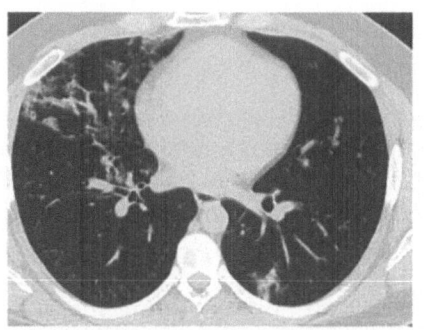 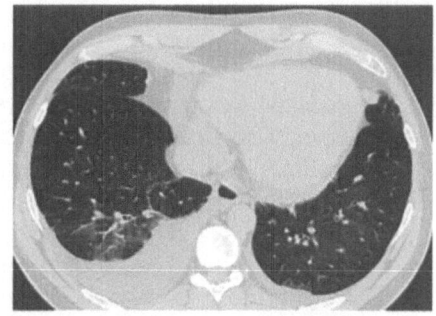

(a) COVID

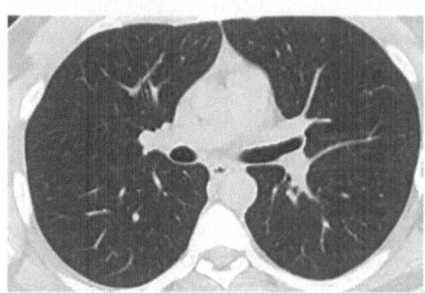 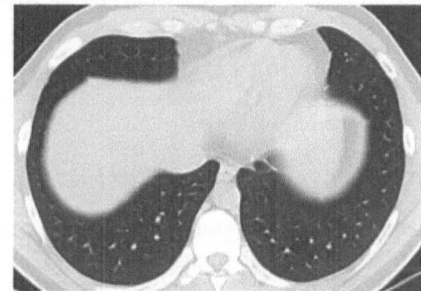

(b) Non-COVID

FIGURE 5.2
Sample CT images from the SARS-COV-2 dataset that we used for evaluation: (a) COVID and (b) non-COVID.

5.4.2 Setting

In this chapter, we use ResNet-50 and DeiT-Tiny as our backbones. We divided the dataset into 80% for training purposes and 20% for validation purposes. Images are resized to $224 \cdot 224$. For adversarial pretraining, the proposed method FFP is compared with a series of AT baselines, i.e., FGSM[1], FreeAT[3], TRADES[2]. We choose AdamW optimizer with a cosine annealing learning rate of 0.0001 with 10 decay steps. Attacks are conducted for 10 steps with step size of 2/255 and l_∞ perturbation budget $\epsilon = 8 / 255$. We set radius $r = 9$, regularization eps $= 0.001$ with a kernel size of 16. For resnet50, we trained the model for 300 epochs, and for DeiT, we trained 600 epochs. We set different pruning rates k to lighten the model (the pruned network layer retains a parameter of k%). The training parameters of the pruning process are the same as those of the pretraining, and the number of training rounds and learning rate can be appropriately reduced when fine-tuning.

5.5 Results

The results section demonstrates the effectiveness of the proposed FFP framework through comprehensive adversarial testing and robust model pruning experiments. FFP has achieved improved adversarial robustness across various attack methods and strengths, outperforming baseline models on both ResNet-50 and DeiT-Tiny backbones. The framework also retained high accuracy with significant model pruning, achieving up to 99% weight reduction while maintaining performance superior to traditional pruning methods. Visualization using GradCAM++ showed that FFP enhances interpretability by focusing on lesion areas. An ablation study confirmed the contributions of key FFP components, Feature-preserving regularization (FPR) and hybrid metric-based optimization (HMO), in boosting robustness and interpretability, making FFP a promising approach for efficient and reliable medical image analysis.

5.5.1 Adversarial Pretraining

To evaluate the performance of our proposed method, we employ a wide range of white box adversarial attacks with a l_∞ threat model: FGSM[1] and PGD[2]. As reported in Table 5.1, we achieve the best comprehensive

TABLE 5.1

Comparison of Our Adversarial Training Approach (FFP) with TRADES, FGSM, and FreeAT

ResNet50

Method	Clean	10-PGD (4/255)	10-PGD (8/255)	100-PGD (8/255)	FGSM (8/255)	10-PGD (16/255)	Time
Base	0.9819	\	\	\	\	\	66 m 36s
TRADES	0.9416	0.9195	0.8873	0.8832	0.8953	0.8269	879 m 59 s
FGSM	0.9819	0.9235	0.7867	0.7625	0.8551	0.4305	294 m 59 s
FreeAT	0.9356	0.8954	0.837	0.829	0.8531	0.7123	170 m 56 s
FFP (Ours)	**0.9537**	**0.9195**	**0.8692**	**· 0.8632**	**0.8813**	**0.7767**	**211m 53 s**

DeiT-Tiny

Method	Clean	10-PGD (4/255)	10-PGD (8/255)	100-PGD (8/255)	FGSM (8/255)	10-PGD (16/255)	Time
Base	0.9517	\	\	\	\	\	124 m
TRADES	0.9497	0.9074	0.8289	0.827	0.8551	0.6962	614 m 51 s
FGSM	0.9638	0.1751	0.0684	0.0362	0.996	0.0241	69 m 3 s
FreeAT	0.9457	0.8692	0.7325	0.6881	0.8148	0.5654	122 m 16s
FFP (Ours)	**0.9638**	**0.9014**	**0.8149**	**0.7762**	**0.8813**	**0.6962**	**151 m 2 s**

performance on the resnet-50 and DeiT under different attack methods and attack intensities. Results demonstrate that, for Resnet-50, we have achieved an average improvement of 0.074%, 3.847%, and 1.556%, respectively, on clean samples, samples attacked by PGD-10 ($\epsilon = 8 / 255$) and FGSM ($\epsilon = 8 / 255$) compared with three SOTA baselines. For DeiT-Tiny, we gain an average improvement of 1.699%, 4.380%, and 5.259%, respectively, on clean samples attacked by PGD-10 ($\epsilon = 8 / 255$) and FGSM ($\epsilon = 8 / 255$), compared with two SOTA baselines (except FGSM). Although FGSM has the shortest training time, it does not perform well on adversarial samples, especially those under strong attacks. When training based on the DeiT model, FGSM can hardly resist PGD attack. Compared with TRADES, our method can save 4–5 times of training time while maintaining a comparable performance and has higher accuracy in clean samples and samples attacked by a small perturbation budget. Research shows that the performance of FreeAT is close to that of PGD on natural images, while our experiments show that the acceleration of FreeAT on medical images will sacrifice more performance. Our method can focus on the details of the steep gradient area of the medical image while accelerating the training, thus achieving better clean accuracy and robust accuracy than FreeAT.

5.5.2 Robust Model Pruning

Table 5.2 shows the lung CT data of novel coronavirus under three pruning ratios and two network architectures set of experimental results. The results indicate that, compared to the LWM pruning algorithm, our construction framework can maintain more robust weights without sacrificing clean accuracy. On the Deit-Tiny model, our method can still achieve a clean sample accuracy of 92.56%, a PGD-10 adversarial accuracy of 74.25%, and a FGSM

TABLE 5.2

Comparison of Our Robust Pruning Framework with LWM

Model	k	FFP (Ours)			LWM			Parameters	File Size
		Clean	10-PGD	FGSM	Clean	10-PGD	FGSM		
ResNet50	1.00	0.9638	0.8149	0.8813	0.9638	0.8149	0.8813	100.00%	94.4M
	0.10	0.9336	0.8813	0.8933	0.4426	0.4426	0.4426	48.75%	86.2M
	0.05	0.9235	0.8531	0.8571	0.4426	0.4426	0.4426	45.90%	48.9M
	0.01	0.9235	0.8753	0.8813	0.4426	0.4426	0.4426	43.62%	19.2M
DeiT-Tiny	1.00	0.9638	0.8149	0.8813	0.9638	0.8149	0.8813	100.00%	22.1M
	0.10	0.9537	0.8511	0.8672	0.9517	0.7386	0.8430	11.13%	11.5M
	0.05	0.9457	0.7847	0.7666	0.9456	0.7002	0.7786	6.19%	5.91M
	0.01	0.9256	0.7425	0.7384	0.8531	0.5915	0.6056	2.24%	1.45M

adversarial accuracy of 73.84% at a high pruning rate of 0.01 (i.e., with 99% weight removed). Compared to LWM, our method has improved robust accuracy by 7.25%, 15.10%, and 13.28%, respectively, with a greater improvement compared to low pruning rates. In addition, networks pruned using our method are more likely to converge at very high pruning rates. For the ResNet-50 network, when the pruning rates are 0.1, 0.05, and 0.01, LWM cannot converge, but our method can maintain excellent performance of the pruned model.

5.5.3 Visualization

We investigated the influence of our method on the interpretability of convolutional neural networks. The visualization tool we have chosen is GadCAM++. From Figure 5.3, it can be seen that our adversarial training method FFP can better focus on the lesion area. From Figure 5.4, it can be seen that our pruning algorithm maintains good interpretability at a high pruning rate of 0.01.

5.5.4 Ablation Study

To further gain insights into the performance of our method, we performed an ablation study based on FreeAT for the reinforcement module of FFP

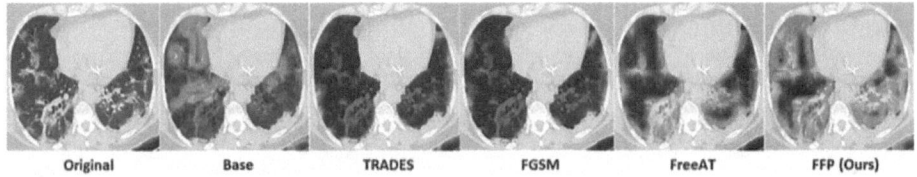

Original   Base   TRADES   FGSM   FreeAT   FFP (Ours)

FIGURE 5.3
GradCAM++ results of different adversarial training methods (Deit-Tiny).

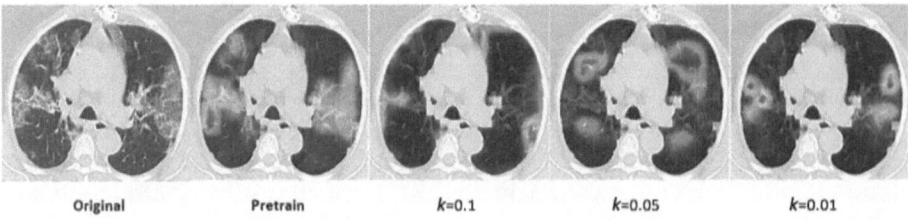

Original   Pretrain k=0.1 k=0.05 k=0.01

FIGURE 5.4
GradCAM++ results of different pruning algorithms (Deit-Tiny), where k represents pruning rate.

TABLE 5.3

Results of Ablation Experiment: Effectiveness of Two Key Enhancement
Components in the FFP Framework Are Validated

HMO	FPR	Clean	PGD-10	FGSM
×	×	0.9356	0.8370	0.8531
√	×	0.9396	0.8511	0.8712
×	√	0.9477	0.8531	0.8753
√	√	0.9537	0.8692	0.8813

framework, including FPR (feature-preserving regularization) and HMO
(hybric metric-based optimization). As shown in Table 5.3, both components
improve the generalization, robustness, and interpretability of the model.
First, we study the impact of HMO on adversarial training, that is, whether
it produces better robustness and curtails the vulnerability of the network.
One can observe that HMO improves the adversarial accuracy (1.41% for
PGD-10 and 1.81% for FGSM). Note that the clean accuracy for FreeAT-HMO
is approximately the same as FreeAT, which indicates that HMO may have a
limited effect on standard accuracy but has a substantial impact on robustness. Second, we investigate the impact of FRP on adversarial training. We
know from these results that FPR for adversarial training can improve the
clean accuracy (1.21%) and robust accuracy (1.61% for PGD-10, 1.81%) of the
model at the same time. In addition, incorporating the two components
together can further boost the performance (1.81% for clean, 3.22% for PGD-
10, and 2.82% for FGSM).

5.6 Conclusion

In this chapter, we propose a free and freature-preserving (FFP) framework
to improve the model-wise adversarial robustness in medical image classification task. The feature-preserving regularization is first introduced to inject
a priori knowledge of organ contour and lesion texture into networks. We
further optimize the min–max problem via distance metric. In addition, We
accelerate the adversarial training by synchronously updating the gradient.
Finally, we train the pruning mask based on the optimization target of FFP
to compress the model size. We experimentally validate FFP framework on
two model architectures against recent baseliness; results demonstrate that
our method significantly improves the adversarial robustness and interpretability in medical imaging diagnosis.

References

[1] S. Qiu, P. Joshi, M. I. Miller, C. Xue, X. Zhou, C. Karjadi, G. H. Chang, A. S. Joshi, B. Dwyer, S. Zhu, M. C. Kaku, Y. Zhou, Y. J. Alderazi, A. Swaminathan, S. Kedar, M. Saint-Hilaire, S. H. Auerbach, J. Yuan, E. Sartor, R. Au, and V. B. Kolachalama, "Development and validation of an interpretable deep learning framework for alzheimer's disease classification," *Brain*, vol. 143, pp. 1920–1933, 2020.

[2] F. Li, Y. Wang, T. Xu, L. Dong, L. Yan, M. Jiang, X. Zhang, H. Jiang, Z. Wu, and H. Zou, "Deep learning-based automated detection for diabetic retinopathy and diabetic macular oedema in retinal fundus photographs," *Eye*, vol. 36, pp. 1433–1441, 2021.

[3] W. Zhao, W. Jiang, and X. Qiu, "Deep learning for COVID-19 detection based on CT images," *Scientific Reports*, vol. 11, 2021.

[4] E. Hussain, M. Hasan, M. A. Rahman, I. Lee, T. Tamanna, and M. Z. Parvez, "Corodet: A deep learning based classification for COVID-19 detection using chest X-ray images," *Chaos, Solitons, and Fractals*, vol. 142, p. 110495, 2020.

[5] I. J. Goodfellow, J. Shlens, and C. Szegedy, "Explaining and harnessing adversarial examples," *CoRR*, vol. abs/1412.6572, 2015.

[6] S. G. Finlayson, I. S. Kohane, and A. Beam, "Adversarial attacks against medical deep learning systems," *ArXiv*, vol. abs/1804.05296, 2018.

[7] X. Ma, Y. Niu, L. Gu, Y. Wang, Y. Zhao, J. Bailey, and F. Lu, "Understanding adversarial attacks on deep learning based medical image analysis systems," *Pattern Recognition*, vol. 110, p. 107332, 2021.

[8] A. Madry, A. Makelov, L. Schmidt, D. Tsipras, and A. Vladu, "Towards deep learning models resistant to adversarial attacks," *ArXiv*, vol. abs/1706.06083, 2018.

[9] N. Ye and Z. Zhu, "Bayesian adversarial learning," in *NeurIPS*, 2018.

[10] H. R. Zhang, Y. Yu, J. Jiao, E. P. Xing, L. E. Ghaoui, and M. I. Jordan, "Theoretically principled trade-off between robustness and accuracy," *ArXiv*, vol. abs/1901.08573, 2019.

[11] Z. Li, X. Zhang, H. Müller, and S. Zhang, "Large-scale retrieval for medical image analytics: A comprehensive review," *Medical Image Analysis*, vol. 43, pp. 66–84, 2018.

[12] M. Xu, T. Zhang, Z. Li, M. Liu, and D. Zhang, "Towards evaluating the robustness of deep diagnostic models by adversarial attack," *Medical Image Analysis*, vol. 69, p. 101977, 2021.

[13] X. Li, D. Pan, and D. Zhu, "Defending against adversarial attacks on medical imaging AI system, classification or detection?" *2021 IEEE 18th International Symposium on Biomedical Imaging (ISBI)*, pp. 1677–1681, 2021.

[14] A. Margeloiu, N. Simidjievski, M. Jamnik, and A. Weller, "Improving interpretability in medical imaging diagnosis using adversarial training," *ArXiv*, vol. abs/2012.01166, 2020.

[15] A. Shafahi, M. Najibi, A. Ghiasi, Z. Xu, J. P. Dickerson, C. Studer, L. S. Davis, G. Taylor, and T. Goldstein, "Adversarial training for free!" in *Neural Information Processing Systems*, 2019.

[16] L. Oakden-Rayner, "Exploring large scale public medical image datasets," *Academic Radiology*, vol. 27, pp. 106–112, 2020.

[17] L. A. Daza, J. C. Pérez, and P. Arbeláez, "Towards robust general medical image segmentation," *ArXiv*, vol. abs/2107.04263, 2021.

[18] V. Sehwag, S. Wang, P. Mittal, and S. S. Jana, "Hydra: Pruning adversarially robust neural networks," *arXiv: Computer Vision and Pattern Recognition*, 2020.

[19] K. Xiang, L. Peng, H. Yang, M. Li, Z. Cao, S. Jiang, and G. Qu, "A novel weight pruning strategy for light weight neural networks with application to the diagnosis of skin disease," *Applied Soft Computing*, vol. 111, p. 107707, 2021.

[20] W. Samek, T. Wiegand, and K.-R. Müller, "Explainable artificial intelligence: Understanding, visualizing and interpreting deep learning models," *ArXiv*, vol. abs/1708.08296, 2017.

6

Grey Prediction Model Based on Fixed-Point Accumulation and Its Application to Predict Natural Gas Futures Contract Price

Lianyi Liu, Junliang Du, and Sifeng Liu

6.1 Introduction

6.1.1 Background and Purpose of the Study

Amid growing global emphasis on environmental protection and a low-carbon economy, natural gas, as an efficient and clean energy source, has become increasingly vital in energy restructuring. Compared to traditional fossil fuels, natural gas offers higher combustion efficiency and lower emissions, making it widely used in power generation, industrial applications, and residential needs [1]. In recent years, global demand for natural gas has surged, particularly in emerging markets and developing countries [2]. However, demand forecasting remains challenging due to the influence of multiple factors, including economic development, climate conditions, seasonal fluctuations, energy prices, and policy interventions.

Accurate natural gas demand forecasting is crucial not only for managing energy supply chains but also for ensuring scientific energy dispatch and effective policy-making. Accurate demand forecasts help optimize supply and demand planning, reduce waste and storage costs, and improve resource efficiency [3]. Especially against the backdrop of global energy transitions, the clean energy profile of natural gas is becoming more pronounced, making demand forecasting a key area of focus for energy management in many countries [4].

While the demand and value of natural gas forecasting are rising, it still faces significant challenges. The complexity of natural gas demand stems from the combined effects of macroeconomic conditions, seasonal changes, policy interventions, and climate variables, leading demand data to exhibit nonlinear and cyclical characteristics [5]. Current time series models, such as ARIMA and exponential smoothing, rely on assumptions of linearity and stationarity, which often fall short in capturing the

DOI: 10.1201/9781032632483-6

complex fluctuations in natural gas demand [6]. To address these limitations, machine learning and deep learning models, such as support vector regression and long short-term memory networks, have been widely applied to natural gas demand forecasting in recent years [7]. However, these models typically rely on large datasets and lack sufficient interpretability, making them challenging to use directly for policy-making [8]. Relying solely on machine learning is insufficient to fully address the complexities of demand forecasting [9].

In contrast, grey forecasting models, known for their suitability for small samples and uncertain systems, are gaining attention in natural gas demand forecasting. Grey models leverage fuzzy modeling to provide stable forecasts in limited and uncertain data environments. However, classic grey models still face limitations when dealing with highly nonlinear and multi-factor-driven systems. Recently, the integration of novel accumulation operators and nonlinear functions has opened new avenues for applying grey forecasting models in complex settings.

Based on these considerations, this study proposes an improved discrete grey model using a fixed-point cumulative operator. By combining grey system theory with buffer operator methods, this model aims to enhance adaptability and predictive accuracy in small-sample environments. By incorporating the nonlinear relationships of multiple factors, this model seeks to capture the dynamic trends in natural gas demand more accurately, offering an innovative approach to addressing the nonlinear and uncertain aspects of natural gas demand forecasting.

6.1.2 Literature Review of Grey Prediction Algorithms

Grey system theory is a combination theory of the automatic control science and operational research mathematical methods, which is often used in the modeling of uncertain systems. Diverging from conventional approaches such as fuzzy mathematics and rough set theory, grey system theory is specifically tailored to address the modeling intricacies inherent in scenarios characterized by limited data and pervasive uncertainty [10]. The notion of a grey system typically pertains to intricate systems besieged by scant information availability, exemplified by ambiguous market conditions or regions with deficient statistical data. Central to the tenets of grey system theory is the meticulous extraction and utilization of available information to navigate the labyrinth of uncertain systems [11]. Traditional prediction methodologies, such as the empirical model [12], moving average model [13], neural network [14], and support vector regression [15], predominantly rely on extensive statistical datasets for modeling and analysis, imposing stringent prerequisites on data types and sample sizes. Nonetheless, during the nascent stages of system development, conventional methodologies often falter in rendering precise analyses owing to a paucity of information. In stark contrast, the grey model exhibits remarkable efficacy, requiring a mere four data points for robust modeling and analysis. This unique advantage under-scores its proficiency in compensating for the shortcomings associated with the analysis of "data-poor" scenarios. The essence of the grey model lies in its treatment of stochastic variables as manifestations of grey actions, repre-senting temporal and spatial fluctuations within a continuum spanning from "white" to "black." By harnessing the mechanisms of accumulation, genera-tion, and whitening differential equations, the grey model unveils the under-lying evolution patterns latent within the data, effectuating a transformative journey from "grey" to "white." This study delves into the iterative process of data accumulation, culminating in the proposal of a novel grey accumulative generating operator aimed at enhancing the adaptive versatility of the grey model within complex systems.

Numerous scholars have made significant contributions to refining the structural underpinnings, delineating modeling conditions, and conducting theoretical analyses, thereby augmenting the theoretical scaffold of the grey model in discrete and nonlinear modeling. Substantial advancements have been achieved across several key domains, as follows:

Optimization of Model System Parameters: The correction of the background value can obtain the more accurate integral solution of the grey model, and can greatly reduce the systematic error [16]. The traditional background value is calculated by fixed geometric trapezoidal area, which has weak structural compatibility and poor generalization performance. A common method is to introduce an adaptive optimization factor α into the background value generation equation $z^{(1)}(k)=\alpha x^{(1)}(k)+(1-\alpha)x^{(1)}(k+1)$, so as to reduce the estima-tion error of the background value [17]. The basic form $(\frac{\mathrm{d}x}{\mathrm{d}t}+ax=b)$ of the grey model consists of two system parameters, development coefficient a, and grey action b. The pursuit of optimal parameter solutions has emerged as a primary objective in enhancing predic-tion efficacy. Liu et al. [18], for instance, innovatively employed the Weibull cumulative distribution function to fashion a double-shape parameter, deviating from conventional static parameters. This novel approach substantially bolstered the grey model's aptitude for fitting impure exponential sequences. Furthermore, the integra-tion of intelligent algorithms for parameter optimization within the grey model has garnered widespread scholarly interest. Tech-niques such as the particle swarm optimization (PSO) algorithm [19], the differential evolution method [20], the mixed gradient descent method [21], and various heuristic algorithms have been explored in this context. The optimization of parameter identifica-tion methodologies represents a critical facet of modeling, neces-sitating judicious selection in alignment with model structure and data characteristics.

Structural Improvement of the Grey Differential Equation: The introduction of the discrete grey model (DGM) [22] represents a significant stride, rectifying the inherent instability plaguing traditional prediction models. Subsequent endeavors have focused on devising more adaptable model structures to cater to the diverse modeling requirements across various data characteristics [23]. Exploiting the interplay between univariate and multivariable, discrete and continuous time models, Wei and Xie [24] introduced a unified framework for research and computation, facilitating the evaluation of multistep advance predictions. Moreover, extensions incorporating Fourier functions, time-delay effects, and seasonal factors [25] have substantially enriched the framework of the grey prediction model, broadening its applicability and efficacy.

Improvement of Buffer Operator: In modeling processes, the output results of systems affected by disruptive influences often deviate from anticipated qualitative analyses, underscoring the necessity of accounting for system disturbances. Confronted with the challenge of erratic growth rates in raw sequence data, the traditional moving average operator exhibits limited adaptability, failing to ensure sequence smoothness. The introduction of a novel fractional buffer operator has demonstrated considerable potential in minimizing prediction errors and exhibits promising performance in applications such as shale gas production forecasting [26]. In essence, the buffer operator serves to mitigate the stochastic interference inherent in the original data, thereby endowing the grey system model with enhanced generalization capabilities.

Optimization of Grey Accumulative Generating Operator: Wu et al. [27] posited that distinctions exist among information, implying that data from disparate time nodes exert varying impacts on future data. In response, they introduced the fractional accumulative generating operator to handle the "in-between" information situated between adjacent data points. Subsequently, Ma et al. [28] advanced a novel conformable fractional grey model, streamlining the fractional calculation process. Furthermore, leveraging the concept of variable weight accumulation, a novel grey generating operator was introduced to modulate the weight of incoming information [29]. Recognizing the tendency for predicted results to exhibit expansion rates exceeding anticipated expectations, a damped accumulative method was devised to refine predictive outcomes [30]. Additional enhancements, including convolution accumulation, reverse accumulation, and generalized accumulation, represent refinements of the first-order accumulation generating operator (1-AGO). Given the pivotal role of the accumulation process in transitioning data information from "grey" to "white," adherence to the "new information priority" [31] principle remains imperative in innovating the grey generating operator.

6.1.3 Contributions of the Study

Given the importance of natural gas demand forecasting in energy management and the limitations of existing methods, this study aims to develop a forecasting model capable of addressing data uncertainty and complex nonlinear relationships to enhance prediction accuracy and applicability. Based on these advancements, grey models have garnered widespread utilization in modeling scenarios characterized by limited data availability. This chapter's principal contribution and innovation reside in the exploration of modified grey models tailored specifically for energy price forecasting. The primary innovations of the proposed modified grey model are delineated as follows: (1) The model meticulously adheres to the modeling principle of "new information priority." Employing variable accumulation weights, the model assigns greater importance to recent information $x^{(0)}(n)$, thereby accentuating the timeliness of data. Subsequently, particle swarm optimization (PSO) is employed to ascertain the optimal accumulative parameters. (2) Leveraging matrix perturbation theory, the paper scrutinizes the impact of original data perturbations on predicted values. (3) In contrast to existing accumulative generating operators, the proposed FPAGO boasts simpler operational guidelines. Through the presentation of three numerical examples, the applicability of FPAGO in addressing practical prediction challenges is empirically demonstrated.

6.2 Preliminaries

In this section, we give the definition of the grey model and some of its important properties. Then the fixed-point axiom of grey system and the effectiveness of basic buffer operator are analyzed.

6.2.1 Original GM (1,1) Model

GM (1,1) is the basic form of the grey model, which has been widely used in the "poor data" forecasting problems in many fields. The modeling process of GM (1,1) mainly includes the steps of 1-AGO, background value generation, differential equation modeling, and response reduction solution. Among them, the data accumulation is the basis of grey model modeling, which ensures that the accumulation sequence meets the grey exponential characteristic of modeling.

Definition 1: ([1]) With the original sequence $X^{(0)} = \left\{ x^{(0)}(1), x^{(0)}(2), \cdots, x^{(0)}(n) \right\}$, the 1-AGO is defined as

$$x^{(1)}(k) = \sum_{i=1}^{k} x^{(0)}(i). \tag{6.1}$$

After the operation of 1-AGO, $X^{(1)}$ can be used in the differential equation modeling of the grey model. Then the main modeling steps of GM (1,1) are as follows:

Step 1: Assume $X^{(1)}$ and $X^{(0)}$ are defined as in Definition 1, $\dfrac{dx}{dt} + ax = b$ is the differential equation of GM (1,1), then we can get that the integration form of GM (1,1) is $\int_{k}^{k+1} x^{(0)}(t)dt = a\int_{k}^{k+1} x^{(1)}(t)dt + \int_{k}^{k+1} bdt$. Thus its approximate discrete form can be given as

$$x^{(0)}(k) + az^{(1)}(k) = b. \tag{6.2}$$

where the parameters a and b are called the growth coefficient and grey action value, respectively. $z^{(1)}(k)$ is the background value in which $z^{(1)}(k+1) = \left(x^{(1)}(k) + x^{(1)}(k+1) \right)/2$.

Step 2: The least square method can be used to estimate the parameters, expressed as

$$\begin{bmatrix} \hat{a} & \hat{b} \end{bmatrix}^{T} = \left(B^{T}B \right)^{-1} B^{T}Y, \tag{6.3}$$

where

$$B = \begin{bmatrix} -z^{(1)}(2) & 1 \\ -z^{(1)}(3) & 1 \\ \vdots & \vdots \\ -z^{(1)}(n) & 1 \end{bmatrix}, \; Y = \begin{bmatrix} x^{(0)}(2) \\ x^{(0)}(3) \\ \vdots \\ x^{(0)}(n) \end{bmatrix}.$$

Step 3: Notice that the initial value is $\hat{x}^{(1)}(1) = x^{(0)}(1)$ and that the response function of GM (1,1) is

$$\hat{x}^{(1)}(k+1) = \left(x^{(0)}(1) - \frac{b}{a} \right) e^{-ak} + \frac{b}{a} \tag{6.4}$$

Step 4: By the inverse operation of 1-AGO, the reduced value can be obtained as

$$\hat{x}^{(0)}(k+1) = \hat{x}^{(1)}(k+1) - \hat{x}^{(1)}(k), \; k = 2,3,\cdots. \tag{6.5}$$

Step 5: The mean absolute percentage error (MAPE) is used to test the accuracy of the prediction results, as follows:

$$\text{MAPE} = \frac{1}{n}\sum_{k=1}^{n}\left|\frac{\hat{x}^{(0)}(k)-x^{(0)}(k)}{x^{(0)}(k)}\right|\times 100\%. \tag{6.6}$$

Compared with other time series forecast algorithms, we can find that the data accumulation operation is a unique modeling tool of the grey model, which enables the grey model to have better prediction performance for exponential trend time series. However, GM (1,1) is only applicable to exponential trend data series. In the face of a nonlinear trend sequence, the fixed 1-AGO operation greatly limits the predictive ability of the model and may lead to inevitable modeling errors. In the process of accumulation, the importance of new information is not reflected. Therefore, it is necessary to properly optimize 1-AGO.

6.2.2 Fixed-Point Axiom and Grey Buffer Operator

The impact disturbance system has always been an important problem in the prediction field, which has become a great obstacle to the quantitative prediction [1]. This is mainly because the collected statistical data is often distorted due to the interference received by the system itself; that is, the system data fails to correctly describe the actual regularity of the system change. In this case, the original data should be preprocessed to eliminate the interference of distorted data.

The fixed-point axiom stipulates that, under the action of sequence operator, the latest data $x(n)$, which is the basis of future trend development, remains unchanged. Thus it can eliminate the system interference of previous imprecise data to the greatest extent. Based on the fixed-point axiom, a simple grey buffer operator is defined as follows:

Definition 2: Assume a raw sequence is $X = \{x(1), x(2), \cdots, x(n)\}$, D_1 is the buffer operator, the sequence $XD_1 = \{x(1)d_1, x(2)d_1, \cdots, x(n)d_1\}$ is the buffer generation sequence, defined as

$$x(k)d_1 = \lambda x(k)+(1-\lambda)x(n) = x(k)+(1-\lambda)(x(n)-x(k)). \tag{6.7}$$

If $\lambda < 1$, then the D_1 is the weakening buffer operator. If $\lambda > 1$, then the D_1 is the strengthening buffer operator.

To verify the validity of the buffer operator, a set of random numbers obeying normal distribution is generated as $X = \{0.8699, 1.1028, 2.0735, 1.8308, 0.5950, 1.9105\}$, and its standard deviation is 0.6192. The effect of the buffer operator on the original sequence is shown in Figure 6.1. As we can

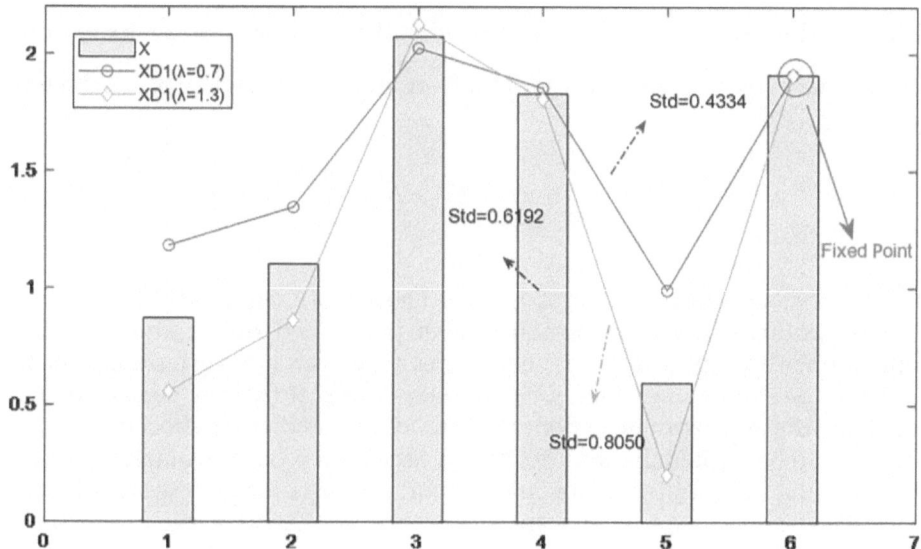

FIGURE 6.1
Mechanism of fixed-point buffer operator.

see, when $\lambda = 0.7$, the new sequence becomes smoother than the original one, and the standard variance of sequence XD_1 is 0.4334. Meanwhile, the latest data $x(n)$ remains unchanged, which serves as the basis for our next prediction.

6.3 Fixed-Point Cumulative Discrete Grey Model

According to the fixed-point axiom, this section gives the definition of fixed-point accumulation and establishes a new grey prediction model. The important properties and parameter solution of the proposed model are also given.

6.3.1 Fixed-Point Accumulation Grey Generating Operator

Reasonable data accumulation generation technology is beneficial to reducing modeling error and improving the accuracy of prediction [32]. The traditional 1-AGO does not conform to the "new information priority" principle, and its fixed model structure also limits the adaptation range of the model. To improve the accuracy of prediction, a modified grey generating operator FPAGO is proposed as follows:

Definition 3: $X^{(\lambda)} = \left\{ x^{(\lambda)}(1), x^{(\lambda)}(2), \cdots, x^{(\lambda)}(n) \right\}$ is the λ-order fixed-point accumulative sequence of $X^{(0)}$, and the λ-order ($0 < \lambda \leq 1$) FPAGO can be represented as

$$x^{(\lambda)}(k) = \lambda \sum_{i=1}^{k} x^{(0)}(i) + k(1-\lambda)x^{(0)}(n), \ k = 1, 2, \cdots, n. \tag{6.8}$$

FPAGO is an optimization of 1-AGO. The 1-AGO regarded data as information points of equal importance, then performed fitting and reduction operations through differential equations. However, it is very unreasonable to have the same data weights for all data points. If the raw sequence does not have the approximate exponential trend, the prediction effect of the grey model will be limited. In order to improve the data processing effect, the new information priority principle is an important basis for grey system theory modeling. By setting a fixed point, the proposed FPAGO is able to adjust the cumulative sequence, so that new information has a greater weight on the predicted results. Meanwhile, the selection of the cumulative parameter λ is an adaptive process, which can ensure that the new sequence is more in line with the modeling needs of exponential fitting than the traditional method. Then the following properties of FPAGO can be concluded:

Property 1: The fixed-point accumulative sequence $X^{(\lambda)}$ is a monotone increasing sequence.

Property 2: The accumulated parameter λ can adjust the weight of the latest data. The smaller λ is, the greater weight it has.

6.3.2 Fixed Point Cumulative Discrete Grey Model

The differential equation $\dfrac{dx}{dt} + ax = b$ is the traditional form of grey model. However, in many practical cases, the fitting effect of the model will be greatly reduced due to systematic errors in the construction of background values (see Eq. [6.2]). Thus we use the DGM [24] instead of the traditional form to establish the fixed-point accumulative discrete grey model (FPDGM). The discrete formula is as follows:

$$x^{(\lambda)}(k+1) = \beta_1 x^{(\lambda)}(k) + \beta_2. \tag{6.9}$$

The system parameters of the Eq. (6.9) is solved by the least square method that

$$\begin{bmatrix} \hat{\beta}_1 & \hat{\beta}_2 \end{bmatrix}^T = \left(\mathbf{B}^T \mathbf{B} \right)^{-1} \mathbf{B}^T \mathbf{Y}. \tag{6.10}$$

where

$$\mathbf{B} = \begin{bmatrix} x^{(\lambda)}(1) & 1 \\ x^{(\lambda)}(2) & 1 \\ \vdots & \vdots \\ x^{(\lambda)}(n-1) & 1 \end{bmatrix}, \mathbf{Y} = \begin{bmatrix} x^{(\lambda)}(2) \\ x^{(\lambda)}(3) \\ \vdots \\ x^{(\lambda)}(n) \end{bmatrix}. \tag{6.11}$$

The initial point is set as $\hat{x}^{(\lambda)}(1) = x^{(0)}(1)$; then the fitting results of FPDGM is given:

$$\hat{x}^{(\lambda)}(k+1) = \hat{\beta}_1 \hat{x}^{(\lambda)}(k) + \hat{\beta}_2, k = 1, 2, \cdots. \tag{6.12}$$

The fitting sequence $\hat{X}^{(\lambda)} = \left\{ \hat{x}^{(\lambda)}(1), \hat{x}^{(\lambda)}(2), \cdots \right\}$ is the fitting results of $X^{(\lambda)}$. Thus the predicted results can be obtained, as follows:

$$\hat{x}^{(0)}(k) = \begin{cases} \dfrac{\hat{x}^{(\lambda)}(k) - \hat{x}^{(\lambda)}(k-1) - (1-\lambda)\hat{x}^{(0)}(n)}{\lambda} & , k = 1, 2, \cdots, n-1, n+1, n+2, \cdots \\ \hat{x}^{(\lambda)}(n) - \hat{x}^{(\lambda)}(n-1) & , k = n \end{cases} \tag{6.13}$$

Unlike 1-AGO, the inverse of FPAGO should first calculate the predicted fixed-point value $\hat{x}^{(0)}(n)$. The fixed point is the basis for us to calculate the fitting results and the next prediction. In addition, when the accumulative parameter of FPDGM model satisfies $\lambda \neq 1$, the predicted result of the initial value satisfies $\hat{x}^{(0)}(1) \neq x^{(0)}(1)$. The traditional grey model takes initial point $\hat{x}^{(0)}(1) = x^{(0)}(1)$ as the basis of the further forecast (see Eq. (4)), but the information of the initial value is not used effectively. A common method is to assume the initial condition as $\hat{x}^{(1)}(1) = x^{(0)}(1) + c$ [17], and the variable c is solved by minimizing the fitting error, which may bring huge computational complexity. Based on the fixed-point axiom, FPDGM can smooth the initial data, and the prediction results depend on the information priority of the fixed point. Therefore, it is clear that the grey prediction model with FPAGO is more reasonable than 1-AGO.

6.3.3 Analysis of Modeling Conditions

The use of each model must meet certain modeling conditions. The quasi-exponential regularity of original sequence acts as an important modeling condition to evaluate the data reliability [33]. For an equidistant data sample, the grey model modeling criteria are as follows:

Lemma 1: ([1]) Assume $Y = \{y_1, y_2, \cdots, y_n\}$ is the raw time series; then it has the following provisions:

1. $\Delta(k) = |y_{k+1} - y_k|$ represents information difference.

2. $\sigma(k) = \dfrac{y_k}{y_{k+1}}$ is the stepwise ratio of the sequence Y. If $\forall k, \sigma(k) \in [a, b]$, $b - a = \delta$, then the sequence Y obeys the grey exponential regularity with absolute grey value. When $\delta < 0.5$, the sequence Y is considered to have a quasi-exponential regularity.

3. $\rho(k+1) = \dfrac{y_{k+1}}{\sum_{i=1}^{k} y_i}$ is the smooth ratio of the sequence Y.

If Y satisfies

$$\frac{\rho(k+1)}{\rho(k)} < 1 \text{ and } \rho(k+1) \in [0, 0.5],$$

the sequence Y is regarded as the quasi-smooth sequence, and its first-order accumulation generating sequence has a quasi-exponential regularity.

The stepwise ratio is an index describing the randomness of data series. After the accumulation generation operation, the randomness of the accumulative data series $X^{(1)}$ will decrease and show the characteristics of approximate exponential regularity. It is generally believed that if the sequence $X^{(0)}$ satisfies that $\sigma(k) = \dfrac{x^{(0)}(k)}{x^{(0)}(k+1)} \in \left(e^{-\frac{2}{n+1}}, e^{\frac{2}{n+1}} \right)$, then the raw data meet the high-precision modeling requirement of the grey model [32].

Theorem 1: Assume $X^{(\lambda)}$ is the λ-order fixed-point accumulated generating sequence of $X^{(0)}$. If the sequence $X^{(\lambda)}$ satisfies the stepwise ratio condition of modeling, then the raw sequence $X^{(0)}$ of FPDGM should meet the condition that $\rho\left(x^{(0)}(k)\right) \in [0, 1]$.

Proof.

According to Lemma 1, $\rho\left(x^{(0)}(k)\right) \in [0, 0.5]$, then the sequence $X^{(\lambda)}$ satisfies that

$$\sigma\left(x^{(\lambda)}(k)\right) = \frac{1}{1 + \rho\left(x^{(0)}(k)\right)} \in \left[\frac{2}{3}, 1 \right].$$

Therefore, we can have

$$0 \leq \frac{x^{(\lambda)}(k+1) - x^{(\lambda)}(k)}{x^{(\lambda)}(k)} \leq 1.$$

According to Property 1, $x^{(\lambda)}(k+1) > x^{(\lambda)}(k)$, so the preceding formula can be decomposed as

$$\lambda x^{(1)}(k+1) + (1-\lambda)(k+1)x^{(0)}(n) \leq \frac{3}{2}\lambda x^{(1)}(k) + \frac{3}{2}k(1-\lambda)x^{(0)}(n).$$

Then we can get

$$\rho\left(x^{(0)}(k+1)\right) = \frac{x^{(0)}(k+1)}{x^{(0)}(k)} \leq \frac{1}{2} + (\frac{k}{2}-1)\frac{1-\lambda}{\lambda}\frac{x^{(0)}(n)}{x^{(1)}(k)} \geq \frac{1}{2} + \max_{\lambda}\left[\min_{k \geq 3}\left((\frac{k}{2}-1)\frac{1-\lambda}{\lambda}\frac{x^{(0)}(n)}{x^{(1)}(k)}\right)\right] = 1.$$

Therefore, the smooth ratio condition of FPDGM is that $\rho\left(x^{(0)}(k)\right) \in [0,1]$.
Proof completed.

From Lemma 1, the modeling of traditional 1-AGO is subject to the smooth ratio requirement that $\rho\left(x^{(0)}(k)\right) \in [0,0.5]$, so the use of traditional models is limited by data. Comparing with 1-AGO, FPAGO has low requirements for modeling the original sequence that the smooth ratio condition $\rho\left(x^{(0)}(k)\right) \in [0,1]$, which can expand the adaptive range of the grey model.

6.3.4 Properties of the FPDGM Model

6.3.4.1 Smoothness Analysis of Accumulative Sequence

For the high accuracy of the prediction results, only non-negative upconcave sequences are suitable for grey models. By improving the smoothness of the sequence, the stepwise ratio of the raw sequence can be reduced. Through reasonable function transformation, the smoothness of the sequence can be improved for modeling accuracy. Wei et al. [34] gave the sufficient and necessary conditions for monotone functions to improve the smoothness of sequences in the grey prediction model.

Lemma 2 ([34]): Assuming $f(x)$ as a differentiable concave or convex function on an interval, the necessary and sufficient condition of $f(x)$ can improve the smoothness of any monotone; increasing/decreasing data sequence is that $f(x)$ is a monotone decreasing function on x. That is

$$\forall x \in [a,b], \frac{xf'(x)}{f(x)} < 1. \tag{6.14}$$

Theorem 2: Assume the sequence $X^{(0)} = \left\{x^{(0)}(1), x^{(0)}(2), \cdots, x^{(0)}(n)\right\}$ is the monotone sequence on the interval $[a,b]$, The accumulative sequence of FPAGO has a higher smoothing ratio than that of 1-AGO.

Proof.

FPAGO can be seen as the combination of the sequence buffering and then first-order accumulation. Then the function transformation of FPAGO can be denoted as

$$f(x^{(0)}(k)) = \lambda x^{(0)}(k) + \lambda x^{(0)}(n).$$

Thus we can easily deduce that

$$\frac{x^{(0)}(k) f'(x^{(0)}(k))}{f(x^{(0)}(k))} = \frac{\lambda x^{(0)}(k)}{\lambda x^{(0)}(k) + \lambda x^{(0)}(n)} < 1.$$

Proof completed.

FPAGO can be regarded as a functional transformation on the basis that a 1-AGO will smooth out the modeling sequence. Reasonable data conversion technology can improve the smoothness of the accumulative sequence, thus reducing the modeling requirements for the raw sequence $X^{(0)}$ (see Theorem 1). In addition, the influence of convexity must be taken into account to ensure that the transformed sequence has non-negative upconcavity during data transformation.

6.3.4.2 Stability Analysis of Solution

An effective forecasting model can predict the future uncertain trend with available information. However, the obtained "known information" often contains noise factors, which affects the stability of the results. Therefore, the stability of the model in the face of unknown factors is an important guarantee for the accuracy of the solution.

Lemma 3 ([35]): Assume $A \in C^{m \times n}$, $b \in C^m$, A^+ is the generalized inverse of A, $B = A + E$ and $c = b + k \in C^m$. Then x and $x + h$ are the solutions of $\min \|Ax - b\|_2$ and $\min \|Bx - c\|_2$, respectively. If $\|A^+\|_2 \|E\|_2 < 1$, then the perturbation bound is

$$\|h\| \le \frac{\kappa_+}{\gamma_+} \left(\frac{\|E\|_2}{\|A\|} \|x\| + \frac{\|k\|_2}{\|A\|} + \frac{\kappa_+}{\gamma_+} \frac{\|E\|_2}{\|A\|} \frac{\|r_x\|}{\|A\|} \right). \tag{6.15}$$

where $\kappa_+ = \|A^+\|_2 \|A\|$, $\gamma_+ = 1 - \|A^+\|_2 \|E\|_2$ and $r_x = b - Ax$.

Lemma 4 ([36]): Let the solution of the DGM $(x^{(1)}(k+1) = \beta_1 x^{(1)}(k) + \beta_2)$ is x. If only a disturbance happens that $\hat{x}^{(0)}(1) = x^{(0)}(1) + \varepsilon$, then the perturbation bound is

$$L\left[x^{(0)}(1)\right] = \sqrt{n-1}|\varepsilon|\frac{\kappa_+}{\gamma_+}\left(\frac{\|x\|}{\|B\|} + \frac{1}{\|B\|} + \frac{\kappa_+}{\gamma_+}\frac{1}{\|B\|}\frac{\|r_x\|}{\|B\|}\right). \tag{6.16}$$

If only a disturbance happens that $\hat{x}^{(0)}(k) = x^{(0)}(k) + \varepsilon, k = 2,3,\cdots,n$, then the perturbation bound is

$$L\left[x^{(0)}(k)\right] = |\varepsilon|\frac{\kappa}{\gamma}\left(\frac{\sqrt{n-k}}{\|B\|}\|x\| + \frac{\sqrt{n-k+1}}{\|B\|} + \frac{\kappa}{\gamma}\frac{\sqrt{n-k}}{\|B\|}\frac{\|r_x\|}{\|B\|}\right). \tag{6.17}$$

Theorem 3: According to the least square method, $\min\|Bx - Y\|_2, x$ is the solution of FPDGM. If only disturbance ε happens on $x^{(0)}(1)$, then the perturbation bound of the solution is

$$L\left[x^{(0)}(1)\right] = \lambda\sqrt{(n-1)}|\varepsilon|\frac{\kappa_+}{\gamma_+}\left(\frac{1}{\|B\|}\|x\| + \frac{1}{\|B\|} + \frac{\kappa_+}{\gamma_+}\frac{1}{\|B\|}\frac{\|r_x\|}{\|B\|}\right). \tag{6.18}$$

If only disturbance happens that $\hat{x}^{(0)}(k) = x^{(0)}(k) + \varepsilon, k = 2,3,\cdots,n-1$, then the perturbation bound of the solution is

$$L\left[x^{(0)}(k)\right] = \lambda|\varepsilon|\frac{\kappa_+}{\gamma_+}\left(\frac{\sqrt{n-k}}{\|B\|}\|x\| + \frac{\sqrt{n-k+1}}{\|B\|} + \frac{\kappa_+}{\gamma_+}\frac{\sqrt{n-k}}{\|B\|}\frac{\|r_x\|}{\|B\|}\right). \tag{6.19}$$

If only disturbance ε happens on $x^{(0)}(n)$, then the perturbation bound of the solution is

$$L\left[x^{(0)}(n)\right] = |\varepsilon|\frac{\kappa_+}{\gamma_+}\left(\frac{\sqrt{\frac{n(n-1)(2n-1)}{6}}(1-\lambda)}{\|B\|}\|x\| + \frac{\sqrt{\frac{n(n-1)(2n-1)}{6}-1}(1-\lambda)^2 + (n-n\lambda+\lambda)^2}{\|B\|} + \frac{\kappa_+}{\gamma_+}\frac{\sqrt{\frac{n(n-1)(2n-1)}{6}}(1-\lambda)}{\|B\|}\frac{\|r_x\|}{\|B\|}\right). \tag{6.20}$$

Proof.

If only disturbance ε happens on $x^{(0)}(1)$, substituting $x^{(0)}(1) = x^{(0)}(1) + \varepsilon$ into Eq. (6.8), we have

$$x^{(\lambda)}(k) = x^{(\lambda)}(k) + \lambda\varepsilon.$$

Then

$$
B + \Delta B = \begin{bmatrix} x^{(r)}(1) & 1 \\ x^{(r)}(2) & 1 \\ \vdots & \vdots \\ x^{(r)}(n-1) & 1 \end{bmatrix} + \begin{bmatrix} \lambda\varepsilon & 0 \\ \lambda\varepsilon & 0 \\ \vdots & \vdots \\ \lambda\varepsilon & 0 \end{bmatrix}, \quad Y + \Delta Y = \begin{bmatrix} x^{(r)}(2) \\ x^{(r)}(3) \\ \vdots \\ x^{(r)}(n) \end{bmatrix} + \begin{bmatrix} \lambda\varepsilon \\ \lambda\varepsilon \\ \vdots \\ \lambda\varepsilon \end{bmatrix}.
$$

Assume the solution of the optimization problem $\min\|Bx - Y\|_2$ is Δx. Considering that the columns of B are linearly independent, $\min\|Bx - Y\|_2$ has a unique solution $x = Y^{\dagger}b$.

Given that

$$
\|\Delta Y\|_2 = \sqrt{n-1}\lambda|\varepsilon|, \ \Delta B^T \Delta B = \begin{bmatrix} (n-1)\lambda^2\varepsilon^2 & 0 \\ 0 & 0 \end{bmatrix}, \ \|\Delta B\|_2 = \sqrt{(n-1)}\lambda|\varepsilon|.
$$

Because $\|B^{\dagger}\|_2 \|\Delta B\|_2 < 1$ and $B^{\dagger}$ are Moore–Penrose, the perturbation bound of the solution can be given by Lemma 3, that is,

$$
\|\Delta x\| \leq \frac{\kappa_+}{\gamma_+}\left(\frac{\|\Delta B\|_2}{\|B\|}\|x\| + \frac{\|\Delta Y\|_2}{\|B\|} + \frac{\kappa_+}{\gamma_+}\frac{\|\Delta B\|_2}{\|B\|}\frac{\|r_x\|}{\|B\|} \right).
$$

So

$$
L\left[x^{(0)}(1)\right] = \lambda|\varepsilon|\frac{\kappa_+}{\gamma_+}\left(\frac{\sqrt{(n-1)}}{\|B\|}\|x\| + \frac{\sqrt{(n-1)}}{\|B\|} + \frac{\kappa_+}{\gamma_+}\frac{\sqrt{(n-1)}}{\|B\|}\frac{\|r_x\|}{\|B\|} \right).
$$

If ε is regarded as a disturbance of $x^{(0)}(2)$, then

$$
\Delta B = \begin{bmatrix} 0 & 0 \\ \lambda\varepsilon & 0 \\ \lambda\varepsilon & 0 \\ \vdots & \vdots \\ \lambda\varepsilon & 0 \end{bmatrix}, \ \Delta Y = \begin{bmatrix} \lambda\varepsilon \\ \lambda\varepsilon \\ \vdots \\ \lambda\varepsilon \end{bmatrix}.
$$

The perturbation bound for the solution of FPDGM is

$$
L\left[x^{(0)}(2)\right] = \lambda|\varepsilon|\frac{\kappa_+}{\gamma_+}\left(\frac{\sqrt{n-2}}{\|B\|}\|x\| + \frac{\sqrt{n-1}}{\|B\|} + \frac{\kappa_+}{\gamma_+}\frac{\sqrt{n-2}}{\|B\|}\frac{\|r_x\|}{\|B\|} \right).
$$

Similarly, if ε is the disturbance happening on $x^{(0)}(k)$, $k = 3, 4, \cdots, n-1$, we can get

$$L\left[x^{(0)}(k)\right] = \lambda|\varepsilon|\frac{\kappa_+}{\gamma_+}\left(\frac{\sqrt{n-k}}{\|B\|}\|x\| + \frac{\sqrt{n-k+1}}{\|B\|} + \frac{\kappa_+}{\gamma_+}\frac{\sqrt{n-k}}{\|B\|}\frac{\|r_x\|}{\|B\|}\right).$$

If ε is the disturbance happening on $x^{(0)}(n)$, then

$$\Delta B = \begin{bmatrix} (1-\lambda)\varepsilon & 0 \\ 2(1-\lambda)\varepsilon & 0 \\ 3(1-\lambda)\varepsilon & 0 \\ \vdots & \vdots \\ (n-1)(1-\lambda)\varepsilon & 0 \end{bmatrix}, \Delta Y = \begin{bmatrix} 2(1-\lambda)\varepsilon \\ 3(1-\lambda)\varepsilon \\ \vdots \\ (n-1)(1-\lambda)\varepsilon \\ (n-n\lambda+\lambda)\varepsilon \end{bmatrix}.$$

The perturbation bound of FPDGM is

$$L\left[x^{(0)}(n)\right] = |\varepsilon|\frac{\kappa_+}{\gamma_+}\left(\frac{\sqrt{\frac{n(n-1)(2n-1)}{6}}(1-\lambda)}{\|B\|}\|x\| + \frac{\sqrt{\left[\frac{n(n-1)(2n-1)}{6}-1\right](1-\lambda)^2+(n-n\lambda+\lambda)^2}}{\|B\|} + \frac{\kappa_+}{\gamma_+}\frac{\sqrt{\frac{n(n-1)(2n-1)}{6}}(1-\lambda)}{\|B\|}\frac{\|r_x\|}{\|B\|}\right).$$

Proof completed.

The matrix disturbance theory verifies that the model can keep the solution stable when the system is disturbed. Lemma 4 gives the stability analysis of the traditional DGM with 1-AGO. From Eq. (6.17), it is clear that the perturbation bound of the solution increases with n. This is the main reason why the grey prediction model cannot carry out large sample prediction [37]. Theorem 3 analyzes the stability of the solution of the FPDGM model. From Eq. (6.19), it can be found that the stability of the FPDGM model is related to the accumulated parameter λ. In addition, the perturbation of the latest point will have the greatest impact on the predictions, so the FPDGM model must guarantee the accuracy of the "fixed point" $x^{(0)}(n)$. Accurate new information is used to reduce the influence of interrupted old information on the prediction results. And the accumulated parameter λ can adaptively adjust the importance of information. From Lemma 4 and Theorem 3, it is obvious that the perturbation bound of the FPDGM is improved compared with the traditional DGM with 1-AGO, and the influence degree of information disturbance can be changed by using the accumulated parameter values. Then the following properties of the perturbation bound of FPDGM can be obtained:

Property 3: For the predicted results, the new information $x^{(0)}(n)$ has a larger perturbation bound than the old information $x^{(0)}(k)$, $k < n$.

Property 4: If ε is a disturbance that happens on $x^{(0)}(k), k < n$, the FPDGM model has a smaller perturbation bound than the DGM model. The smaller the accumulative parameter λ is, the more stable the results of the FPDGM model are.

6.3.5 Solution of Hyperparameter

The selection of the system hyperparameter has an important effect on the forecasting results. In addition to the traditional method, this paper provides a method to solve a more reasonable parameter λ according to the error of the verification set.

The traditional method typically uses the MAPE error between all the fitted data and the actual data to select the hyperparameter. Thus the value of the cumulative parameter λ can be determined by the following nonlinear optimization problem:

$$\min_{\lambda} \text{MAPE} = \frac{1}{n} \sum_{k=1}^{n} \left| \frac{\hat{x}^{(0)}(k) - x^{(0)}(k)}{x^{(0)}(k)} \right| \times 100\%. \tag{6.21}$$

The purpose of this simple method is used to minimize the fitting MAPE of input data. However, the future state of the system may be uncertain and abrupt. Our desire is to be able to use the latest data to test the reasonableness of the hyperparameter. Therefore, if the sample size of the data is sufficient, it is a better way to divide the sample data into training set and verification set reasonably. And then the parameter λ can be identified by the predicted MAPE of recent data, as shown in Figure 6.2. Thus the following nonlinear optimization problem can be established:

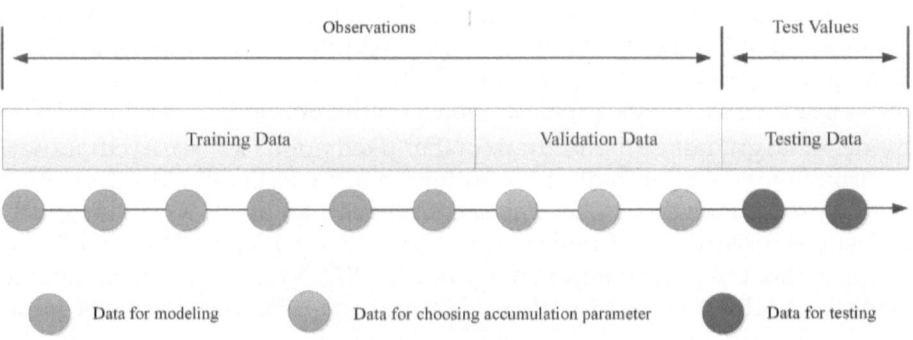

FIGURE 6.2
Partitioning of data sets for accurately estimating the system status.

$$\min_{\lambda} MAPE_{validation} = \frac{1}{n-m+1} \sum_{i=m}^{n} \left| \frac{\hat{x}^{(0)}(i) - x^{(0)}(i)}{x^{(0)}(i)} \right| \times 100\% . \qquad (6.22)$$

To solve this optimization problem, a brute force method can increase the λ from 0 to 1 by 0.001at a time for choosing a satisfactory solution. But this often requires considerable computational resources. Considering that only one hyperparameter of FPDGM model needs to be solved, the heuristic algorithms [30] are convenient to solve the hyperparameter of the FPDGM. Figure 6.3 shows the flowchart of solving the accumulative parameter of FPDGM by the PSO algorithm.

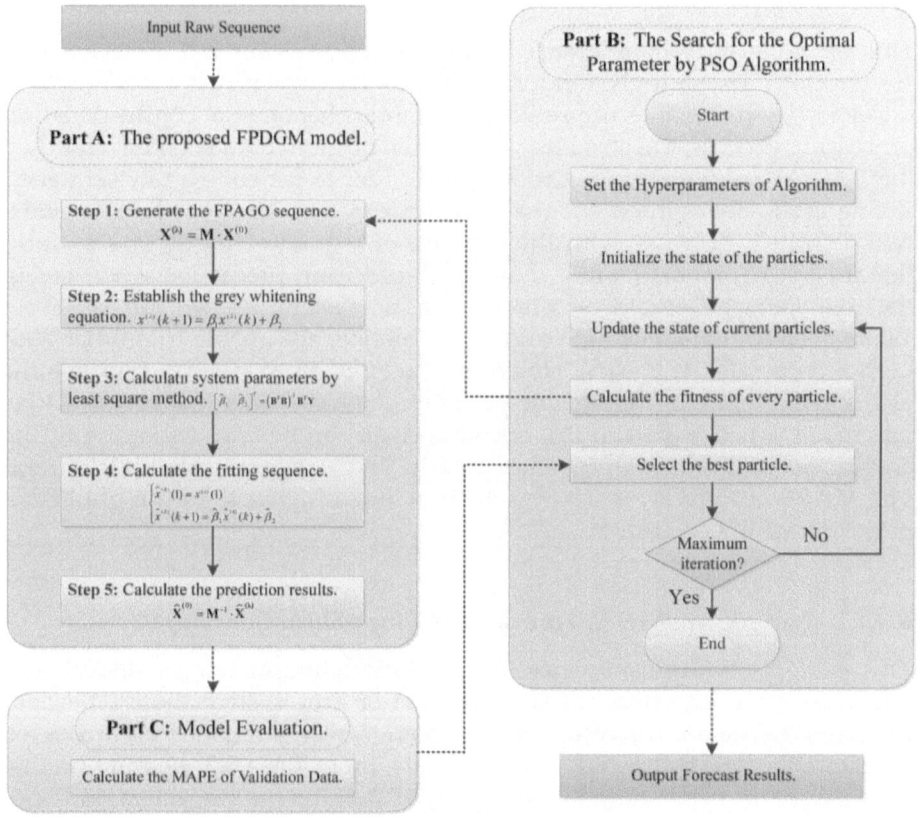

FIGURE 6.3
Flowchart of parameter optimization of FPDGM by PSO algorithm.

6.4 Validation

6.4.1 Practical Examples

The fixed-point axiom provides a new idea for the research of the weighted grey model. To verify the prediction effect of the FPDGM model, this section provides three numerical examples to analyze the prediction performance of FPDGM from different perspectives. Example analysis I shows the fitting effect of the FPDGM model. Example analysis II verifies the predictive stability of the FPDGM in the face of the impact disturbance series. Finally, example analysis III shows the comparison of the FPAGO with other existing grey generating operators.

6.4.1.1 *Example Analysis I: Lorenz Chaotic System Forecasting Example*

This example is from reference [38]. A chaotic system is a deterministic system with a seemingly random irregular movement, whose behavior is uncertain, unrepeatable, unpredictable chaotic phenomena. For the data preprocessing process, the absolute value of the original data is taken, and then the 1-AGO is performed in chronological order to generate a raw sequence. Zhang et al. [38] pointed out that the accuracy of a grey prediction model will definitely decrease with the increase of sequence length, so the traditional GM (1,1) model cannot make high-precision prediction when facing the sequences generated by Lorenz chaotic system. As we can see from Table 6.1, traditional GM (1,1) and DGM models are unable to predict with high accuracy (MAPE>10%). However, the FPDGM model can improve the fitting effect by choosing flexible parameter values. When the accumulative parameter λ is 0.8, 0.5 and 0.3, respectively, it can be found that the fitting accuracy of FPDGM is improved gradually. The best parameter λ is 0.277, and The MAPE of FPDGM is 3.80%, which is much higher than the prediction performance of GM (1,1).

6.4.1.2 *Example Analysis II: Forecast of China's Shale Gas Output*

This example is from reference [26]. The modeling of impact disturbance sequence is an important research content of grey system theory. Because the statistical data is distorted by unknown factors, it must be preprocessed to restore the true characteristics of the data. From Table 6.2, we can find that the fitting and prediction accuracy of GM (1,1) for the impact disturbance series are not ideal, and the raw data does not meet the requirement of the grey model. Therefore, the data must be preprocessed first. According to the method in reference [26], the average buffer operator is used to preprocess the raw data:

TABLE 6.1

Predicted Results of the FPDGM Model with Different Accumulative Parameter

Raw sequence	GM (1,1)	DGM	FPDGM⁰·⁸	FPDGM⁰·⁵	FPDGM⁰·³	FPDGM⁰·²⁷⁷
0.155	0.16	0.16	0.07	0.08	0.14	0.15
1.11	2.29	2.30	1.83	1.46	1.36	1.35
1.92	2.54	2.55	2.15	1.89	1.85	1.85
2.24	2.83	2.84	2.51	2.34	2.35	2.36
3.03	3.15	3.16	2.89	2.81	2.86	2.87
3.3	3.50	3.51	3.30	3.29	3.39	3.40
4.16	3.89	3.90	3.74	3.80	3.92	3.94
4.64	4.33	4.34	4.22	4.32	4.47	4.49
5.18	4.81	4.83	4.73	4.87	5.02	5.04
5.6	5.35	5.37	5.28	5.44	5.59	5.61
6.25	5.95	5.97	5.88	6.03	6.18	6.19
6.39	6.62	6.63	6.52	6.64	6.77	6.79
7.35	7.36	7.38	7.21	7.28	7.38	7.39
8.18	8.18	8.20	7.96	7.94	8.00	8.00
8.57	9.10	9.12	8.76	8.63	8.63	8.63
9.27	10.12	10.14	9.63	9.35	9.27	9.27
MAPE	13.97%	14.11%	12.71%	8.33%	4.32%	**3.81%**

TABLE 6.2

Predicted Results of China's Shale Gas Output

Year	Raw Value	Relative Growth	GM (1,1)	Processed Value: XD_2	Relative Growth	GM (1,1)	FPDGM
2012	0.25	/	0.25	38.12	/	27.76	36.39
2013	2.00	700.00%	18.43	45.70	19.87%	37.45	45.70
2014	13.00	550.00%	29.63	56.62	23.91%	47.01	55.98
2015	44.71	243.92%	47.65	71.16	25.68%	59.02	67.03
2016	78.82	76.29%	76.62	84.39	18.58%	74.09	78.91
2017	89.95	14.12%	123.20	89.95	6.59%	93.02	91.67
Fitting MAPE			**165.96%**			4.21%	**3.31%**
	108.81	20.97%	198.10		/	116.78	105.37
Forecast MAPE			**82.06%**			7.32%	**3.16%**

$$x(k)d_2 = XD_2 = \frac{1}{n-k+1}\sum_{i=k}^{n} x(i). \tag{6.23}$$

After buffering, the original raw of inconsistent growth rate becomes smooth. For the preprocessed sequence XD_2, GM (1,1) has high fitting accuracy and its fitting MAPE is 4.21%. Then the parameter solving of FPDGM is done in the traditional method (see Eq. [6.21]), and $\lambda = 0.4979$. As we can see, the FPDGM has the smaller prediction MAPE than GM (1,1). Based on the fixed-point axiom, the prediction MAPE of FPDGM is reduced from 7.32% of the traditional GM (1,1) to 3.16%. Therefore, it is clear that FPDGM can better adapt to the impact disturbance series modeling and improve the model accuracy.

6.4.1.3 Example Analysis III: Annual Electricity Consumption Forecast in China

Data of this example is from the reference [39]. Annual data on electricity consumption in China tends to grow monotonically and has the high smoothness, so the data can be adapted to the direct modeling of the grey model. The data from 2005 to 2016 were used for modeling, leaving 2 data points from 2017 to 2018 as tests. In addition to GM (1,1), DGM and non-homogeneous discrete grey model (NDGM) [40], we combine three existing grey generating operators with DGM models to construct three optimized discrete grey models. The formula and the abbreviations of the modified models are shown in Table 6.3. Since the sample size for the observations is greater than 8, the validation set can be used to perform the selection of the accumulative parameter of FPDGM. The FPDGM model with accumulative parameter λ selected by the fitting error of all data samples (see Eq. [6.21]) is denoted as FPDGM[a]. And the FPDGM model with validation set (see Eq. [6.22]) is denoted as FPDGM[b]. Then three data points from 2014 to 2016 are used as the validation set. Then the parameter optimization process of FPDGM[b] is

TABLE 6.3

Modified Grey Generating Operator

Accumulative Generating Operator	Formula	DGM with the Grey Generating Operator
Fractional accumulation [27]	$x^{(r)}(k) = \sum_{i=1}^{k} \binom{k-i+r-1}{k-i} x^{(0)}(i), 0 < r \leq 1$	F-DGM
New information priority accumulation [29]	$x^{(\xi)}(k) = \sum_{i=1}^{k} \xi^{k-i} x^{(0)}(i), \ 0 < \xi \leq 1$	NIP-DGM
Damping accumulation [30]	$x^{(\zeta)}(k) = \sum_{i=1}^{k} \frac{x^{(0)}(i)}{\zeta^{i-1}}, \ 0 < \zeta \leq 1$	D-DGM
Fixed-point accumulation	$x^{(\lambda)}(k) = \lambda \sum_{i=1}^{k} x^{(0)}(i) + k(1-\lambda) x^{(0)}(n)$	FPDGM

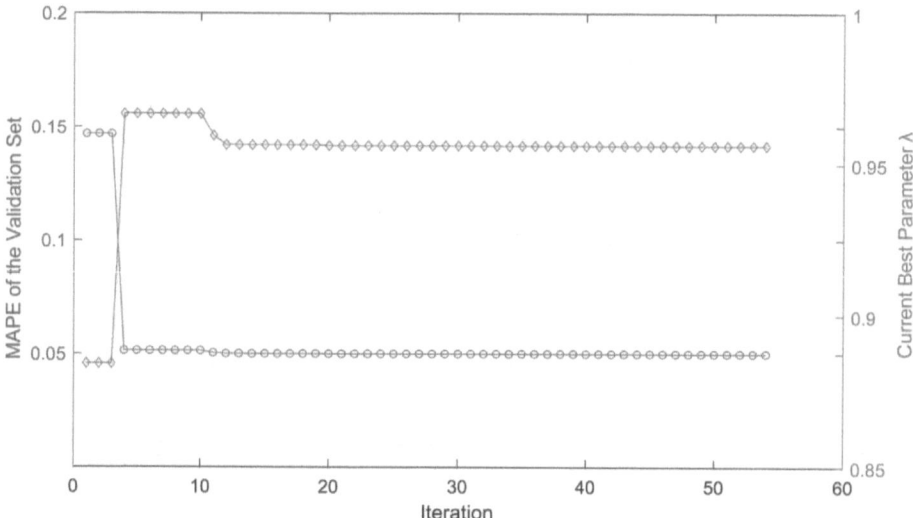

FIGURE 6.4
Optimal parameter optimization of FPDGM by the PSO algorithm.

shown in Figure 6.4. We can see that, after 20 iterations of the PSO algorithm, the optimal parameter minimizes the prediction error can be found. With the optimal parameter $\lambda = 0.9562$, we can make the next prediction.

The prediction results of the eight models are shown in Figure 6.5 and Table 6.4. The DGM with four modified grey generating operators all have better fitting MAPEs than the traditional three 1-AGO grey models. However, the performance of their prediction results is uncertain. Since the raw data approximates the quasi-exponential data (see Lemma 1), the accumulative parameter $\lambda >$ of the FPDGM[a] model is 1, and its prediction result is equivalent to that of the DGM model. This is obviously unreasonable that the FPDGM[a] model fails to correctly estimate the importance of the new information on the future state of the system. In contrast, the FPDGM[b] can make more accurate predictions by reasonably estimating the system state from the predicted errors in the validation set. Compared to other comparison models, the FPDGM[b] has the lowest forecast MAPE (3.42%). Therefore, when facing limited information for modeling, it is crucial to consider the different value of available information.

6.4.2 Validation with Benchmark Datasets

The Occam's razor principle tells us, "Under similar generalization error conditions, simpler [solutions] tend to be more effective." There is no need to waste time to determine whether you can achieve great results with fewer

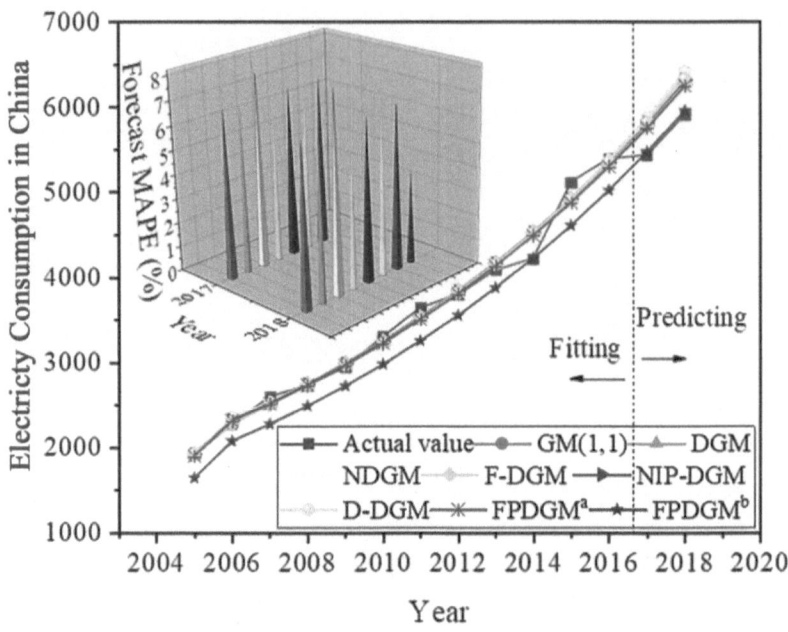

FIGURE 6.5

Predicted performance of the eight models on the electricity consumption in China.

TABLE 6.4

Predicting Results of the Grey Models

Date	Actual Value	GM (1,1)	DGM	NDGM	F-DGM	NIP-DGM	D-DGM	FPDGM[a]	FPDGM[b]
2005	1911	1911	1911	1911	1911	1911	1911	1911.00	1918.82
2006	2272	2312.92	2315.32	2342.35	2272.00	2314.24	2303.38	2315.32	2341.41
2007	2596	2514.72	2517.31	2532.63	2502.19	2516.70	2505.80	2517.31	2545.48
2008	2726	2734.14	2736.92	2741.85	2737.42	2736.73	2726.00	2736.92	2765.28
2009	2941	2972.69	2975.68	2971.91	2985.42	2975.85	2965.55	2975.69	3002.00
2010	3298	3232.07	3235.28	3224.88	3249.98	3235.71	3226.16	3235.28	3256.96
2011	3635	3514.07	3517.52	3503.04	3533.82	3518.11	3509.66	3517.52	3531.56
2012	3794	3820.68	3824.39	3808.90	3839.33	3825.01	3818.08	3824.39	3827.32
2013	4083	4154.04	4158.03	4145.22	4168.77	4158.54	4153.60	4158.03	4145.85
2014	4223	4516.49	4520.77	4515.03	4524.45	4521.00	4518.61	4520.77	4488.93
2015	5117	4910.56	4915.15	4921.67	4908.78	4914.90	4915.69	4915.15	4858.43
2016	5390	5339.01	5343.95	5368.80	5324.30	5342.97	5347.66	5343.95	5256.39
Fitting MAPE		2.17%	2.18%	2.17%	2.13%	2.18%	**2.12%**	2.18%	2.44%
2017	5430	5804.85	5810.15	5860.45	5773.72	5808.18	5817.60	5810.15	5685.01
2018	5916	6311.33	6317.02	6401.07	6259.96	6313.75	6328.83	6317.02	6146.65
Forecast MAPE		6.79%	6.89%	8.06%	6.07%	6.89%	7.06%	6.89%	**4.30%**

resources. Therefore, we chose benchmark datasets to evaluate the superiority of the FPDGM model against the existing algorithms.

6.4.2.1 Benchmark Datasets

The M4-competition datasets are used as benchmark datasets to test the forecast performance of the FPDGM. The M4 competition [41] is an open competition that evaluates the predictive performance of participating statistical algorithms or machine learning algorithms using the given training and test sample datasets,1 specifically designed for time series forecasting research. The M4 dataset has the following characteristics:

Multi-Frequency Coverage: The M4 dataset comprises 100,000 time series spanning five distinct frequencies: yearly (23,000 series), quarterly (24,000 series), monthly (48,000 series), weekly (359 series), and daily (4,227 series). This wide range of frequencies makes it well-suited for evaluating a model's predictive performance across different time scales.

Diverse Domains: The time series in the dataset are sourced from various application domains, primarily including finance, economics, demographics, industry, and other areas. This diversity reflects the complexity and variability across fields, supporting a comprehensive evaluation of model applicability and robustness in different sectors.

Varying Series Lengths: Series lengths range from a few dozen to several hundred data points, assessing models on both short- and long-term forecasts.

Data Stability and Volatility: Differences in seasonality, trend, and stability across series challenge model adaptability and highlight generalizability.

This paper is to verify the effectiveness of the FPDGM in the small sample prediction problems, so the original data samples need to be segmented. We selected the first 10,000 annual samples (Y1~Y10000) and kept only the first 13 data of all samples. Then, for each sample, the first 10 data are used for modeling analysis, leaving the last 3 data to test the 1-step, 2-step, and 3-step prediction errors of the model, as shown in Figure 6.6.

6.4.2.2 Model and Parameter Settings

In addition to the grey models, the simple exponential smoothing model (SES), the moving average method (MA), and the naive forecasting method (NF) are used as the benchmark models. These traditional statistical methods are simple to model and do not require much computational resources.

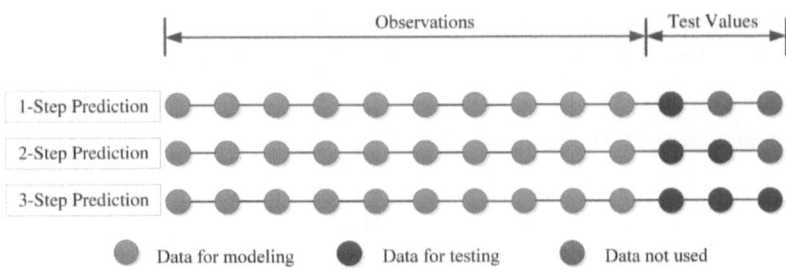

FIGURE 6.6
Multistep verification of time series predictions.

Then the fractional grey model (FGM (1,1)) [27], conformable fractional grey model (CFGM (1,1)) [28], and new information propriety grey model (NIPGM (1,1)) [29] are used as comparison. For the fairness of the calculation results, these three models and the FPDGM model are all solved with the parameter solution of Eq. (6.21).

6.4.2.3 Experimental Results and Analysis

A summary of the results of $10,000$ data samples is shown in Table 6.5. It can be seen that the traditional GM (1,1) algorithm has its unique advantage over other statistical methods for the small sample prediction problem. FPDGM has the best one-step prediction performance with an average prediction MAPE of 7.94%. The average prediction accuracy of all models decreases as the number of prediction steps increases. And the three-step forecast average MAPE of the FPDGM is greater than 10%, which may be no longer reliable. Then the maximum error shows the worst performance of the models in $10,000$ samples. SES has the smallest maximum error, which proves that the simple method is also highly stable. In addition, the performance of the other six grey models is similar. Therefore, we can conclude that FPDGM has better predictive stability and more accurate prediction results compared to the traditional models.

6.5 Forecast of International Natural Gas Futures Contract Price

6.5.1 Data Sources

Natural gas is a kind of precious nonrenewable energy. The futures price of natural gas is mainly affected by international energy price, supply–demand relationship, season, monetary policy and other factors. In order to fully verify the generalization of the FPDGM model, this case selects the international

TABLE 6.5

Predictive Performance of the Models on 10000 Sample Sets

Accuracy Criteria		SES			MA			NF		
		1-Step	2-Step	3-Step	1-Step	2-Step	3-Step	1-Step	2-Step	3-Step
MAE	Average	238.17	304.89	373.79	290.85	354.53	422.67	225.06	292.90	362.47
	Maximum	1.37E+04	1.37E+04	1.38E+04	1.48E+04	1.31E+04	1.26E+04	1.28E+04	1.26E+04	1.22E+04
MAPE	Average	9.74%	12.54%	15.11%	12.32%	14.90%	17.37%	9.25%	12.11%	14.71%
	Maximum	4.31	4.02	3.92	4.31	4.68	4.51	4.94	4.07	3.93
RMSE	Average	238.17	326.15	411.78	290.85	373.75	457.80	225.06	314.80	401.41
	Maximum	13705.68	14370.25	14940.42	14838.00	13223.32	12673.88	12762.00	14370.25	14940.42

Accuracy Criteria		GM (1,1)			DGM			FGM (1,1)		
		1-Step	2-Step	3-Step	1-Step	2-Step	3-Step	1-Step	2-Step	3-Step
MAE	Average	270.81	333.73	408.09	250.50	303.61	362.07	255.56	336.10	438.25
	Maximum	1.45E+05	2.20E+05	3.48E+05	6.72E+04	9.89E+04	1.51E+05	1.45E+05	2.20E+05	3.48E+05
MAPE	Average	10.59%	14.07%	16.13%	9.22%	11.67%	13.30%	10.64%	14.87%	17.84%
	Maximum	177.20	327.33	357.86	82.12	146.56	156.82	177.20	327.33	357.87
RMSE	Average	270.81	354.64	449.16	250.50	322.91	397.25	255.56	361.10	491.48
	Maximum	144950.53	232763.42	397615.24	67177.17	103852.75	170432.93	144952.62	232767.02	397621.86

Accuracy Criteria		CFGM (1,1)			NIPGM (1,1)			FPDGM		
		1-Step	2-Step	3-Step	1-Step	2-Step	3-Step	1-Step	2-Step	3-Step
MAE	Average	249.89	300.13	355.30	252.36	325.22	416.04	229.73	278.79	330.20
	Maximum	1.44E+04	1.45E+04	1.93E+04	1.45E+05	2.20E+05	3.48E+05	1.27E+04	1.20E+04	1.30E+04
MAPE	Average	8.72%	10.47%	12.05%	10.13%	13.93%	16.52%	7.94%	9.73%	11.24%
	Maximum	4.99	6.79	6.62	177.20	327.33	357.86	4.93	5.02	5.13
RMSE	Average	249.89	318.34	388.51	252.36	348.86	465.11	229.73	297.58	363.33
	Maximum	14408.27	14691.92	20597.64	144950.69	232763.69	397615.75	12671.73	12003.96	14245.10

natural gas futures contract price for prediction. The used data can be downloaded free from the website (http://www.eia.gov/dnav/ng/hist/rng c1w.htm).

6.5.2 Compared Models and Parameter Settings

The case intercepts the transaction price data of 1009 consecutive natural weeks. Using the sliding window method, the data of every ten consecutive weeks is taken as a sample, and a total of 1000 experimental samples are generated. Then, for each sample, the first seven data points are used for modeling, and the last three data points are used as tests to verify the single-step and multistep prediction ability of the grey model in the small sample prediction problem. The FPDGM model are all solved with the parameter solution of Eq. (6.21). GM (1,1) and FGM (1,1) models are used as comparison models, and the prediction results are evaluated by MAPE, mean absolute error (MAE), and mean square error (MSE).

$$\text{MAE} = \frac{1}{m} \sum_{i=n+1}^{n+m} \left| \hat{x}^{(0)}(i) - x^{(0)}(i) \right| \tag{6.24}$$

$$\text{MSE} = \frac{1}{m} \sum_{i=n+1}^{n+m} \left(\hat{x}^{(0)}(i) - x^{(0)}(i) \right)^2 \tag{6.25}$$

6.5.3 Predicted Results of Natural Gas Futures Contract Price

Table 6.6 lists the predicted average error and maximum error of 1000 groups of samples. It's obvious that the grey models can reasonably forecast the short-term changes of international natural gas futures contract price. Although the uncertainty of the data fluctuates greatly, the average prediction error of the models is acceptable (MAPE < 10%). The average prediction error of the FPDGM model is the smallest in comparative models, that is, the MAPE of one-step prediction is 4.96%. Figure 6.7 shows the single-step prediction result curve of the three models. In addition, the Diebold–Mariano (DM) test [42] is used to evaluate the model performance of the prediction results in Figure 6.7. The model comparison results are shown in Table 6.7. The results of the DM test show that the prediction performance of the grey model is significantly improved after introducing the proposed fixed-point accumulation operator. FPDGM has better generalization and more accurate prediction results than the existing GM (1,1) and FGM (1,1) models.

6.5.4 Practical Implications

This study develops a FPDGM model for forecasting international natural gas futures contract prices, with a focus on validating its generalization and

TABLE 6.6

Error Statistics of Grey Models

Error Criterion		GM (1,1)			FGM (1,1)			FPDGM		
		1-Step	2-Step	3-Step	1-Step	2-Step	3-Step	1-Step	2-Step	3-Step
MAE	Average	0.29	0.36	0.43	0.25	0.34	0.43	0.23	0.32	0.4
	Maximum	3.72	4.66	5.47	2.78	4.89	9.04	3.4	5.21	7.11
MSE	Average	0.2	0.33	0.52	0.15	0.32	0.61	0.14	0.3	0.51
	Maximum	13.85	22.55	31.84	7.75	31.17	120.99	11.59	30.39	59.92
MAPE	Average	6.11%	7.62%	9.07%	5.31%	7.19%	9.13%	4.96%	6.74%	8.46%
	Maximum	42.57%	55.22%	65.55%	29.47%	50.18%	79.87%	48.55%	84.51%	124.80%

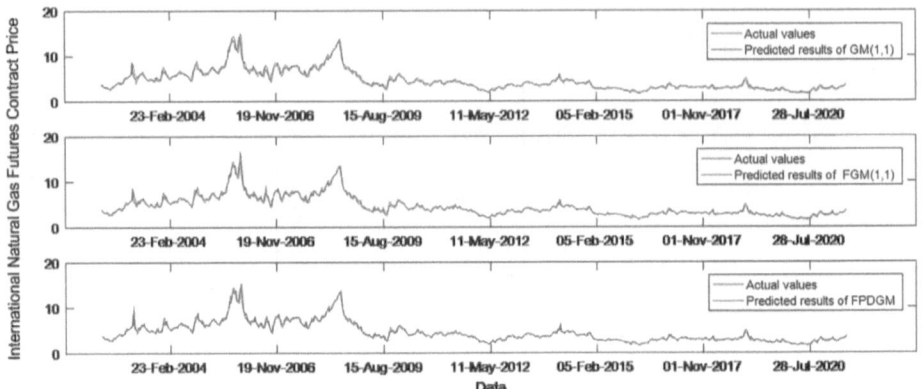

FIGURE 6.7
Forecast results of international natural gas futures contract prices.

TABLE 6.7

DM Test of Prediction Results of Three Models

	FPDGM vs GM (1,1)		FPDGM vs. FGM (1,1)		FGM (1,1) vs. GM (1,1)	
Error Criterion	DM Statistic	*p* Value	DM Statistic	*p* Value	DM Statistic	*p* Value
MAE	−8.52	0.00	−2.94	0.00	−5.44	0.00
MSE	−3.57	0.00	−0.52	0.61	−3.69	0.00
MAPE	**−10.51**	**0.00**	**−4.11**	**0.00**	−6.21	0.00

Note: Model I vs. model II. If the DM statistical value is less than 0, it indicates that the prediction performance of model I is better than that of model II; If the *p* value of DM test is less than 0.05, it indicates that the statistical results are significant.

accuracy in small-sample prediction scenarios. Natural gas, as a nonrenewable energy source, not only plays a crucial role in the energy markets but also has significant implications for the global economy, environmental policy, and international trade. Hence accurate forecasting tools are essential for market stability, energy policy formulation, and corporate risk management.

The FPDGM model demonstrates superior performance in forecasting under high uncertainty, achieving an average MAPE of less than 10%, significantly outperforming the traditional GM (1,1) and FGM (1,1) models in both prediction accuracy and generalization capacity. This advantage extends beyond natural gas markets and may be applicable in other markets with similar characteristics, such as oil and metals futures, where prices are similarly influenced by factors like supply–demand dynamics, policy shifts, and seasonal fluctuations. The practical applications of the FPDGM model include several potential use cases:

Short-Term Trading Decisions: Traders can leverage the FPDGM model to capture short-term price trends more accurately, enhancing decision-making precision and market responsiveness.

Long-Term Price Forecasting: By extending the FPDGM model's multi-step forecasting capabilities, policymakers can use it as a tool for developing adaptive supply–demand strategies to manage market volatility.

Risk Management and Portfolio Optimization: Given the high volatility in energy markets, accurate price forecasting models like the FPDGM model provide institutional investors and fund managers with more diversified strategy options for effective risk control.

6.6 Conclusions

In this paper, we proposed a novel fixed-point accumulative grey generating operator (FPAGO) and then built the fixed-point discrete grey model (FPDGM). It has been proved that the proposed FPAGO can increase the smoothness of the accumulative sequence and thus increase the adaptive range of the grey model. Meanwhile, the solution of the constructed improved grey prediction model has higher stability than its traditional form. In addition, to accurately estimating the future state of the system, a parameter solution based on minimizing forecast error of validation set is proposed.

Numerical examples are used to validate the performance of the proposed FPDGM model. Based on the experimental results, the following conclusions can be drawn: (1) A reasonable parameter selection is beneficial for the FPDGM model to achieve better prediction results. (2) The validation set can effectively prevent the model from overfitting and make accurate prediction. (3) FPAGO can be used in combination with extended structures of the grey model. Based on the fixed-point axiom, the proposed FPDGM can have higher accuracy than other existing models in forecasting the natural gas futures contract price.

While the proposed FPAGO significantly enhances the grey model's performance in small sample forecasting, certain limitations warrant discussion: (1) The FPDGM model's performance is sensitive to parameter choices, which may require significant computational effort for optimization, particularly for large datasets or those with high volatility. (2) The current model assumes a fixed-point applicable to the entire sequence, which may not be ideal for highly nonstationary data. (3) Integrating different grey generating operators could leverage their respective advantages, which is a promising direction for further improving prediction accuracy across diverse datasets. These limitations suggest potential avenues for future research. Subsequent work will focus on developing variable structures, refining data processing techniques to better handle perturbation, and exploring the combined use of different grey generating operators.

The M4-competition datasets are available at the website https://github.com/Mcompetitions/M4-methods.

Note

1   The M4-competition datasets are available at the website https://github.com/Mcompetitions/M4-methods.

References

[1]   Jin B, Xu X. Price forecasting through neural networks for crude oil, heating oil, and natural gas. *Measurement: Energy*, 2024, 1(1): 100001.

[2]   Anser MK, Khan KA, Umar M, et al. Formulating sustainable development policy for a developed nation: Exploring the role of renewable energy, natural gas efficiency and oil efficiency towards decarbonization. *International Journal of Sustainable Development & World Ecology*, 2024, 31(3): 247–263.

[3]   He X, Chen G, Wu J, et al. Deep shale gas exploration and development in the southern Sichuan Basin: New progress and challenges. *Natural Gas Industry B*, 2023, 10(1): 32–43.

[4]   Ediger VŞ, Berk I. Future availability of natural gas: Can it support sustainable energy transition? *Resources Policy*, 2023, 85: 103824.

[5]   Guo T, Wang Y, Tan B, et al. Research on productivity of stimulated natural gas hydrate reservoir. *Renewable Energy*, 2024, 225: 120240.

[6]   Shaari MS, Majekodunmi TB, Zainal NF, et al. The linkage between natural gas consumption and industrial output: New evidence based on time series analysis. *Energy*, 2023, 284: 129395.

[7]   Tiwari AK, Sharma GD, Rao A, et al. Unraveling the crystal ball: Machine learning models for crude oil and natural gas volatility forecasting. *Energy Economics*, 2024, 134: 107608.

[8]   Tian N, Shao B, Bian G, et al. Application of forecasting strategies and techniques to natural gas consumption: A comprehensive review and comparative study. *Engineering Applications of Artificial Intelligence*, 2024, 129: 107644.

[9]   Lu Q, Liao J, Chen K, et al. Predicting natural gas prices based on a novel hybrid model with variational mode decomposition. *Computational Economics*, 2024, 63(2): 639–678.

[10] Liu S, Lin Y. *Grey Systems: Theory and Applications*. London: Springer, 2010.

[11] Liu L, Liu S, Fang Z, et al. The recursive grey model and its application. *Applied Mathematical Modelling*, 2023, 119: 447–464.

[12] Tian D, Zhao X, Gao L, et al. Estimation of water quality variables based on machine learning model and cluster analysis-based empirical model using multi-source remote sensing data in inland reservoirs, South China. *Environmental Pollution*, 2024, 342: 123104.

[13] Tarmanini C, Sarma N, Gezegin C, et al. Short term load forecasting based on ARIMA and ANN approaches. *Energy Reports*, 2023, 9: 550–557.

[14] Smyl S. A hybrid method of exponential smoothing and recurrent neural networks for time series forecasting. *International Journal of Forecasting*, 2020, 36(1): 75–85.

[15] Cai W, Wen X, Li C, et al. Predicting the energy consumption in buildings using the optimized support vector regression model. *Energy*, 2023, 273: 127188.

[16] Ye L, Xie N, Boylan JE, et al. Forecasting seasonal demand for retail: A Fourier time-varying grey model. *International Journal of Forecasting*, 2024.

[17] Wei B, Xie N, Hu A. Optimal solution for novel grey polynomial prediction model. *Applied Mathematical Modelling*, 2018, 62: 717–727.

[18] Liu XM, Xie NM. A nonlinear grey forecasting model with double shape parameters and its application. *Applied Mathematics and Computation*, 2019, 360: 203–212.

[19] Xu Y, Lin T, Du P. A hybrid coal prediction model based on grey Markov optimized by GWO–a case study of Hebei province in China. *Expert Systems with Applications*, 2024, 235: 121194.

[20] Li W, Su Q, Hu Z. A grey prediction evolutionary algorithm with a surrogate model based on quadratic interpolation. *Expert Systems with Applications*, 2024, 236: 121261.

[21] Shaikh F, Ji Q, Shaikh PH, et al. Forecasting China's natural gas demand based on optimised nonlinear grey models. *Energy*, 2017, 140(1): 941–951.

[22] Xie NM. Explanations about grey information and framework of grey system modeling. *Grey Systems: Theory and Application*, 2017, 7(2): 179–193.

[23] Zeng B, Meng W, Tong M. A self-adaptive intelligence grey predictive model with alterable structure and its application. *Engineering Applications of Artificial Intelligence*, 2016, 50: 236–244. https://doi.org/10.1016/j.engappai.2015.12.011.

[24] Wei B, Xie N. On unified framework for discrete-time grey models: Extensions and applications. *ISA Transactions*, 2020, 107: 1–11.

[25] Wang ZX, Wang ZW, Li Q. Forecasting the industrial solar energy consumption using a novel seasonal GM (1,1) model with dynamic seasonal adjustment factors. *Energy*, 2020, 200: 117460.

[26] Zeng B, Zhou M, Liu X, et al. Application of a new grey prediction model and grey average weakening buffer operator to forecast China's shale gas output. *Energy Reports*, 2020, 6: 1608–1618.

[27] Wu LF, Liu SF, Yao LG, et al. Grey system model with the fractional order accumulation. *Communications in Nonlinear Science and Numerical Simulation*, 2013, 18(7): 1775–1785.

[28] Ma X, Wu WQ, Zeng B, et al. The conformable fractional grey system model. *ISA Transactions*, 2020, 96: 255–271.

[29] Ding S, Cai Z, Ye J, et al. A unified new-information-based accumulating generation operator based on feature decoupling for multi-characteristic time series forecasting. *Applied Soft Computing*, 2024, 154: 111310.

[30] Liu L, Chen Y, Wu L. The damping accumulated grey model and its application. *Communications in Nonlinear Science and Numerical Simulation*, 2021, 95: 105665.

[31] Zhou W, Tao H, Ding S, et al. Electricity consumption and production forecasting considering seasonal patterns: An investigation based on a novel seasonal discrete grey model. *Journal of the Operational Research Society*, 2023, 74(5): 1346–1361.

[32] Zhu H, Xiao X, Huang X, et al. Time-lead nonlinear grey multivariable prediction model with applications. *Applied Mathematical Modelling*, 2023, 123: 464–483.

[33] Zeng B, Duan H, Bai Y, Meng W. Forecasting the output of shale gas in China using an unbiased grey model and weakening buffer operator. *Energy*, 2018, 151: 238–249.

[34] Wei Y, Zhang Y. A criterion of comparing the function transformations to raise the smooth degree of grey modeling data. *The Journal of Grey System*, 2007, 19(1): 91–98.

[35] Stewart GW. On the perturbation of pseudo-inverses, projections and linear least squares problems. *SIAM Review*, 1977, 19(4): 634–662.

[36] Wu L, Liu S, Yao L. Discrete grey model based on fractional order accumulate. *Systems Engineering-Theory & Practice*, 2014, 34(7): 1822–1827.

[37] Guo JH, Xiao XP, Yang JW. Effect on grey model's smoothness and accuracy by using function transformation. *Control and Decision*, 2015, 30(07): 1251–1256.

[38] Zhang Y, Xu Y, Wang Z. GM (1,1) grey prediction of Lorenz chaotic system. *Chaos, Solitons & Fractals*, 2009, 42(2): 1003–1009.

[39] Xie WL, Wu WZ, Liu C, Zhao J. Forecasting annual electricity consumption in China by employing a conformable fractional grey model in opposite direction. *Energy*, 2020, 202: 117682.

[40] Javed SA, Liu S. Predicting the research output/growth of selected countries: Application of Even GM (1, 1) and NDGM models. *Scientometrics*, 2018, 115: 395–413. https://doi.org/10.1007/s11192-017-2586-5.

[41] Makridakis S, Spiliotis E, Assimakopoulos V. The M4 competition: Results, findings, conclusion and way forward. *International Journal of Forecasting*, 2018, 34(4): 802–808.

[42] Diebold FX, Mariano RS. Comparing predictive accuracy. *Journal of Business & Economic Statistics*, 2002, 20(1): 134–144.

7

Large Language Models in Medical Image Understanding

Ghada Khoriba, Muhammad Nouman, and Essam A. Rashed

7.1 Introduction

Medical image analysis involves a series of tasks to assist physicians in qualitative and quantitative analyses of lesions or anatomical structures. These tasks can significantly improve the accuracy and reliability of medical diagnoses and prognoses. These tedious tasks were traditionally completed by experienced physicians or medical physicists and were marred by two major problems: low efficiency and bias (Huilin et al., 2023). In recent years, many deep learning (DL) medical applications have been proposed for the automatic analysis of various imaging modalities, including magnetic resonance imaging (MRI), computed tomography (CT), ultrasound (US), or histopathological images (Puttagunta and Ravi, 2021).

Large vision models (LVMs) could enhance medical imaging research by significantly improving image synthesis, reconstruction, and segmentation and enabling precise surgical scene reconstruction. These advanced capabilities make LVMs crucial tools in medical imaging, where their proficiency in processing large datasets facilitates accurate and exhaustive interpretation of medical images—an essential aspect of diagnosing and treating various diseases. Additionally, LVMs can assist in generating clinical documentation, such as radiology reports, thereby streamlining healthcare workflows and improving patient outcomes. Despite their promise, generic LVMs trained on diverse datasets filled with everyday images often struggle with domain-specific tasks, particularly in medical imaging. However, when tailored to medical contexts, LVMs can substantially enhance image analysis, leading to quicker and more accurate diagnoses and, ultimately, better patient care.

Several tasks are commonly considered in this track, such as medical image captioning (MIC), diagnostic captioning (DC), and automatic medical report generation. The image captioning task involves tackling two fundamental questions: visual understanding and linguistic processing, as they represent the convergence of computer vision and NLP. Diagnostic captioning is

DOI: 10.1201/9781032632483-7

a subset of MIC that goes further to provide a diagnostic interpretation of the image. This involves describing what is seen and judging what those observations mean regarding a diagnosis (Reale-Nosei et al., 2024). Using LLMs and LVMs highlights the significant advantage of focusing on attention mechanisms and utilizing them through the Transformers architecture. Hence, methodologies relying on attention scores can remain relatively independent of specific MIC and DC methods as long as these methods are grounded in the Transformer architecture.

7.1.1 Medical Image Understanding

Medical image understanding has emerged as a cornerstone of modern medical imaging and radiation therapy, fundamentally shaping the landscape of diagnosis, treatment planning, and patient care (Shen et al., 2017). With the rapid advancements in generative artificial intelligence (GenAI), particularly in LLMs and LVMs, there is a growing potential to enhance the analysis and interpretation of medical images significantly. These cutting-edge models, which represent a convergence of language and vision processing capabilities, offer new avenues for linking visual data with textual understanding in medical contexts (Hartsock and Rasool, 2024). Integrating LLMs with LVMs makes it possible to generate detailed descriptions, annotations, and even preliminary diagnostic insights directly from medical images.

Moreover, the incorporation of noninvasive imaging modalities such as X-ray, positron emission tomography (PET), CT, MRI, and US has improved the accuracy and significance of medical therapies. Medical image processing (MIP) has played a key role in promoting these techniques, improving the capability to predict, detect, analyze, and evaluate diseases. The data derived from MIP are now being utilized in machine learning (ML) and DL models, leading to the development of intelligent systems that augment medical decision-making and improve the accuracy of image interpretation—an area traditionally vulnerable to human error and subjectivity. The pursuit of precision in medical imaging has driven a significant body of work in this field, underscoring the critical importance of accuracy in delivering high-quality healthcare (Abhisheka et al., 2024).

Multimodal large language models (MLLMs) mark a significant paradigm shift in artificial general intelligence (AGI) research. MLLMs are models based on LLMs that can receive and reason with multimodal information, extending beyond the traditional single "language modality" to include "image," "speech," and other "multimodal" data (Zhang et al., 2024b). Gemini (Gemini Team, 2023) and GPT-4 (Achiam et al., 2023) are notable examples. These models could be utilized for automated image interpretation and report generation, improved diagnostic accuracy, and assistance in medical education and training. However, deploying foundation models in medical image analysis requires a rigorous examination of their trustworthiness, encompassing privacy, robustness, reliability, explainability, and fairness. Explainability is crucial in medical image analysis, especially when applying foundation models in healthcare, due to the demand for trustworthy and actionable decision-making in clinical settings (Shi et al., 2024).

7.1.2 AI in Healthcare

Artificial intelligence (AI) is increasingly being integrated into healthcare, offering potential improvements in diagnostics, treatment, patient care, and operational efficiency (Bai et al., 2024; Chen et al., 2024; He et al., 2024; Hussain et al., 2024; Liu et al., 2023; Qin et al., 2022; Shin et al., 2017; Singhal et al., 2023a; Thirunavukarasu et al., 2023; Zhang et al., 2023a). This section explores the key ways AI can contribute to public health, drawing insights from recent research findings. AI models, particularly DL and ML, improve diagnostics, prevention, and treatment but face privacy and patient autonomy challenges (Bhattamisra et al., 2023; Okeibunor et al., 2023). Examples of medical imaging tasks in healthcare are shown in Figure 7.1. AI techniques, such as NLP and spatial modeling, have improved public health surveillance. This kind of research analyzes large volumes of data from social media and other sources to predict disease outbreaks and understand barriers to care while addressing algorithmic biases in health data analysis (Flores et al., 2023; Olawade et al., 2023). Addressing biases in AI algorithms is crucial to avoid misrepresenting populations and exacerbating health disparities.

In addition, AI and digital health technology can improve primary healthcare service delivery in resource-poor settings (Saif-Ur-Rahman et al., 2023). AI has demonstrated the potential to enhance clinical efficiency and cost-effectiveness by reducing specialists' time and improving patient outcomes (Jiao et al., 2023). (Sharma et al., 2024) propose a mHealth-based patient monitoring system (mHealth-PMS) based on AI for Healthcare 4.0 (Jayaraman et al., 2020).

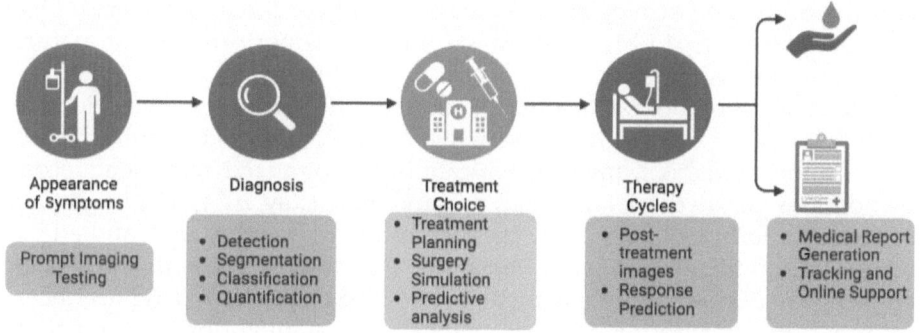

FIGURE 7.1
Overview of medical imaging tasks in healthcare: from diagnosis to treatment monitoring.

AI has the potential to significantly improve healthcare service outcomes through enhanced disease detection, risk prediction, and health monitoring. However, addressing ethical concerns, biases, and public perception issues is essential for successfully integrating AI into healthcare. Continued research and collaboration are necessary to maximize AI's benefits while mitigating its challenges.

7.1.3 Purpose of This Chapter

The primary objective of this chapter is to provide a comprehensive introduction to the key concepts, recent advancements, and emerging trends in LLMs within the realm of medical image understanding. As this area of research is rapidly evolving, we aim to highlight the foundational principles that underpin the use of LLMs in this field and explore their potential applications. By presenting this information concisely yet informatively, we strive to offer readers a clear understanding of how these advanced models are shaping the future of medical imaging and diagnostics.

7.2 Large Language Models

The current state of LLMs in the medical field reveals many applications, from clinical decision support and patient communication to medical education and research analysis. However, several key challenges and limitations exist, such as the lack of domain-specific knowledge, limited understanding of medical terminology, potential biases and errors, and scalability issues. Despite these challenges, there is a promising future for LLMs in the medical field, with opportunities for integration with other AI technologies, the development of domain-specific models, improved transparency and explainability, and strategies to address ethical concerns and biases. Over the past few years, LLMs have shown impressive performance on natural language processing tasks.

LLMs can revolutionize healthcare through applications such as biomedical information retrieval, question answering, medical text summarization, information extraction, medical education, personalized treatment recommendations, predictive health analytics, and more (Ray, 2024). The limitations of LLMs include hallucinations, fairness and bias, privacy, legal and ethical concerns, and the need for comprehensive evaluations. The author adds new challenges, such as adapting to medical knowledge, personalizing healthcare information, interpreting complex medical data, augmenting doctor–patient communication, and addressing dynamic healthcare policies (Ray, 2024). Knowledge graphs could be used to minimize the hallucinations. A system that includes a knowledge update crawler to keep the medical knowledge base current, ensuring that the system's guidance remains accurate and up-to-date, is presented in (Dou et al., 2024).

7.3 Large Vision Models

LVMs have advanced considerably, entangling visual recognition and language understanding to generate content that is not only coherent but also contextually attuned. Constructing large-scale annotated medical image datasets for training deep networks is challenging due to data acquisition complexities, high annotation costs, and privacy concerns (Cheplygina et al., 2019; Kaissis et al., 2020). Vision language pretraining has emerged as a promising approach for developing foundational models that support various AI tasks. LVMs have shown impressive skills in understanding and generating image descriptions (Nguyen et al., 2023). A large margin local estimate (LMLE) model for medical image classification is presented in (Song et al., 2015). The LMLE model is independent of the feature design and was applied to ILD classification in lung HRCT images, phenotype classification, and regression in brain MR images. (Li et al., 2024b) proposed LViT, which utilizes text embeddings to improve medical image segmentation performance. LViT performs superior segmentation in semi-supervised settings and outperforms other state-of-the-art methods. BiomedGPT (Zhang et al., 2024a) is an open-source, lightweight vision–language foundation model for various biomedical tasks. It achieved state-of-the-art results in 16 out of 25 experiments. It demonstrated impressive performance in radiology applications, with a low error rate of 3.8% in visual question answering and 8.3% in generating complex radiology reports. BiomedGPT achieved state-of-the-art results in 16 out of 25 experiments while maintaining a computing-friendly model scale.

7.4 Techniques and Methods

The application of LLMs represents a significant advancement in the rapidly evolving field of medical imaging. These highly advanced models, developed and standardized for natural language processing applications, are now undergoing training to comprehend medical data sets that encompass both textual and graphical information. This section examines the specialized approaches and tools required to properly leverage the strengths of LLMs to improve the analysis of medical datasets.

The use of LLMs for medical imaging also poses difficulties, primarily due to the inherent attributes of medical images. Managing the complexities of these models demands the rigorous preparation of the input data to make it suitable for supported models. Also, a complex and specific modification is required for the models' architecture to be compatible with medical imaging tasks. This section will describe the process for reformulating these large language models to integrate with medical images seamlessly. We will delve into the application of various stages of data preprocessing, from basic ones such as data cleaning and normalization to more complex ones. All steps are essential in preparing the data for analysis to ensure that the integrated model produces accurate and efficient outputs.

Moreover, we will discuss the application of advanced strategies such as transfer learning and fine-tuning (Pham et al., 2018). These strategies are crucial when someone intends to fine-tune the pretrained language models for unique medical tasks. The discussion will provide awareness of the methods of optimizing hyperparameters. This is crucial in determining whether the models are well-tuned and aligned to the medical imaging data characteristics.

To present the current and future development of LLMs for medical imaging, this chapter will focus on a concise theoretical outline of current LLMs, followed by real-world applications that demonstrate the practical usefulness of the concepts and, finally, true case studies that give sound insight into how LLMs can actively be used and further developed today. This section aims to help readers gain all the essential information and methodologies that would allow them to move from theoretical ideas to their practical implementation in solving the given task in medical practice. It can potentially change the existing paradigm of diagnostics and treatment.

7.4.1 Data Preprocessing

Data preprocessing is the foundational step for integrating large language models (LLMs) within medical imaging systems. It improves the quality and consistency of textual and image data. This preparation is critical to enabling simple and robust analysis because it allows for blending different well-suited data types for combined analysis. This section discusses the essential procedures involved in preprocessing in detail to demonstrate how preprocessing helps enhance the performance of the models. The data preprocessing pipeline for medical applications involving LLMs incorporates several steps, as depicted in Figure 7.2. These steps are crucial to preparing both the textual and visual data for correct analysis.

7.4.1.1 Textual Data Preprocessing

Medical texts like patient report documents, doctors' prescriptions, and diagnostic documents contain clinical information. However, we also have

a.) Textual Data Preprocessing Workflow.

1. Cleaning and Normalization.
- Remove noise (e.g., extra formatting, headers).
- Standardize terms and abbreviations (e.g., HTN to hypertension).

2. Tokenization and Lemmatization.
- **Tokenization:** Split text into smaller parts (tokens).
- **Lemmatization:** Reduce words to their base forms.

3. Semantic Tagging.
- Label key medical terms (e.g., symptoms, diagnoses, treatments).
- Map text to clinical categories for context).

4. Vectorization.
- Transform text into numerical vectors.
- Techniques include Word2Vec, GloVe, and BERT-based embeddings.

b.) Visual Data Preprocessing and Annotation Workflow.

Manual Annotation

Experts mark areas of interest (e.g., lesions, tumors), ensures high-quality ground truth data

Semi-Automated Annotation

Smart-assist: Model provides initial annotation, refined by experts

Tools-sync: Interactive annotation with real-time algorithmic adjustments

Fully Automated Annotation

Deep learning models (e.g., U-net, mask R-CNN) perform annotation without expert input, scalable and time-efficient for large datasets

FIGURE 7.2
Data preprocessing workflows for medical imaging applications.

issues with the format, use of terms, symbols, and noises (Savova et al., 2010). Adequate preprocessing of these texts is essential when integrating or analyzing them with medical imaging data using LLMs.

Cleaning and Normalization: Text cleaning involves removing extra formatting, correcting typographical errors, and eliminating irrelevant sections like headers or footers. It is necessary to minimize noise and increase the concentration of any health-related information. The purpose of this process is to focus solely on health-related information that is crucial for accurate analysis. Normalization goes further by standardizing terms or abbreviations among patients' medical records (Meystre et al., 2017). For instance, acronyms such as HTN for hypertension or DM for diabetes mellitus are spelled out so that there is no misunderstanding. This method eliminates noise and replaces standard terms, ensuring the model receives only data in a consistent format. Additionally, it ensures a smooth and accurate analysis.

In a clinical facility, notes can be provided to radiologists containing a blend of common, normalized language and non-normalized abbreviations. Standardizing these terms effectively ensures that the different names for the variables do not affect the model when the LLM analyzes the data. It leads to more accurate results, analyses, and predictions. The following Python code can be used to preprocess medical texts. It expands all medical abbreviations, making the language less complex and more specific. The cleaning and normalization Python code example is in Figure 7.3.

Medical text cleaning impacts healthcare by transforming raw text data into a structured form. It influences the analysis of patient data and the effectiveness of electronic health record systems. This change is essential as an appropriate foundation for providing efficient and individualized patient care regarding their health status.

Tokenization and Lemmatization: Tokenization is the process of breaking down a text into parts known as tokens. Tokenization implies erasing the punctuation marks and dividing the text into tokens, making it convenient for machine learning models. Lemmatization, a more complex process than tokenization, reduces words to their base form, known as a lemma. By taking these tokens out of their stemmed form (lemma), lemmatization makes it easier to analyze them even more (Jiang et al., 2019; Liu et al., 2015). The reason

```
sample_text = """
Ms. Khan complained of persistent cough and expressed concern about her
cholesterol levels. Med history: COPD, high LDL.
Prescribed medications are Simvastatin 40 mg once at night, and
Salbutamol as needed.
Scheduled for annual physical exam next month.
"""
def clean_and_normalize_text(text):          ──► Clean and normalize text
    abbreviations = {                         ◄─┐ Mapping medical
        "COPD": "Chronic Obstructive Pulmonary Disease",│ abbreviations to
        "LDL": "Low-Density Lipoprotein",     │ their expanded
        "mg": "milligrams",                   │ forms
        "med": "medical",                     │
        "Simvastatin": "Simvastatin",         │
        "Salbutamol": "Salbutamol"            │
                                              └─►
    }

    pattern = re.compile(r'\b(' + '|'.join    ◄─┐ regular
(re.escape(key) for key in abbreviations.keys()) + r')\b')│ expression to
    text = pattern.sub(lambda match: abbreviations│ replace
[match.group()], text)                        └ abbreviations
    text = re.sub(r"\s+", " ", text).strip()  ──► Simplify and
                                                  standardize text

    return text
normalized_text = clean_and_normalize_text(sample_text)
```

FIGURE 7.3

Python code example for text cleaning and normalization.

is that the differences in each word form make each token unique. Tokenization and lemmatization aid in the extraction of essential details such as symptoms, diagnosis, and medications when handling discharge summaries or clinical notes. This structural data can easily be linked to patient outcomes or clinical parameters. Breaking down sentences into base words simplifies the structure. It allows models to analyze each word separately, which helps detect symptoms or diagnoses. A Python code example is in Figure 7.4.

Tokenization and lemmatization techniques are beneficial for improving text data in medicine. Using text tokenization and lemmatizing the tokens aids in opening the level of analysis to semantic similarity and categorization.

Semantic Tagging: Semantic tagging is an advanced technique for adding meanings or classifying words in a text. Semantic annotation of domain-specific data requires text mapping based on clinical importance, such as symptoms, diagnosis, or treatment (Névéol et al., 2018). Studies such as Abdelaziz et al. (2023), Demir et al. (2023). and Rimjhim and Dandapat (2023) suggest that data preprocessing involves steps like feature identification, extraction, and assignment, with semantic tagging crucial for improving accuracy and performance in various applications. Semantic tagging is primarily motivated by the structured context around clinical data, enabling language models to better understand and categorize medical information. Consider an example

```
import nltk
from nltk.tokenize import word_tokenize        Import libraries for NLP,
from nltk.stem import WordNetLemmatizer         download tokenizer model
nltk.download('punkt')                          and database for lemmatization
nltk.download('wordnet')

sample_text = """
Ms. Khan complained of persistent cough and was worried about her
cholesterol levels.
After reviewing her medical history of Chronic Obstructive Pulmonary
Disease and high Low-Density Lipoprotein,
the doctor prescribed Simvastatin 40 milligrams nightly and Salbutamol as
required.
"""
def tokenize_and_lemmatize(text):               Function to
    tokens = word_tokenize(text)                tokenize and
    lemmatizer = WordNetLemmatizer()            lemmatize text,
    lemmas = [lemmatizer.lemmatize(token) for   tokenize text into
token in tokens]                                words, lemmatize
    return lemmas                               each word to its
                                                base form
lemmatized_text = tokenize_and_lemmatize(sample_text)
```

FIGURE 7.4
Python code example for tokenization and lemmatization.

(a clinical decision support system); tagging "chest pain" as the symptom and "aspirin" as a treatment will enable the model to associate the symptom better with the relevant treatments. This reduces the time needed to organize medical texts to reflect clinical reasoning and thus improves diagnosis and recommendation accuracy.

This is the case with medical questions tagged and processed by LLMs since it helps build a better structured context in which the LLM can accurately recognize other medical concepts. This process allows LLMs to categorize data, making identifying and interpreting medicine-related texts easier.

For instance, clinical decision support systems often use semantic tagging and medication reconciliation to identify pertinent clinical data from unformatted text. Diagnosing the illness and recommending corrective action becomes easier when you key in a symptom code such as "chest pain, complaints" or a treatment code like "aspirin use."

Some semantic tagging systems rely on machine learning algorithms such as conditional random fields (CRF) or neural networks to tag medical terms automatically (Zhu et al., 2018). These models are developed from the annotated corpora available for clinical data usage and use POS tags and medical ontologies like UMLS. Further improvements in transformer-based language models have demonstrated better prediction accuracy than conventional techniques (Devlin et al., 2018). Indeed, these models can offer contextual details and utilize prelearned knowledge from extensive biomedical corpora.

Semantic tagging aims to define and compare named entities (people, organizations, diseases, etc.) appearing in the text to their types. For example, it assigns "Chronic Obstructive Pulmonary Disease" as a category of a medical description or "Ms. Khan" as an individual. In the Python code example (Figure 7.5), we utilize Python's spaCy (a popular NLP tool) to apply semantic tagging to medical text.

Semantic tagging is not the process of transforming text into a new form. It generates a set of labels linked to parts of the text. Each entity is identified and classified into one of the categories. Semantic tags are a way to tell the model what a specific part of the text means in a coded manner. However, semantic tagging does not include any extra or altered semantic details of the text. It only provides information about the text. This extra layer of information is useful to help the model enhance the level of accuracy where a basic understanding of the text is concerned.

The spaCy loads the medium-sized English model. It is effective at recognizing entities from English text. In this stage, the process takes the lemmatized text for semantic analysis. This integration presents an end-to-end, fine-grained text analysis process, from text preprocessing to deep understanding at the linguistic level. Before extracting entities from the text, the output from the NLP model is analyzed to determine the entities present in the text based on the context and terminology.

```
!pip install spacy                                    ◄┐ Install spaCy, downloaded
!python -m spacy download en_core_web_md               │ and loaded the English
import spacy                                           │ model for NLP tasks
nlp = spacy.load('en_core_web_md')                    ◄┘

lemmatized_text_string = " ".join([
    "Ms.", "Khan", "complained", "of", "persistent", "cough", "and",
"was", "worried",
    "about", "her", "cholesterol", "levels.", "After", "reviewing",
"her", "medical",
    "history", "of", "Chronic", "Obstructive", "Pulmonary", "Disease",
"and", "high",
    "Low-Density", "Lipoprotein,", "the", "doctor", "prescribed",
"Simvastatin", "40",
    "milligrams", "nightly", "and", "Salbutamol", "as", "required."
])
def semantic_tagging(text):                           ◄┐ Function to pe-
    doc = nlp(text)                                    │ -rform semantic
    tagged_entities = [(entity.text, entity.label_) for│ tagging on
entity in doc.ents]                                    │ lemmatized text
    return tagged_entities
tagged_entities = semantic_tagging(lemmatized_text_string)─►
```

FIGURE 7.5
Python code example for semantic tagging.

In the spaCy model (Honnibal and Montani, 2017), named entity recognition (NER), the code ORG usually refers to "organization." However, entities that do not represent organizations may mistakenly use this model. This is due to the inherent challenges of categorizing entities in medical data. In the output, entities like "Chronic Obstructive Pulmonary Disease" and "Simvastatin" have been tagged as "ORG," which is incorrect in a clinical or medical context. This misclassification shows one of the problems of applying general NLP models in medicine. The model may not possess adequate medical domain knowledge to analyze such specific terms. However, it is advisable to use NLP models trained on medical texts or at least enhance general ones with knowledge from the medical field. Such adaptations can improve the model and help it better identify specific medical entities in the domains.

Vectorization: LLMs can process text input by converting it into numbers or vectors (Mikolov, 2013). In medical documents, vectorization lets the models identify patterns and correlations between the data. Vectorization enables a degree of quantification of the words used in patient feedback. Earlier studies in medical text analysis have used BoW and TF-IDF, basic approaches to vectorization. However, it cannot manage semantic relations, the context of meaning between terms, or text data (Zhang et al., 2018). Recently, methods like Word2Vec and GloVe have been used for vectorization to enhance the process, especially when capturing semantic similarity and syntactic patterns (Chiu et al., 2016; Pennington et al., 2014).

Moreover, transformer-based language models such as BERT and its versions, like BioBERT and Clinical BERT, have indeed brought changes in converting text into vectors (Alsentzer et al., 2019; Lee et al., 2020). These models can produce "contextualized word embeddings," which would decode medical terms and provide better analysis of clinical texts compared to other models—appropriate vectorization aids in various areas, ranging from disease detection to finding prescriptive treatments.

There are two main approaches to converting text into vectors. The first translates each word to its vector, while the second reduces the entire document to a single vector. Table 7.1 summarizes the variation between

TABLE 7.1

Comparison of Word-Level and Document-Level Vectorization

	Word-Level Vectorization	Document-Level Vectorization
Definition	It converts each word into a vector representation.	It converts an entire document into a single vector.
Dimensionality	Each word is represented by a vector of fixed dimensions.	The document is represented by a single vector, which might be an average or aggregate of word vectors.
Context sensitivity	Traditional methods (e.g., Word2Vec, GloVe) lack context sensitivity; more advanced embeddings from transformers (BERT, GPT) provide context-sensitive vectors for each word occurrence.	Captures the overall context of the document but loses individual word contexts.
Use cases	Ideal for tasks requiring fine-grained analysis such as word similarity, part-of-speech tagging, and named entity recognition.	Suited for tasks where the overall semantic content is more important, such as document classification, and information retrieval.
Advantages	In LLMs, word-level embeddings are crucial for maintaining the richness of language understanding and allow models to leverage context-dependent meanings dynamically.	Simplifies modeling by reducing the input size; useful for quick summaries or when detailed word-level semantics are less critical.
Computational complexity	Higher computational cost for processing as each word is treated separately.	Lower computational overhead post-vectorization since it deals with a single vector per document.
Memory usage	Requires substantial memory to store vectors for each word.	More memory-efficient when dealing with large volumes of text.
Interpretability	Higher interpretability for individual words in the model's decisions.	Lower interpretability of how specific words or phrases affect the overall document's representation.

```
lemmatized_text_string = " ".join([
    "Ms.", "Khan", "complained", "of", "persistent", "cough", "and",
"was", "worried",
    "about", "her", "cholesterol", "levels.", "After", "reviewing",
"her", "medical",
    "history", "of", "Chronic", "Obstructive", "Pulmonary", "Disease",
"and", "high",
    "Low-Density", "Lipoprotein,", "the", "doctor", "prescribed",
"Simvastatin", "40",
    "milligrams", "nightly", "and", "Salbutamol", "as", "required."
])

doc = nlp(lemmatized_text_string)              ◄ Process the lemmatized
word_vectors = {token.text: token.vector for token  text to generate
in doc if  generate token.has_vector}          vectors for each word
```

FIGURE 7.6
Python code example for world-level vectorization.

word-level vectorization and document-level vectorization while highlighting the technical aspects that concern NLP and LLMs. Figure 7.6 shows a word-level vectorization example code.

7.4.1.2 Image Preprocessing and Annotation

The quality and precision of the annotations have a considerable effect on the model's performance. This section describes the techniques used for medical imaging annotations, starting with the manual method.

Manual Annotation: In this process, specialists draw marks, boxes, or circles to underline specific image features. For example, outline a lesion in dermatological images or circle the tumor in an MRI. The primary purpose of manual annotation is to obtain high-quality and accurate datasets, which serve as the ground truth for training diagnostic models. This is essential for developing models to assist in patient prognosis and aid in clinical decisions (Alsentzer et al., 2019). Experts often employ software to delineate ROIs in medical images. These could be simple rectangles, detailed contours, or pixel masks, depending on the problem domain of the annotations. However, as medical experts do the manual annotation, it also brings a high degree of subjectivity. Experts make judgments on the subjects based on their experience and knowledge. It is argued that manual approaches enable more precise decisions than automated ones, seeing some information that a piece of software cannot discern (Aljabri et al., 2022). However, manual annotation is time-consuming and requires high labor intensity for handling large datasets. Also, images labeled by different experts may display variations due to varying perceptions regarding the images and their attributes. Interobserver variability, including professional backgrounds, can also impact machine learning algorithm training. Because image annotation requires well-trained medical personnel, it is not always convenient. Researchers employ different imaging tools, including 3D Slicer, ITK-Snap (see Figure 7.7), OsiriX MD, Labellerr, Encord, and LabelBox, or tools developed in MATLAB and Python for manual annotation purposes.

These tools can manage multimodal image data (MRI, CT, PET, etc.) and require the basic facilities of 3D view and annotation in complex cases.

Semi-Automated Annotation: Semi-automated annotation methods in medical imaging combine human experience and computational support. This approach can aid in expediting the annotation process and reducing the likelihood of check errors. Such techniques are helpful in medical imaging because manually creating annotations is time-consuming and costly. We divided the semi-automated annotation techniques into two classifications.

Smart-Assist Annotation: In this process, a human expert fine-tunes the already developed algorithms and aims to annotate the images automatically. Experts use machine learning models based on regression models derived from an annotated database to identify areas of interest. For instance, radiologists refine potential lesions or tumors identified by models in neuroimaging.

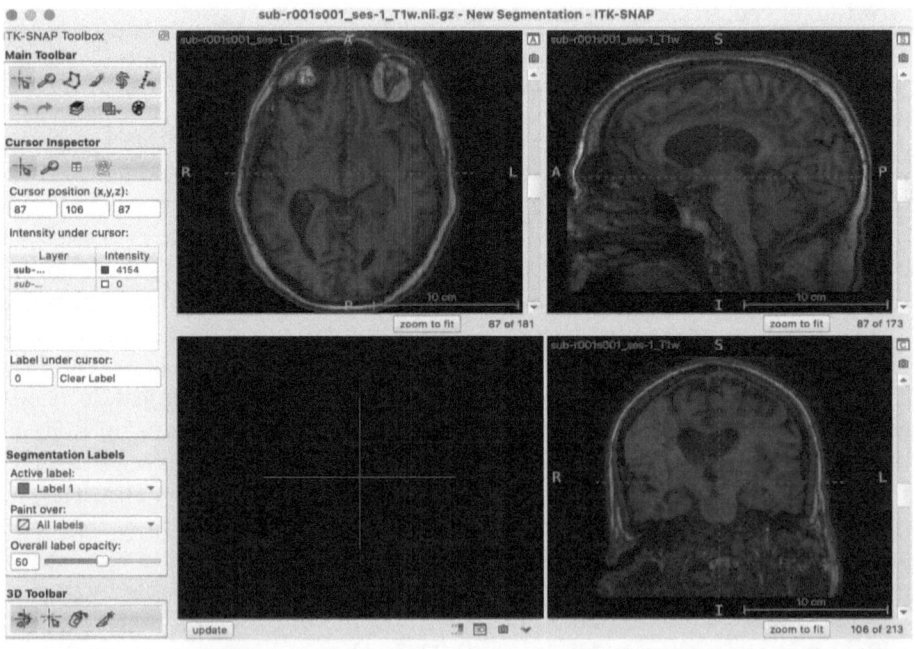

FIGURE 7.7
ITK-SNAP (Yushkevich et al., 2006) user interface for manually segmenting a stroke lesion. This single visualization accurately captures the level of detail required in the manual annotation of biomedical images, which forms the foundation for building robust machine learning models.

This method relies on the computational capability of models to accomplish the first and most time-consuming steps of annotation, letting highly knowledgeable professionals do the final adjustment and assessment.

2. Tools-Sync Annotation: In this approach, experts use software tools to interact with the algorithm in real-time. For example, the annotator provides the input for segmentation, and the algorithm calculates the remaining segmentation results based on that input. The functionalities in ITK-SNAP create the annotation in the organ or lesion analysis, while the software approximates the organ or lesion's boundary. It remains fair to mention that the proposed interactive approach allows the final annotations to incorporate the advantages of manual workflow and algorithmic assistance (see Figure 7.8).

Semi-automated methods offer advantages in terms of efficiency and less of a work burden for experts. These techniques are helpful because they use predictive algorithms that provide first-set annotations and reduce the time spent on detailed annotations. This efficiency gain enables medical professionals to spend more time reviewing and refining these annotations rather than building them from scratch. In addition, semiautomated tools reduce the human errors that arise from fatigue. Manual expertise and speed in algorithm execution also permit working with larger datasets, which is essential for creating stable AI models in diagnostics and analytics.

Fully Automated Annotation: Deep learning solutions for image annotation have recently developed new fully automated approaches. These approaches can annotate the images without expert intervention. In the current scenario, where medical data volumes are generating exponentially, such automated approaches seem ideal. These approaches increase efficiency in handling enormous quantities of medical images and generating quality annotations in less time. Automatic annotation relies on deep learning models, specifically CNNs or convolutional neural networks. These models are particularly adept at recognizing grid-like data, such as images, which makes them suitable for medical use. Elaborate architectures like U-Net, V-Net, and Mask R-CNN have extended it for medical image segmentation and object detection (Ronneberger et al., 2015; Shu et al., 2020).

Deep learning in medical imaging systems is one of the most notable features of fully automated annotation. This allows for real-time annotation of scans during the imaging process and can alert radiologists to areas of interest. In such cases, real-time analysis improves diagnosis speed and accuracy (Topol, 2019). The advantages of fully automated systems are considerable, as shown in Figure 7.8.

- **Scalability:** They can handle large datasets that cannot be processed manually.

- **Speed:** Automatic annotations minimize the time it takes to process a dataset.

- **Consistency:** These systems provide a degree of annotation standardization that human annotators can hardly achieve.

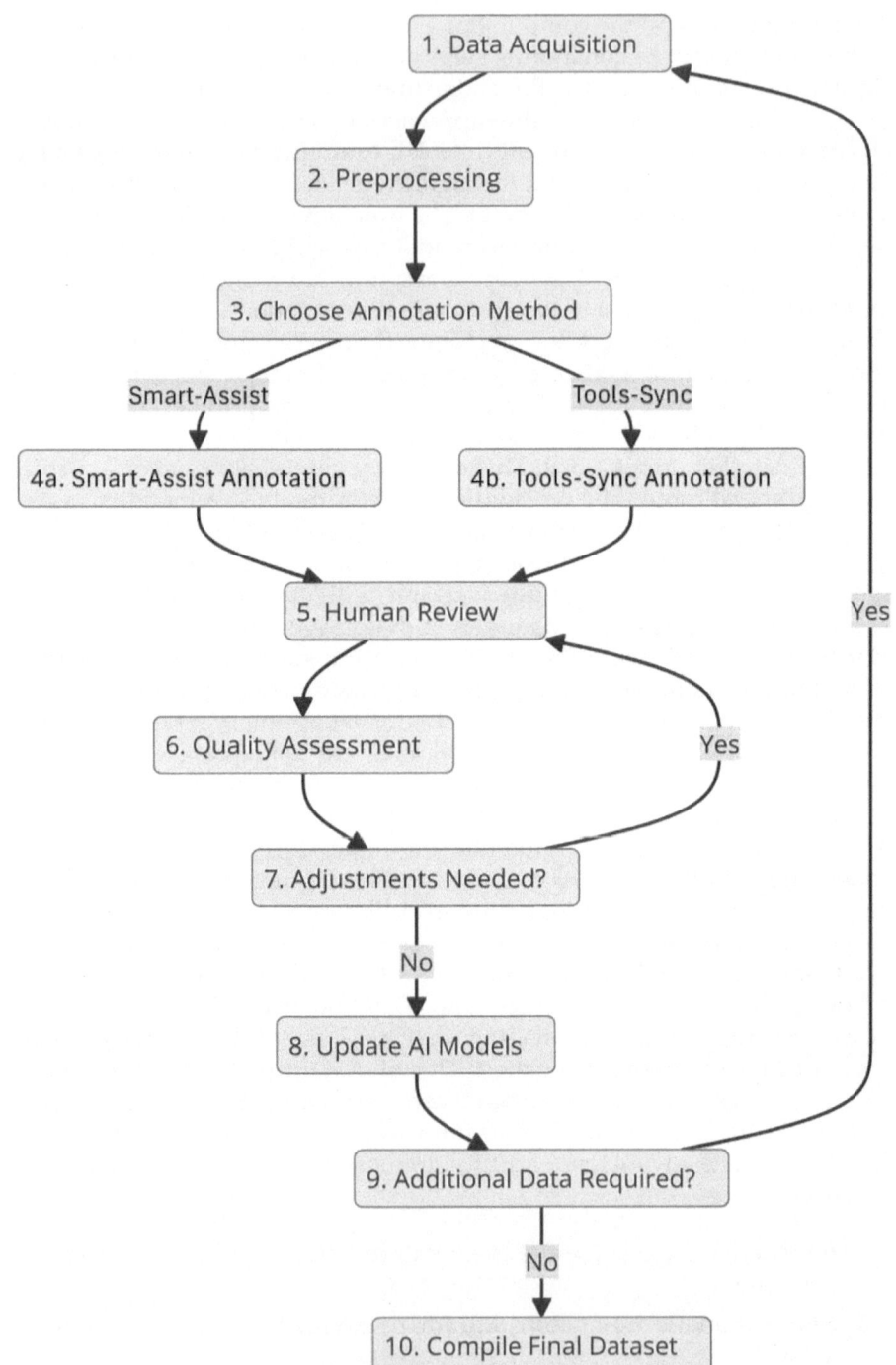

FIGURE 7.8
Flowchart shows steps for semi-automated annotation techniques in medical image annotation.

However, there are still challenges in deploying fully automated annotation systems:

Accuracy: The interpretation of medical images can be complicated for systems due to their various levels of abstraction.

Data Quality: The effectiveness of these systems are directly linked to the quality and diversity of available training data.

Ethical and Legal Implications: Reducing human intervention in diagnosis raises important legal and ethical concerns.

Recent studies seek to identify solutions to these problems. For example, emerging strategies for integrating multiple AI models, such as ensemble and federated learning, can improve accuracy and resilience (Rieke et al., 2020). Furthermore, researchers developed methods like few-shot and self-supervised learning to lessen the requirement for massive, labeled data sets (Chen et al., 2020). In practical applications, there has been an increased development of fully automated annotation systems directly in medicine. Radiologists use AI-based systems to help detect tumors or bone fractures. Digital pathology also involves using AI to assist pathologists in identifying tissues with several types of diseases. Imaging systems use NLP to generate detailed descriptions and annotations from images. Moreover, other healthcare domains, like surgical skills and medical services tailored to specific patient conditions, also utilize NLP.

7.4.2 Model Adaption and Configuration

Adopting LLMs for medical imaging is complex because of the model's complexity and capabilities. We need to tailor LLM models for specific medical applications. The LLM models, primarily designed for text-based data processing, require modifications. Such changes enable LLMs to handle vast amounts of imaging data. Essentially, the modifications made to LLMs aim to achieve three key objectives: (1) improving diagnostic outcomes, (2) ensuring task automation, and (3) advancing treatment plans.

These models can interpret the medical text with corresponding images, such as the radiology report with the patient's scanned images. This capability eradicates the gap between text and image analyses. This approach is more advanced and efficient than traditional ones (Bhayana, 2024). It extends the model knowledge base with modality-specific conditions. This process involves training the LLM to search for specific characteristics and features.

- Specific types of anomalies.
- Various noise patterns.
- Typical anatomical structures and pathological patterns.

Further refinement of the LLMs for each modality enables the identification of certain features distinctive to the different modalities. Multiple modalities make detecting patterns that are challenging to recognize in text or images easier, enhancing the model's viability and real-world applicability. One of the requirements for LLM adaptation is the ability to process text with image information.

LLM makes comprehensive and accurate medical diagnostic models. Combining text and image data forms the foundation of LLM adaptation for medical imaging. This process involves:

- Preparing LLMs to "recognize" medical images and analyze them.
- Assisting in the understanding of relevant medical texts.
- Developing models to integrate and analyze findings from both image and text data.

This approach produces a practical model based on visual and textual analysis (Hu et al., 2024) and can identify patterns that human experts may overlook. For instance, we train an LLM to identify breast cancer symptoms from mammography and patient health reports. By combining the textual and visual data, the model can detect subtle signs that may not be apparent with the usual approach. This enables models to identify signs that conventional assessments may overlook, enabling an early and accurate diagnosis. This adapted approach paves the way for additional architectural enhancements and standardizes the models to fit specific medical scenarios better.

7.4.3 Transfer Learning and Fine-Tuning

The cheXReport (Zeiser et al., 2024) is a fully transformer-based encoder–decoder framework designed to generate chest X-ray reports. It uses Swin Transformer blocks (Liu et al., 2021b) in the encoder and decoder, improving the extraction and integration of visual and textual features from chest X-ray images. CheXReport is evaluated on the publicly available MIMIC-CXR dataset comprising 377110images and corresponding free-text reports. Specifically, CheXReport achieves state-of-the-art performance on the MIMIC-CXR dataset, outperforming other leading models on BLEU-4 and ROUGE metrics.

LVLMs have emerged as powerful tools in computer vision, extending the capabilities of LLMs. These advanced systems utilize a pretrained visual encoder to embed visual features, which the LLM then processes to extract image descriptions and perform diagnoses. In recent years, several specialized LVLMs have been developed and pretrained for various medical image analysis applications. One such model is an instruction prompt-tuned version of Flan-PaLM specialized for the medical domain (Singhal et al., 2023a). Another notable advancement is the Large Language and Vision Assistant for BioMedicine (LLaVA-Med) (Li et al., 2024a), which aims to integrate visual and textual information in biomedical contexts. LLaVA-Med++ (Xie et al., 2024) LLaVA-Med++ achieves state-of-the-art performance in two of the three VQA benchmarks and ranks third in the remaining. Pretraining on MedTrinity-25M improves performance by approximately 10.75% on VQA-RAD, 6.1% on SLAKE, and 13.25% on PathVQA compared to the model trained without it. For ultrasound imaging, researchers have introduced LLaVA-Ultra, a Large Chinese Language and Vision Assistant designed to interpret and analyze ultrasound images (Guo et al., 2024). Additionally, the Med-MoE model (Jiang et al., 2024) employs a Mixture of Domain-Specific Experts' approaches to create lightweight medical vision-language models, potentially improving efficiency and performance in specialized medical tasks.

TABLE 7.2

Medical Image Understanding Datasets

Dataset	Tasks	Size	Details
CheXpert (Irvin et al., 2019)	Automated chest X-ray interpretation	224,316	Chest radiographs of 65,240 patients with both frontal and lateral views available.
VQA-RAD (Lau et al., 2018)	Visual Question Answering in Radiology	3,515	Question–answer pairs on 315 radiology images
PathVQA (He et al., 2020)	Medical Visual Question Answering	32,799	Open-ended questions from 4,998 pathology images where each question is manually checked to ensure correctness.
PMC-VQA (Zhang et al., 2023b)	Medical Visual Question Answering	227 K	VQA pairs of 149k images that cover various modalities or diseases.
PMC-OA (Lin et al., 2023)	Language-Image Pre-training using Biomedical Documents	1.65 M	Biomedical image-text pairs
MIMIC-III (Johnson et al., 2016)	Medical Code Prediction	112K	Clinical reports records (average length 709.3 tokens) and 1,159 top-level ICD-9 codes. Data includes vital signs, medications, laboratory measurements, observations, survival data, and more.
VietMed-Sum (Le-Duc et al., 2024)	Real-time speech Summarization for Medical Conversations, English-translated and Vietnamese	24,357	Utilize LLM and human annotators collaboratively to create gold standard and synthetic summaries for medical conversation summarization.

(continued)

TABLE 7.2 (*Continued*)

Medical Image Understanding Datasets

Dataset	Tasks	Size	Details
MultiMedQA (Singhal et al., 2023b)	Medical question answering	About 202K	Includes the MedQA (Jin et al., 2021), MedMCQA (Pal et al., 2022), PubMedQA (Jin et al., 2019), MMLU clinical topics (Hendrycks et al., 2021), LiveQA (Abacha et al., 2017), and Medication QA (Singhal et al., 2023c) datasets
MedConceptsQA (Ben Shoham and Rappoport, 2024)	Benchmark for medical concepts questions answering	Over 800K	Questions of various medical concepts across different vocabularies: diagnoses, procedures, and drugs
SLAKE (Liu et al., 2021a)	Medical visual question answering	7,000	With 642 images, Comprehensive semantic labels annotated by experienced physicians, and a new structural medical knowledge base for Med-VQA
QUILT-1M (Ikezogwo et al., 2024)	Medical visual question answering	1M	Histopathology paired image-text samples
MedPromptX-VQA (Shaaban et al., 2024)	medical visual question Answering	6,485	Distinct patients records n-context visual question answering dataset encompassing interleaved image and EHR data derived from MIMIC-IV and MIMIC-CXR databases.
OVQA (Huang et al., 2022)	Medical visual question answering	19,020	Medical visual question question and answer pairs generated from 2,001 medical images collected from 2,212 EMRs in orthopedics.
MedTrinity-25M (Xie et al., 2024)	Medical visual question answering, medical report generation	25M	Large-scale multimodal dataset for medicine, covering over 25 million images across ten modalities, with multigranular annotations for more than 65 diseases

7.5 Medical Imaging Applications

Medical image analysis is a critical field in healthcare, enabling precise diagnosis, medical report generation, and chatbots for disease monitoring. Recent advancements in deep learning, federated learning, and transformer models have significantly enhanced the capabilities of medical image analysis, offering improved accuracy, efficiency, and privacy.

7.5.1 Disease Diagnosis

Medical image understanding is critical in disease diagnosis, utilizing advanced deep learning modeling to enhance accuracy and efficiency.

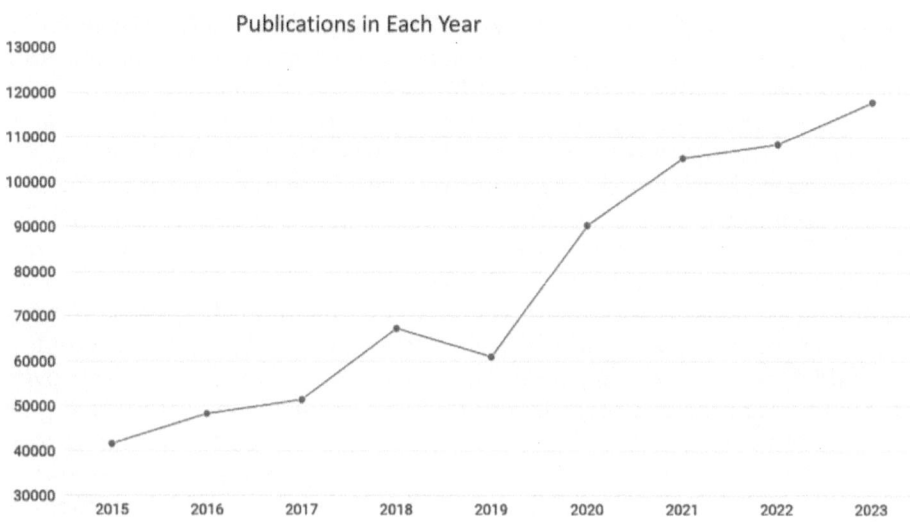

FIGURE 7.9
Number of publications till 2023. (Criteria "Medical Image Understanding for Disease Diagnosis," Data Source [Science and Inc., 2024]).

Figure 7.9 shows a positive trend in the number of publications, especially in recent years, with a significant acceleration after 2019. This highlights the growing research interest and increasing investments in medical image understanding for disease diagnosis.

Deep learning has shown significant success in cancer diagnosis using various medical imaging modalities, including X-ray, ultrasound, CT, MRI, PET, and histopathological images. Techniques like transfer learning, ensemble learning, and vision transformers are particularly effective (Jiang et al., 2023). The main challenges include the need for high-quality labeled datasets, model explainability, and generalization, especially for rare cancers and multimodal image fusion. The Hercules model proposed by (Abdar et al., 2023), a deep hierarchical attentive multilevel fusion model with uncertainty quantification, improves medical image classification accuracy in retinal OCT, lung CT, and chest X-ray datasets compared to other methods.

7.5.2 Medical Report Generation

LVMs enhance medical report generation using advanced vision–language pretraining, efficient fine-tuning strategies, and domain-specific adaptations. These models address challenges in data annotation and improve the accuracy and coherence of generated medical reports, demonstrating significant potential in the medical field. Customizing off-the-shelf general-purpose large-scale pretrained models, such as vision transformers and language models, can significantly improve medical report generation. This approach leverages the strengths of models like EVA-ViT-g and ChatGLM-6B to enhance the generation of medical reports by focusing on efficient transfer learning and parameter tuning (Yang et al., 2023). MedEPT, a parameter-efficient medical report generation approach, improves performance using less trainable parameters and 30% less training time than previous methods (Li, 2023).

Nakaura et al. presented a comparative assessment done on a retrospective study involving 28 patients (Nakaura et al., 2024). Results show that GPT–3.5 and GPT-4 can generate radiology reports with high readability and reasonable image findings from concise keywords; however, concerns persist regarding the accuracy of impressions and differential diagnoses, thereby requiring verification by radiologists. There were no significant differences in qualitative scores about grammar, readability, image findings, and overall quality between radiologists and GPT–3.5 or GPT-4 ($p > 0.05$). However, qualitative scores of the GPT series in impression and differential diagnosis scores were significantly lower than those of radiologists ($p < 0.05$). Saab et al. (Saab et al., 2024) investigated the capabilities of Gemini models in medical applications. Gemini models are specialized AI models that integrate multiple data types, such as textual and image data, to improve diagnosis and treatment predictions. The study highlights their potential in advancing precision medicine.

7.5.3 Medical Chatbots

XrayGPT integrates vision and language models to analyze and summarize chest radiographs effectively. This model aligns visual and textual data, improving the understanding and interpretation of radiographic images (Thawakar et al., 2023). Medical chatbots could be used in medical education. Hirano et al. (Hirano et al., 2024) assess the performance of GPT-4 Turbo with Vision (GPT-4TV) by comparing its ability to process both text and image input with that of the text-only GPT-4 Turbo (GPT-4T) in the context of the Japan Diagnostic Radiology Board Examination (JDRBE). GPT-4TV correctly answered 62 questions (45%), whereas GPT-4T correctly answered 57 questions (41%). A statistical analysis found no significant performance difference between the two models ($P = 0.44$). The GPT-4TV responses received significantly lower legitimacy scores from both radiologists than the GPT-4T responses. Huatuo is a model fine-tuned with a vast corpus of Chinese medical knowledge (Wang et al., 2023). The paper explores how incorporating traditional and contemporary Chinese medical information enhances the model's performance in medical-related question-answering and decision-making tasks.

7.5.4 Medical Image Segmentation

LVM-Med, a self-supervised vision model trained on large-scale medical datasets, significantly improves performance on various medical imaging tasks. It bridges the gap between natural and medical image domains through effective self-supervised learning techniques (Nguyen et al., 2023). The segment anything model (SAM) demonstrates remarkable performance in medical image segmentation by leveraging self-prompting techniques. This approach significantly improves segmentation accuracy with minimal data, outperforming fine-tuning methods by over 15% (Wu et al., 2023).

7.6 Challenges and Limitations

Medical image analysis is critical to modern healthcare, enabling precise diagnosis, treatment planning, and disease monitoring. However, despite significant advancements, several challenges and limitations hinder the full potential of medical image analysis, particularly when using LLMs and LVMs.

7.6.1 Data Privacy and Security

LLMs reveal significant variations in privacy protection capabilities across different architectures. In (Sun et al., 2024), the Enron email dataset analysis demonstrates that specific models, such as Oasst-12b, ERNIE, Baichuan-13b, and the Llama2 series, exhibit robust privacy safeguards, with Llama2 variants showing exceptional resistance to email address disclosure. Conversely, models like GPT-4, ChatGPT, and Vicuna display vulnerability to privacy leakage, particularly under five-shot prompting conditions, with Total Disclosure scores frequently exceeding 48%. A positive correlation between model size and privacy risk was observed within similar architectural families, as evidenced by higher disclosure rates in larger models.

Furthermore, prompting techniques significantly influence privacy leakage, with five-shot prompting scenarios generally resulting in increased Total and Conditional Disclosure scores compared to zero-shot configurations. The vulnerability of few-shot learning models to backdoor attacks was examined (Liu et al., 2024). This study emphasizes that these models are susceptible due to their limited data exposure. This research underscores the need for more resilient training techniques to mitigate such risks. Fast adversarial training enhanced with prior-guided knowledge to strengthen model defense mechanisms is explored in (Jia et al., 2024). This approach leverages prior information to accelerate training while maintaining defense effectiveness and addressing security issues in sensitive applications like medical imaging. On a broader scale, Xu et al., 2024 conducted a comprehensive analysis of jailbreak attacks and their defenses in large language models. This study is relevant to medical image analysis due to the increasing integration of these models in automated reporting and diagnostic systems. It highlights potential risks and defenses against adversarial manipulations. The work of

Clusmann et al. (2023) and Thirunavukarasu et al. (2023) provided forward-looking perspectives on the role of large language models in medicine. They discussed the implications of using such models for privacy, security, and regulatory compliance in medical systems, highlighting the importance of aligning technological advancements with ethical considerations.

7.6.2 Data Generalization and Variability

Medical image analysis is crucial for accurate diagnosis and treatment planning. However, the variability and generalization of data across different imaging systems and conditions pose significant challenges. Many deep learning segmentation methods struggle with unseen data due to cross-domain distribution shifts. Techniques like Bayesian modeling (BayeSeg) and domain-aware dual attention networks have been proposed to enhance generalizability by modeling domain-stable and domain-specific features separately (Gao et al., 2023; Lai et al., 2023). The domain-aware dual attention network effectively segmented medical images in unseen domains, outperforming existing advanced approaches. Such research aims to bridge the gap between current capabilities and the need for reliable, generalizable medical image understanding in clinical settings; however, it's still a challenge.

7.6.3 Accuracy and Hallucination Prevention

Hallucination prevention in medical language models is a critical area of research, particularly in medical applications where accuracy and reliability are paramount. Diverse sources and types of hallucinations in multilingual settings and the proposed strategies to mitigate them are discussed in Guerreiro et al. (2023). A model introspection technique to detect and understand when and why these hallucinations occur is presented in Xu et al. (2023). By analyzing internal states and activations of the model, they develop methods to identify hallucinated outputs. The study also provides insights into improving the reliability and faithfulness of neural machine translation systems by focusing on introspection and detecting hallucinations.

7.6.4 Uncertainly Quantification

Uncertainty quantification methods are essential for determining the confidence level of deep learning model predictions in radiologic image analysis. These methods help identify when a model lacks sufficient information, allowing medical experts to reassess uncertain cases and build trust in AI systems (Faghani et al., 2023). It is essential to consider uncertainty evaluation to assess structural reliability, codified design, performance-based design, and risk-based decision-making. Ma et al. (2023) proposed a trustworthy deep learning framework, TRUDLMIA, for medical image analysis. It addresses challenges like limited data availability, class imbalance, and model trustworthiness. The framework combines supervised and self-supervised learning, utilizes a novel surrogate AUC margin loss function, and aims to build high-performing and high-trust models. The trustworthiness of medical image analysis can be significantly enhanced by implementing explainable AI frameworks, trustworthy deep learning models, uncertainty quantification methods, and privacy-preserving techniques such as federated and continual learning. These approaches collectively address the core concerns of transparency, reliability, and data privacy, fostering greater confidence in AI-driven medical diagnostics and treatment planning.

7.6.5 Model Interpretability and Explainability

It is important that an AI model has its predictions explained for clinical use. Medical practitioners need to comprehend the reasoning behind the decisions made by the AI model. Current LLM and LVM models lack transparency, making it difficult for clinicians to understand how predictions are made. The application of explainable AI (XAI) methods, such as attention maps and feature importance, enhances the interpretability of the conclusions clinicians could derive regarding model decision-making. Additionally, meeting the interpretability requirements will be key to meeting the ethical and regulatory expectations associated with healthcare.

7.7 Future Perspectives

Integrating LLMs in medical image understanding promises to revolutionize the field by enabling more precise and personalized healthcare solutions. Future advancements may focus on enhancing the interpretability and transparency of these models, addressing current limitations related to data biases and ethical concerns. The synergy between LLMs and multimodal data, such as combining imaging with clinical notes or bioinformatic data, could also lead to more comprehensive diagnostic tools. Regarding the potential for LLMs to support real-time decision-making, automating complex image analysis tasks and facilitating cross-disciplinary collaboration will likely drive significant innovations, ultimately improving patient outcomes and medical practice efficiency.

7.8 Acknowledgements

This work was supported by JST, PRESTO Grant Number JPMJPR23P7, Japan.

References

Alistair EW Johnson et al. 2016. MIMIC-III, a Freely Accessible Critical Care Database. *Scientific Data* 3 (2016), 160035. https://doi.org/10.1038/sdata.2016.35

Ankit Pal et al. 2022. MedMCQA: A Large-Scale Multi-subject Multi-choice Dataset for Medical Domain Question Answering. *Conference on Health, Inference, and Learning (Proceedings of Machine Learning Research)*, 248–260.

Arun James Thirunavukarasu et al. 2023. Large Language Models in Medicine. *Nature Medicine* 29, 8 (2023), 1930–1940. https://doi.org/10.1038/s41591-023-02448-8

Asma Ben Abacha, Eugene Agichtein, Yuval Pinter, and Dina Demner-Fushman. 2017. Overview of the Medical Question Answering Task at TREC 2017 LiveQA. *Text REtrieval Conference (TREC) 2017*, Gaithersburg, MD.

Aurélie Névéol et al. 2018. Clinical Natural Language Processing in Languages Other than English: Opportunities and Challenges. *Journal of Biomedical Semantics* 9 (2018), 1–13. https://doi.org/10.1186/s13326-018-0179-8

Bang Yang et al. 2023. PCLmed at ImageCLEFmedical 2023: Customizing General-Purpose Foundation Models for Medical Report Generation. *CLEF 2023: Conference and Labs of the Evaluation Forum*. CEUR-WS.org.

Barsha Abhisheka et al. 2024. Recent Trend in Medical Imaging Modalities and Their Applications in Disease Diagnosis: A Review. *Multimedia Tools and Applications* 83, 14 (2024), 43035–43070. https://doi.org/10.1007/s11042-023-17326-1

Billy Chiu et al. 2016. How to Train Good Word Embeddings for Biomedical NLP. *Proceedings of the 15th Workshop on Biomedical Natural Language Processing*, 166–174.

Bo Liu et al. 2021a. SLAKE: A Semantically-Labeled Knowledge-Enhanced Dataset for Medical Visual Question Answering. In *2021 IEEE 18th International Symposium on Biomedical Imaging (ISBI)*. IEEE, 1650–1654.

Congzhen Shi et al. 2024. A Survey on Trustworthiness in Foundation Models for Medical Image Analysis. *arXiv preprint* arXiv:2407.15851 (2024). https://doi.org/10.48550/arXiv.2407.15851

Chunyuan Li et al. 2024a. Llava-Med: Training a Large Language-and-Vision Assistant for Biomedicine in One Day. *Advances in Neural Information Processing Systems* 36 (2024).

Dan Hendrycks et al. 2021. Measuring Massive Multitask Language Understanding. *International Conference on Learning Representations*.

Di Jin et al. 2021. What Disease Does this Patient Have? A large-scale open domain question answering dataset from Medical Exams. *Applied Sciences* 11, 14 (2021), 6421. https://doi.org/10.3390/app11146421

David B Olawade et al. 2023. Using Artificial Intelligence to Improve Public Health: A Narrative Review. *Frontiers in Public Health* 11 (2023). https://doi.org/10.3389/fpubh.2023. 1196397

Digital Science and Research Solutions Inc. 2024. Medical Image Understanding for Disease Diagnosis in Full Data. https://app.dimensions.ai. Source: https://app.dimensions.ai, Exported: September 08, 2024.

Dinggang Shen et al. 2017. Deep Learning in Medical Image Analysis. *Annual Review of Biomedical Engineering* 19, 1 (2017), 221–248. https://doi.org/10.1146/annurev-bioeng-071516-044442

Duy MH Nguyen et al. 2023. LVM-Med: Learning Large-Scale Self-Supervised Vision Models for Medical Imaging via Second-order Graph Matching. In *Proceedings of the 37th Conference on Neural Information Processing Systems (NeurIPS 2023)*. Neural Information Processing Systems. https://doi.org/10.5555/3666122.3667334

Emily Alsentzer et al. 2019. Publicly Available Clinical BERT Embeddings. *arXiv preprint* arXiv:1904.03323 (2019). https://doi.org/10.48550/arXiv.1904.03323

Eric J Topol. 2019. High-Performance Medicine: The Convergence of Human and Artificial Intelligence. *Nature Medicine* 25, 1 (2019), 44–56. https://doi.org/10.1038/s41591-018-0300-7

Fan Bai et al. 2024. M3D: Advancing 3D Medical Image Analysis with Multi-Modal Large Language Models. *arXiv preprint* arXiv:2404.00578 (2024). https://doi.org/10.48550/arXiv.2404.00578

Felipe André Zeiser et al. 2024. CheXReport: A Transformer-Based Architecture to Generate Chest X-Ray Reports Suggestions. *Expert Systems with Applications* 255 (2024), 124644. https://doi.org/10.1016/j.eswa.2024.124644

Fenglin Liu et al. 2023. A Medical Multimodal Large Language Model for Future Pandemics. *NPJ Digital Medicine* 6, 1 (2023), 226. https://doi.org/10.1038/s41746-023-00952-2

Gabriel Reale-Nosei et al. 2024. From Vision to Text: A Comprehensive Review of Natural Image Captioning in Medical Diagnosis and Radiology Report Generation. *Medical Image Analysis* 97 (2024), 103264. https://doi.org/10.1016/j.media.2024.103264

Gemini Team. 2023. Gemini: A Family of Highly Capable Multimodal Models. *arXiv preprint* arXiv:2312.11805 (2023). https://doi.org/10.48550/arXiv.2312.11805

Georgios A Kaissis et al. 2020. Secure, Privacy-Preserving and Federated Machine Learning in Medical Imaging. *Nature Machine Intelligence* 2, 6 (2020), 305–311. https://doi.org/10.1038/s42256-020-0186-1

Guergana K Savova et al. 2010. Mayo Clinical Text Analysis and Knowledge Extraction System (cTAKES): Architecture, Component Evaluation and Applications. *Journal of the American Medical Informatics Association* 17, 5 (2010), 507–513. https://doi.org/10.1136/jamia.2009.001560

Haochun Wang et al. 2023. Huatuo: Tuning Llama Model with Chinese Medical Knowledge. *arXiv preprint* arXiv:2304.06975 (2023). https://doi.org/10.48550/arXiv.2304.06975

Hieu Pham et al. 2018. Efficient Neural Architecture Search via Parameters Sharing. *International Conference on Machine Learning*. PMLR, 4095–4104.

Hoo-Chang Shin et al. 2017. Natural Language Processing for Large-Scale Medical Image Analysis Using Deep Learning. *Deep Learning for Medical Image Analysis* (2017), 405–421. https://doi.org/10.1016/B978-0-12-810408-8.00023-7

Huilin Lai et al. 2023. Domain-Aware Dual Attention for Generalized Medical Image Segmentation on Unseen Domains. *IEEE Journal of Biomedical and Health Informatics* 27 (2023), 2399–2410. https://doi.org/10.1109/JBHI.2023.3251380

Ibrahim Abdelaziz et al. 2023. DataRinse: Semantic Transforms for Data Preparation Based on Code Mining. *Proceedings of the VLDB Endowment* 16, 12 (2023), 4090–4093. https://doi.org/10.14778/3611540.3611628

Iryna Hartsock and Ghulam Rasool. 2024. Vision-Language Models for Medical Report Gener-ation and Visual Question Answering: A review. *arXiv preprint* arXiv:2403.02469 (2024). https://doi.org/10.48550/arXiv.2403.02469

Jacob Devlin et al. 2018. BERT: Pre-training of Deep Bidirectional Transformers for Language Understanding. *arXiv preprint* arXiv:1810.04805 (2018). https://doi.org/10.48550/arXiv.1810.04805

Jan Clusmann et al. 2023. The Future Landscape of Large Language Models in Medicine. *Com-Munications Medicine* 3, 1 (2023), 141.

Jason J Lau et al. 2018. A Dataset of Clinically Generated Visual Questions and Answers About Radiology Images. *Scientific Data* 5 (2018), 180251. https://doi.org/10.1038/sdata.2018.251

Jeffrey Pennington et al. 2014. Glove: Global Vectors for Word Representation. *Proceedings of the 2014 Conference on Empirical Methods in Natural Language Processing (EMNLP)*, 1532–1543.

Jeremy Irvin et al. 2019. CheXpert: A Large Chest Radiograph Dataset with Uncertainty Labels and Expert Comparison. *Proceedings of the AAAI Conference on Artificial Intelligence*, Vol. 33, 590–597.

Jian-Hua Shu et al. 2020. An Improved Mask R-CNN Model for Multiorgan Segmentation. *Mathematical Problems in Engineering* 2020, 1 (2020), 8351725. https://doi.org/10.1155/2020/8351725

Jinhyuk Lee et al. 2020. BioBERT: A Pre-Trained Biomedical Language Representation Model for Biomedical Text Mining. *Bioinformatics* 36, 4 (2020), 1234–1240. https://doi.org/10.1093/bioinformatics/btz682

Joseph Chukwudi Okeibunor et al. 2023. The Use of Artificial Intelligence for Delivery of Essential Health Services Across WHO Regions: A Scoping Review. *Frontiers in Public Health* 11 (2023). https://doi.org/10.3389/fpubh.2023.1102185

Josh Achiam et al. 2023. GPT-4 Technical Report. *arXiv preprint* arXiv:2303.08774 (2023). https://doi.org/10.48550/arXiv.2303.08774

Kai Ma et al. 2023. Towards Building a Trustworthy Deep Learning Framework for Medical Image Analysis. *Sensors* 23 (2023). https://doi.org/10.3390/s23198122

Kai Zhang et al. 2024a. A Generalist Vision–Language Foundation Model for Diverse Biomedical Tasks. *Nature Medicine* (2024), 1–13.

Karan Singhal et al. 2023a. Large Language Models Encode Clinical Knowledge. *Nature* 620, 7972 (2023), 172–180. https://doi.org/10.1038/s41586-023-06291-2

Karan Singhal et al. 2023b. Large Language Models Encode Clinical Knowledge. *Nature* 619, 7972 (2023), 316–323. https://doi.org/10.1038/s41586-023-06291-2

Karan Singhal et al. 2023c. Large Language Models Encode Clinical Knowledge. *Nature* 620, 7972 (2023), 172–180.

Khai Le-Duc et al. 2024. Real-time Speech Summarization for Medical Conversations. *arXiv preprint* arXiv:2406.15888 (June 2024). https://doi.org/10.48550/arXiv.2406.15888

Khaled Saab et al. 2024. Capabilities of Gemini Models in Medicine. *arXiv preprint* arXiv:2404.18416 (2024). https://doi.org/10.48550/arXiv.2404.18416

KM Saif-Ur-Rahman et al. 2023. Artificial Intelligence and Digital Health in Improving Primary Health Care Service Delivery in LMICs: A Systematic Review. *Journal of Evidence-Based Medicine* 16, 3 (2023), 303–320. https://doi.org/10.1111/jebm.12547

Kubilay Can Demir et al. 2023. Deep Learning in Surgical Workflow Analysis: A Review of Phase and Step Recognition. *IEEE Journal of Biomedical and Health Informatics* 27, 11 (2023), 5405–5417. https://doi.org/10.1109/JBHI.2023.3311628

Lei Zhang et al. 2018. Deep Learning for Sentiment Analysis: A Survey. *Wiley Interdisciplinary Reviews: Data Mining and Knowledge Discovery* 8, 4 (2018), e1253. https://doi.org/10.1002/widm.1253

Lichao Sun et al. 2024. Trustllm: Trustworthiness in Large Language Models. *arXiv preprint* arXiv:2401.05561 (2024). https://doi.org/10.48550/arXiv.2401.05561

Lidia Flores et al. 2023. Addressing Bias in Artificial Intelligence for Public Health Surveillance. *Journal of Medical Ethics* (2023). https://doi.org/10.1136/jme-2022-108875

Mai A Shaaban et al. 2024. MedPromptX: Grounded Multimodal Prompting for Chest X-ray Diagnosis. *arXiv preprint arXiv:2403.15585* (2024). https://doi.org/10.48550/arXiv.2403.15585

Manar Aljabri et al. 2022. Towards a Better Understanding of Annotation Tools for Medical Imaging: A Survey. *Multimedia Tools and Applications* 81, 18 (2022), 25877–25911. https://doi.org/10.1007/s11042-022-12100-1

Matthew Honnibal and Ines Montani. 2017. *spaCy 2: Natural language understanding with bloom embeddings, convolutional neural networks and incremental parsing.* github.

Min Jiang et al. 2019. Combining Contextualized Embeddings and Prior Knowledge for Clinical Named Entity Recognition: Evaluation Study. *JMIR Medical Informatics* 7, 4 (2019), e14850. https://doi.org/10.2196/14850

Mingzhe Hu et al. 2023. Reinforcement Learning in Medical Image Analysis: Concepts, Applications, Challenges, and Future Directions. *Journal of Applied Clinical Medical Physics* 24, 2 (2023), e13898. https://doi.org/10.1002/acm2.13898

Mingzhe Hu et al. 2024. Advancing Medical Imaging with Language Models: Featuring a Spotlight on ChatGPT. *Physics in Medicine & Biology* 69, 10 (2024), 10TR01. https://doi.org/10.1088/1361-6560/ad387d

Moloud Abdar et al. 2023. Hercules: Deep Hierarchical Attentive Multilevel Fusion Model With Uncertainty Quantification for Medical Image Classification. *IEEE Transactions on Industrial Informatics* 19 (2023), 274–285. https://doi.org/10.1109/TII.2022.3168887

Muralikrishna Puttagunta and S Ravi. 2021. Medical Image Analysis Based on Deep Learning Approach. *Multimedia Tools and Applications* (2021). https://doi.org/10.1007/s11042-021-10707-4

Nicola Rieke et al. 2020. The Future of Digital Health with Federated Learning. *NPJ Digital Medicine* 3, 1 (2020), 1–7. https://doi.org/10.1038/s41746-020-00323-1

Nuno M Guerreiro et al. 2023. Hallucinations in Large Multilingual Translation Models. *Transactions of the Association for Computational Linguistics* 11 (2023), 1500–1517. https://doi.org/10.1162/tacl_a_00615

Ofir Ben Shoham and Nadav Rappoport. 2024. MedConceptsQA: Open Source Medical Concepts QA Benchmark. *arXiv e-prints* arXiv:2405 (2024).

Olaf Ronneberger et al. 2015. U-net: Convolutional Networks for Biomedical Image Segmentation. In *Medical Image Computing and Computer-Assisted Intervention–MICCAI 2015: 18th International Conference, Munich, Germany, October 5–9, 2015, Proceedings, Part III 18.* Springer, 234–241.

Omkar Thawakar et al. 2023. XrayGPT: Chest Radiographs Summarization Using Medical Vision-Language Models. *ArXiv* abs/2306.07971 (2023). https://doi.org/10.48550/arXiv.2306.07971

Partha Pratim Ray. 2024. Timely Need for Navigating the Potential and Downsides of LLMs in Healthcare and Biomedicine. *Briefings in Bioinformatics* 25, 3 (May 2024), bbae214. https://doi.org/10.1093/bib/bbae214

Paul A Yushkevich et al. 2006. User-Guided 3D Active Contour Segmentation of Anatomical Structures: Significantly Improved Efficiency and Reliability. *NeuroImage* 31, 3 (2006), 1116–1128. https://doi.org/10.1016/j.neuroimage.2006.01.015

Prem Prakash Jayaraman et al. 2020. Healthcare 4.0: A Review of Frontiers in Digital Health. *Wiley Interdisciplinary Reviews: Data Mining and Knowledge Discovery* 10, 2 (2020), e1350. https://doi.org/10.1002/widm.1350

Qi Li. 2023. Harnessing the Power of Pre-trained Vision-Language Models for Efficient Medical Report Generation. *Proceedings of the 32nd ACM International Conference on Information and Knowledge Management* (2023). https://doi.org/10.1145/3583780.3614961

Qi Wu et al. 2023. Self-Prompting Large Vision Models for Few-Shot Medical Image Segmentation. In *MICCAI Workshop on Domain Adaptation and Representation Transfer*. Springer, 156–167.

Qiao Jin et al. 2019. PubMedQA: A Dataset for Biomedical Research Question Answering. *Proceedings of the 2019 Conference on Empirical Methods in Natural Language Process-ing and the 9th International Joint Conference on Natural Language Processing (EMNLP-IJCNLP)*, 2567–2577.

Qile Zhu et al. 2018. GRAM-CNN: A Deep Learning Approach with Local Context for Named Entity Recognition in Biomedical Text. *Bioinformatics* 34, 9 (2018), 1547–1554. https://doi.org/10.1093/bioinformatics/btx815

Qiuhui Chen et al. 2024. Med3DInsight: Enhancing 3D Medical Image Understanding with 2D Multi-Modal Large Language Models. *arXiv preprint* arXiv:2403.05141 (2024). https://doi.org/10.48550/arXiv.2403.05141

Rajesh Bhayana. 2024. Chatbots and Large Language Models in Radiology: A Practical Primer for Clinical and Research Applications. *Radiology* 310, 1 (2024), e232756. https://doi.org/10.1148/radiol.232756

Rimjhim and Sourav Kumar Dandapat. 2023. Tagging Multi-label Categories to Points of Interest From Check-in Data. *IEEE Transactions on Emerging Topics in Computational Intelligence* 7 (2023), 1191–1204. https://doi.org/10.1109/TETCI.2022.3229338

Shahriar Faghani et al. 2023. Quantifying Uncertainty in Deep Learning of Radiologic Images. *Radiology* 308, 2 (2023), e222217. https://doi.org/10.1148/radiol.222217

Shangqi Gao et al. 2023. BayeSeg: Bayesian Modeling for Medical Image Segmentation with Interpretable Generalizability. *Medical image analysis* 89 (2023), 102889. https://doi.org/10.48550/arXiv.2303.01710

Shengyu Liu et al. 2015. Drug Name Recognition: Approaches and Resources. *Information* 6, 4 (2015), 790–810. https://doi.org/10.3390/info6040790

Songtao Jiang et al. 2024. MoE-TinyMed: Mixture of Experts for Tiny Medical Large Vision-Language Models. *arXiv preprint* arXiv:2404.10237 (2024). https://doi.org/10.48550/arXiv.2404.10237

Stephane M Meystre et al. 2017. Clinical Data Reuse or Secondary Use: Current Status and Potential Future Progress. *Yearbook of Medical Informatics* 26, 01 (2017), 38–52. https://doi.org/10.15265/IY-2017–007

Subrat Kumar Bhattamisra et al. 2023. Artificial Intelligence in Pharmaceutical and Health-Care Research. *Big Data and Cognitive Computing* 7 (2023), 10. https://doi.org/10.3390/bdcc7010010

Sunil Kumar Sharma et al. 2024. Mobile Healthcare (m-Health) Based on Artificial Intelligence in Healthcare 4.0. *Expert Systems* 41, 6 (2024), e13025. https://doi.org/10.1111/exsy.13025

Takeshi Nakaura et al. 2024. Preliminary Assessment of Automated Radiology Report Generation with Generative Pre-Trained Transformers: Comparing Results to Radiologist-Generated Reports. *Japanese Journal of Radiology* 42 (2024), 190–200. https://doi.org/10.1007/s11604-023-01487-y

Ting Chen et al. 2020. A Simple Framework for Contrastive Learning of Visual Representations. *International Conference on Machine Learning. PMLR*, 1597–1607.

Tomas Mikolov. 2013. Efficient Estimation of Word Representations in Vector Space. *arXiv preprint* arXiv:1301.3781 (2013). https://doi.org/10.48550/arXiv.1301.3781

Veronika Cheplygina et al. 2019. Not-So-Supervised: A Survey of Semi-Supervised, Multi-Instance, and Transfer Learning in Medical Image Analysis. *Medical Image Analysis* 54 (2019), 280–296. https://doi.org/10.1016/j.media.2019.03.009

Walayat Hussain et al. 2024. Revolutionising Healthcare with Artificial Intelligence: A Bibliometric Analysis of 40 Years of Progress in Health Systems. *Digital Health* 10 (2024), 20552076241258757. https://doi.org/10.1177/20552076241258757

Weijia Xu et al. 2023. Understanding and Detecting Hallucinations in Neural Machine Translation via Model Introspection. *Transactions of the Association for Computational Linguistics* 11 (2023), 546–564. https://doi.org/10.1162/tacl_a_00563

Weiqi Jiao et al. 2023. The Economic Value and Clinical Impact of Artificial Intelligence in Healthcare: A Scoping Literature Review. *IEEE Access* 11 (2023), 123445–123457. https://doi.org/10.1109/ACCESS.2023.3327905

Weixiong Lin et al. 2023. PMC-CLIP: Contrastive Language-Image Pre-training using Biomedical Documents. *arXiv preprint* arXiv:2303.07240 (March 2023). https://doi.org/10.48550/arXiv.2303.07240

Wisdom Ikezogwo et al. 2024. Quilt-1m: One Million Image-Text Pairs for Histopathology. *Advances in Neural Information Processing Systems* 36 (2024).

Xiaojun Jia et al. 2024. Improving Fast Adversarial Training With Prior-Guided Knowledge. *IEEE Transactions on Pattern Analysis and Machine Intelligence* 46, 9 (2024), 6367–6383. https://doi.org/10.1109/TPAMI.2024.3381180

Xiaoman Zhang et al. 2023b. PMC-VQA: Visual Instruction Tuning for Medical Visual Question Answering. *arXiv preprint* arXiv:2305.10415 (May 2023). https://doi.org/10.48550/arXiv.2305.10415

Xiaoman Zhang et al. 2023a. Knowledge-Enhanced Visual-Language Pre-training on Chest Radiology Images. *Nature Communications* 14, 1 (2023), 4542. https://doi.org/10.1038/s41467-023-40260-7

Xiaoyan Jiang et al. 2023. Deep Learning for Medical Image-Based Cancer Diagnosis. *Cancers* 15 (2023). https://doi.org/10.3390/cancers15143608

Xinwei Liu et al. 2024. Does Few-Shot Learning Suffer from Backdoor Attacks? *Proceedings of the AAAI Conference on Artificial Intelligence*, Vol. 38, 19893–19901.

Xuechen Guo et al. 2024. LLaVA-Ultra: Large Chinese Language and Vision Assistant for Ultrasound. *Proceedings of the 32nd ACM International Conference on Multimedia*, 8845–8854.

Xuehai He et al. 2020. PathVQA: 30000+ Questions for Medical Visual Question Answering. *arXiv preprint* arXiv:2003.10286 (2020). https://doi.org/10.48550/arXiv.2003.10286

Yang Song et al. 2015. Large Margin Local Estimate With Applications to Medical Image Classification. *IEEE Transactions on Medical Imaging* 34 (2015), 1362–1377. https://doi.org/10.1109/TMI.2015.2393954

Yefan Huang et al. 2022. OVQA: A Clinically Generated Visual Question Answering Dataset. *Proceedings of the 45th International ACM SIGIR Conference on Research and Development in Information Retrieval*, 2924–2938.

Yuichiro Hirano et al. 2024. GPT-4 Turbo with Vision Fails to Outperform Text-Only GPT-4 Turbo in the Japan Diagnostic Radiology Board Examination: Correspondence. *Japanese Journal of Radiology* (2024). https://doi.org/10.1007/s11604-024-01561-z

Yunfei Xie et al. 2024. MedTrinity-25M: A Large-Scale Multimodal Dataset with Multigranular Annotations for Medicine. *arXiv preprint* arXiv:2408.02900 (2024). https://doi.org/10.48550/arXiv.2408.02900

Yutao Dou et al. 2024. ShennongMGS: An LLM-Based Chinese Medication Guidance System. *ACM Transactions on Management Information Systems* (April 2024). https://doi.org/10.1145/3658451

Yuting He et al. 2024. Foundation Model for Advancing Healthcare: Challenges, Opportunities, and Future Directions. *arXiv preprint* arXiv:2404.03264 (2024). https://doi.org/10.48550/arXiv.2404.03264

Yutong Zhang et al. 2024b. Potential of Multimodal Large Language Models for Data Mining of Medical Images and Free-text Reports. *arXiv preprint* arXiv:2407.05758 (2024). https://doi.org/10.48550/arXiv.2407.05758

Ze Liu et al. 2021b. Swin Transformer: Hierarchical Vision Transformer Using Shifted Windows. In *Proceedings of the IEEE/CVF International Conference on Computer Vision*, 10012–10022.

Zihan Li et al. 2024b. LViT: Language Meets Vision Transformer in Medical Image Segmentation. *IEEE Transactions on Medical Imaging* 43, 1 (2024), 96–107. https://doi.org/10.1109/TMI.2023.3291719

Zihao Xu et al. 2024. A Comprehensive Study of Jailbreak Attack Versus Defense for Large Language Models. *Findings of the Association for Computational Linguistics ACL 2024*, 7432–7449.

Ziyuan Qin et al. 2022. Medical Image Understanding with Pretrained Vision Language Models: A Comprehensive Study. *arXiv preprint* arXiv:2209.15517 (2022). https://doi.org/10.48550/arXiv.2209.15517

8

Enhancing Credit Card Fraud Detection with Spatial-Temporal Analysis and Balanced Learning Approaches

Nur Indah Lestari, Walayat Hussain,
José M. Merigó, and Mahmoud Bekhit

8.1 Introduction

The increasing adoption of online shopping and electronic payment systems highlights the necessity for robust fraud detection techniques. Especially in the context of the COVID-19 epidemic, wherein there has been a noticeable surge in the use of digital payment methods and online transactions, criminals engaged in fraudulent activities have identified new ways for conducting their illegal activities [1–3]. Considering this situation, financial institutions need to maintain awareness in detecting and analysing emerging patterns of fraudulent activities. Furthermore, they must develop specific plans to respond appropriately to protect customers who are at risk. Consequently, credit card fraud spiked during this time period, with fraudsters manipulating the economic crisis to target vulnerable individuals and enterprises.

Due to the growing complexity of fraudster techniques, conventional fraud detection systems face challenges in keeping up. These challenges include managing large amounts of data and finding the right balance between security and user experience. In order to effectively identify fraud in the current constantly evolving area, it is necessary to utilise a prompt and visionary strategy that is flexible, robust, and able to navigate the complexities of recent financial fraud.

As depicted by [4], the illustration presented in Figure 8.1 illustrates a conventional framework for detecting fraudulent activities that are commonly implemented in commercial systems. Upon successful card verification, financial institutions such as VISA, MasterCard, and Citibank utilize an online predictive model to evaluate every transaction. In contrast to a basic rule-checking system that emphasizes card blacklists, budgetary assessments, and fraud regulations, the predictive model is constructed to

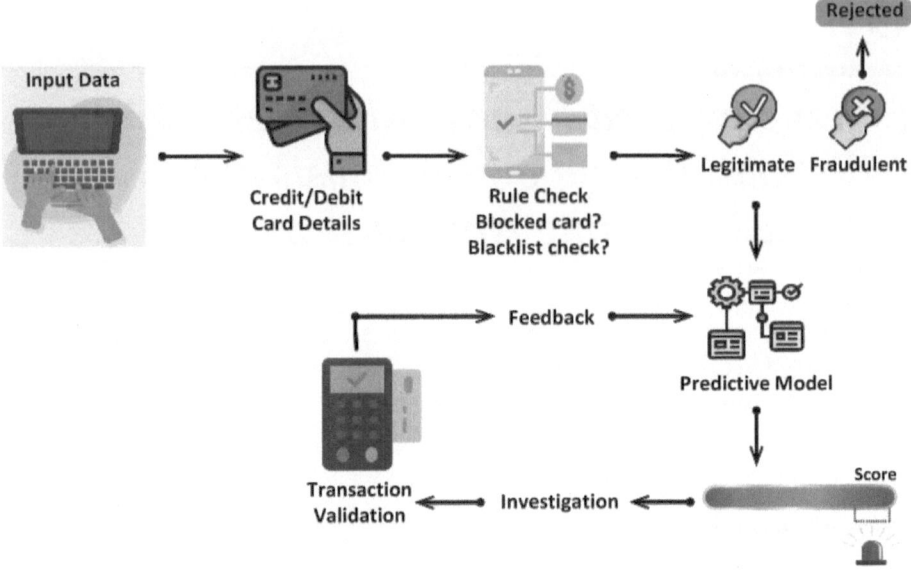

FIGURE 8.1
Framework of credit card fraud detection.

autonomously identify fraudulent patterns and generate a score indicative of the risk of fraud. As a result, investigators are able to concentrate on transactions that pose high risk efficiently and subsequently provide the analysis outcomes to the predictive model for updating purposes systems [5]. Given the dynamic nature of the attacking strategies employed by potential fraudsters, it is compulsory that a well-functioning system can effectively adjust to these evolving attack methods.

Fraudulent transactions frequently display unusual patterns when examined from the perspectives of space and time, encouraging the incorporation of spatial and temporal analysis into fraud detection. For example, conventional detection methods may fail to notice a possible case of fraud if there is a rapid sequence of transactions from distant places. The same principle applies regarding suspicious patterns of transactions that occur at inconvenient times. The system can identify fraudulent actions and grasp their context and method of operation due to these analyses, which improves the overall efficacy of the detection procedure.

The integration of spatial-temporal analysis in credit card detection systems for fraud has great potential. Through this approach, such systems may obtain another level of accuracy and precision that was previously unachievable using conventional approaches. The combination of these features enables a sophisticated detection process that can effectively adjust to the constantly shifting methods used by fraudsters. It guarantees an enhanced, adaptable, and accurate method for detecting fraud that can recognize complex and intricate patterns that signal fraudulent activity.

The main contribution of this chapter is to design and assess an innovative system for detecting credit card fraud by combining machine learning and deep learning techniques, balancing, geolocation monitoring, and temporal attention systems and advanced balancing techniques in order to consider the data imbalance challenge in datasets. This system aims to solve the weaknesses of current fraud detection techniques, which frequently encounter difficulties in adjusting to the swiftly changing strategies employed by fraudsters in the worldwide financial arena.

This chapter is structured as follows: The Introduction addresses the problem of credit card fraud and the necessity for efficient detection techniques. The Literature Review analyses current methodologies and highlights research shortcomings. The Research Methodology defines the analytical approaches and machine learning methodologies applied. The Results and Discussion section evaluates model efficacy and examines implications for fraud detection. The Conclusions summarise the principal findings and outline the study's contributions to the world of digital banking security.

8.2 Literature Review

This section explores the literature on systems that identify credit card fraud. It focuses explicitly on tracing the development of credit card fraud detection. It also covers the evolution from basic techniques to advanced, technology-driven alternatives. A conventional fraud detection system typically incorporates an automated fraud detection model and a manual review operation conducted by the organization's investigator [6]. The automated fraud detection technique is designed to monitor and evaluate every transaction that comes in using data mining methods, resulting in a scoring system [7, 8]. The manual process involves corporate investigators' examining transactions that are suspicious and have been flagged by an automated fraud detection system due to their high fraud scores. The investigators then provide responses indicating whether the transactions are illegal or valid [9]. An automated fraud detection system may be constructed with either expert-driven approaches, data-driven methods, or a mix of both [10].

Spatial analysis has become essential in numerous scientific fields, including epidemiology and geoscience, where it pertains to examining the characteristics, locations, and interconnections of elements within spatial data. It comprises the investigation and construction of models to depict spatial trends and patterns. Spatial analysis plays a crucial role in detecting credit card fraud by identifying transaction location abnormalities. This enables the identification of potentially fraudulent activities when cardholders conduct transactions in distant or uncommon areas that differ from their regular routine.

Fraudsters often act in certain areas to efficiently move cash between their accounts and optimise their earnings within a short time frame instead of regularly changing their transaction locations. This behaviour sets them apart from authorised customers in terms of geographical patterns [11–13]. Hence the spatial transactional behaviour of users is an additional crucial factor in identifying fraudulent attributes. Additionally, the transactional behaviour of users is a crucial component in temporal analysis for identifying fraudulent attributes. Users' transactional behaviours tend to evolve over time [14, 15]. The transactional behaviour of genuine customers is notably developing with their living conditions and income levels. Conversely, in order to counteract the evolving transactional patterns of authentic users and the perpetual revisions to credit card fraud detection models, fraudulent actors consistently modify their methods of operation [11].

Various strategies and approaches have been developed and applied to identify credit card fraud. Examining the complex, thorough, and constantly evolving character of fraud is essential to comprehending the effectiveness and suitability of these numerous methods.

The comparative study of the existing literature demonstrates that various approaches have been utilised in the field of credit card fraud detection. In addition, this comparison demonstrates that while the literature describes the variety of approaches that have already been applied in identifying credit card fraud, gaps in the existing literature still need to be filled. One gap is that these approaches could be further improved by simultaneously integrating the spatial-temporal element, resampling technique, machine learning, and deep learning.

Although a substantial amount of study has focused on credit card fraud detection systems, notable gaps and shortcomings need more investigation and advancement. A significant deficiency in the existing body of research is the lack of a comprehensive framework that integrates spatial analysis, temporal analysis, resampling methods, and the collective capabilities of both machine learning and deep learning algorithms. An integrated approach is crucial for improving fraud detection systems' precision, accuracy, and effectiveness. An advanced system would possess the ability to not only accurately detect fraudulent activity but also to adapt to the changing nature of credit card fraud, eventually enhancing the security of financial transactions. The existence of these gaps emphasises the need for more thorough and unified strategies that can effectively tackle the intricacies of fraud detection in the present-day digital landscape.

TABLE 8.1

Critical Evaluation of Existing Literature of Credit Card Fraud Detection System Approaches

Source	Spatial-Temporal Analysis		Imbalance Technique	Machine Learning	Deep Learning
	Spatial	Temporal			
Abd El-Naby et al. [16]	✗	✗	✓	✓	✗
Afriyie et al. [17]	✗	✗	✓	✓	✗
Almazroi and Ayub [18]	✗	✗	✓	✓	✓
Barz et al. [19]	✓	✓	✗	✓	✗
Cheng et al. [4]	✓	✓	✗	✓	✓
de Sá et al [6]	✗	✗	✗	✓	✗
Esenogho et al. [20]	✗	✗	✓	✓	✓
Fanai and Abbasimehr [21]	✗	✓	✓	✓	✓
Ghaleb et al. [22]	✓	✗	✓	✓	✓
Gupta et al. [23]	✗	✗	✓	✓	✗
Khalid et al. [24]	✗	✓	✓	✓	✓
Li et al [25]	✗	✗	✓	✓	✓
Lucas et al. [26]	✗	✓	✗	✓	✗
Lunghi et al. [27]	✗	✓	✓	✓	✓
Nguyen et al. [28]	✗	✗	✓	✓	✓
Ni et al. [29]	✗	✗	✓	✓	✗
Xie et al. [11]	✓	✓	✗	✓	✓
Xie et al. [30]	✗	✓	✗	✓	✓
Xie et al. [31]	✗	✓	✗	✓	✓
Zhu et al. [32]	✓	✗	✓	✓	✓

8.3 Research Methodology

This section outlines the methods for detecting credit card fraud, beginning with the processing of data, which includes providing an overview of the information and preparing it for modeling. This section also encompasses the process of exploratory data analysis (EDA) in order to gain insights into the qualities of the data, followed by the building of a model, wherein the methods used are described. It also explores various resampling approaches that aim to mitigate class imbalance. It also assesses the efficacy of the model by using classification performance indicators.

8.3.1 Proposed Approach

The proposed approach used in this chapter is shown in Figure 8.2. The methodology begins by analysing the unprocessed history user data,

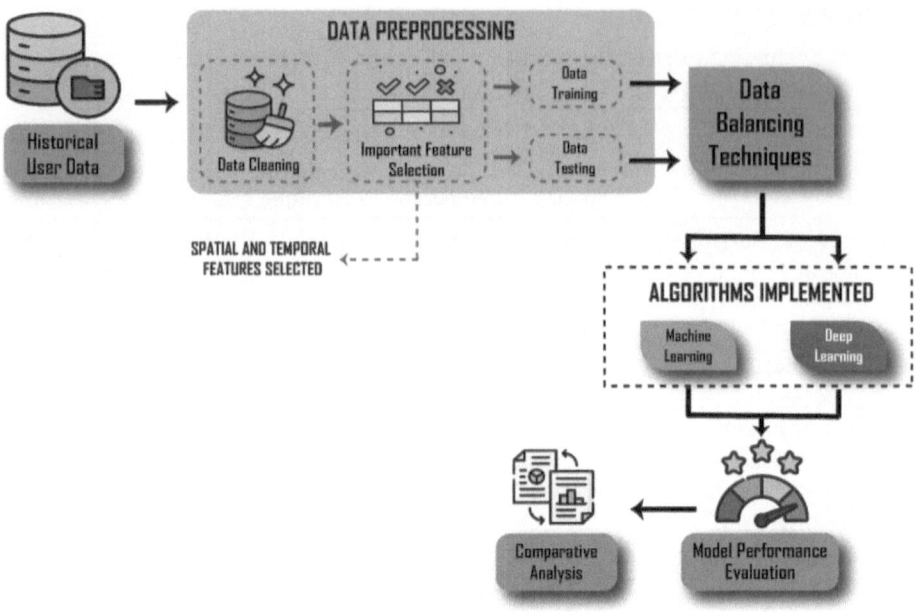

FIGURE 8.2
Framework for detecting credit card fraud using spatial–temporal data and machine learning, from data collection through model evaluation.

performing data processing on the historical user data, and then assessing several machine learning and deep learning algorithms. The first step involves subjecting the raw historical user data to a thorough data cleaning procedure to eliminate any inconsistencies, inaccuracies, or unnecessary data, hence ensuring the dataset's quality. Following that, an important feature selection phase is conducted, explicitly focusing on the indispensable spatial and temporal attributes for our analysis. After the dataset is refined, it is divided into sets for training and testing. This partition enables us to train our models efficiently while allocating a portion of the data for future evaluation of their predicting capabilities. Subsequently, the data balancing techniques are implemented to ensure a balanced portrayal of classes within the dataset, mitigating any possible biases that may compromise the correctness of our model. Various algorithms, including both machine learning and deep learning, are implemented to develop fraud detection models. Following the training process, a comparative analysis is conducted to evaluate and compare the performance of each algorithm systematically. This phase is of the utmost importance, as it enables us to determine each algorithm's robustness and comparative efficacy when implemented on our dataset.

8.3.2 Data Processing

The dataset utilized in this research encompasses a variety of simulated credit card transactions, including both authentic and fraudulent activities. The dataset comprises transactions that occur between January 1, 2019, and December 31, 2020, providing an extensive examination of temporal trends. By capturing the interactions of 1000 consumers with 80 distinct merchants, this dataset offers a wealth and variety of transactional information.

The data was produced utilizing the Sparkov Data Generation utility, a specialized instrument developed for the purpose of simulating authentic credit card transaction data. This GitHub-hosted utility, which was created by Brandon Harris, functions as a resilient instrument for generating synthetic datasets that simulate real-world transactional patterns exceptionally well. Using predefined merchant and consumer categories, the transactions were generated with the assistance of the "faker" Python library. By following this methodology, a diverse and authentic dataset is obtained, comprising various consumer profiles that differ in terms of location, gender, age, and transactional attributes like quantities and frequency.

The data has been split into two main files: fraudTrain.csv, which comprises training data and primarily consists of transactions and labels, and fraudTest.csv, a distinct set of transactions provided for model evaluation in the interest of testing.

Data cleaning is crucial for the integrity of the model. The "trans_date_trans_time" column is converted to a date-time object and then into a numerical format for analysis. Missing values are addressed using forward filling. This step is critical for maintaining the continuity and relevance of the data. Our data cleaning process involved handling missing values and inconsistencies. We employed a forward-fill method (fillna (method="ffill")) to address missing values, maintaining the sequential integrity of the dataset. Additionally, the trans_date_trans_time column, initially in date-time format, was converted to a numeric format for analytical compatibility. This transformation was crucial for integrating time-based features into our models.

The target variable, which distinguishes between legitimate and fraudulent transactions, was precisely delineated and kept distinct from the feature set. This separation is crucial for supervised learning models, in which the model's objective is to make predictions regarding the target variable. In our feature engineering phase, we focused on the features trans_date_trans_time, lat, and long, which are pivotal in identifying fraud patterns. We used one-hot encoding (pd.get_dummies) to convert categorical variables into a machine-readable format. This step is essential in preparing the data for input into machine learning models, ensuring that each feature contributes effectively to the model's predictive power.

8.3.3 Data Analysis

Our research investigates the spatial patterns of fraudulent transactions, a crucial step in the fight against financial fraud. Collecting and analysing location data associated with fraudulent transactions is the first stage, which provides the opportunity to identify "hotspots" of fraudulent activity. This knowledge assists in identifying regions or locations that are particularly susceptible to fraud. Having identified these potential locations, the next step is to utilize advanced mapping tools. These tools graphically depict the geographical distribution of fraud, thereby generating a clear picture of the fraud landscape.

Visual representation facilitates the understanding of spatial patterns of fraud, emphasizing the urgency and specific areas of focus of our anti-fraud strategies. When spatial data is integrated, it can provide a comprehensive perspective on fraudulent activity, greatly enhancing the effectiveness of fraud prevention techniques. By integrating these insights into the research, you have the potential to provide a valuable viewpoint on addressing financial crime at both the local and global levels.

Figure 8.3 illustrates the occurrence of transactions over a period of time, differentiating between fraudulent and non-fraudulent transactions. Analysing the evolution of fraud patterns over time assists in detecting periods of increased risk, which may be associated with spatial susceptibility. Observing unique surges in fraudulent transactions may indicate the existence of coordinated fraud activities in particular places.

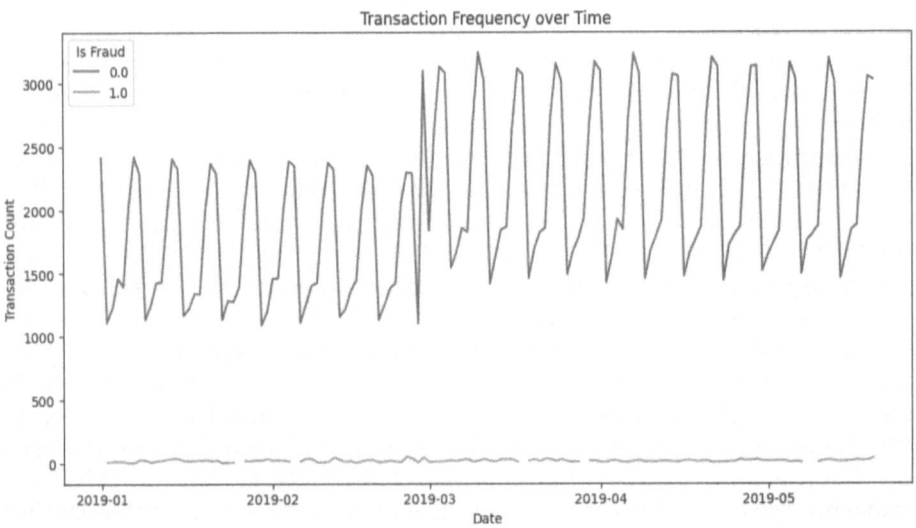

FIGURE 8.3
Transaction frequency over time.

Integrating location data with time patterns enables a comprehensive understanding of fraudulent conduct from multiple perspectives. By examining the timing and location of fraudulent activities, one can acquire a more complete comprehension of the matter. The analysis can provide information to guide preventive measures. For example, if there is a sudden increase in fraudulent activities on specific days, it would be prudent to introduce extra verification measures during transactions on those days.

8.3.4 Implemented Methods

Our research study integrates several types of machine learning models to tackle the problem of credit card fraud, with a particular focus on the use of ensemble and boosting techniques in improving prediction accuracy and mitigating overfitting. Random Forest and CatBoost are very effective in dealing with categorical data and mitigating overfitting using innovative methodologies. Additionally, methods like AdaBoost and XGBoost aim to improve the performance of models, focusing on fixing the problems caused by complicated and unbalanced datasets that are common in fraud detection situations. The use of logistic regression with Ridge Classifier offers a robust statistical framework for addressing binary classification tasks, using regularization strategies to mitigate the risk of overfitting. In the context of fraud detection, the Gaussian naive Bayes approach is used, which utilizes probabilistic principles and assumes feature independence to enhance efficiency.

The entire approach to fraud detection is shown by the integration of many methods, ranging from stochastic gradient descent to the Extra Trees Classifier. This comprehensive strategy utilizes the advantages of each model to manage extensive and complicated datasets successfully, emphasizing the significance of flexibility and accuracy in combating digital fraud.

8.3.5 Data Balancing Techniques

This study investigates and uses different resampling techniques to address class imbalance in credit card fraud detection. Initially, we replicate minority class instances using random over-sampling (ROS) to adjust class distribution. SMOTE produces synthetic samples to increase dataset variety and reduce overfitting risks. Also, adaptive synthetic sampling (ADASYN) is used to provide synthetic data for underrepresented classes, focusing on harder instances to learn. Random under-sampling is examined to reduce the number of majority class samples, making the dataset more manageable. However, this method may lose crucial information. These methods address class imbalance, which is crucial to detecting complex fraud patterns, to improve model performance.

8.3.6 Performance Metrics

To address class imbalance, a variety of assessment criteria are used to evaluate a credit card fraud detection model. Precision and accuracy are key to this study. Precision is the ratio of correctly predicted positive events to all positive predictions, while accuracy is the percentage of real positives and negatives across all forecasts. Sensitivity, or recall, is more important when failing to detect a fraudulent transaction has serious consequences. This confirms the model's ability to detect all real fraud. The F1 score, which balances accuracy and recall, is ideal for biassed datasets. However, the AUC-ROC score assesses classification performance across thresholds, which is crucial for distinguishing fraudulent from legitimate transactions. The combination of these measures provides a comprehensive assessment framework, enabling a detailed review of the performance of the model.

8.4 Results and Discussion

This section utilises a range of machine learning and deep learning methodologies, including Random Forest, CatBoost, Bagging, logistic regression, XGB, AdaBoost, Gaussian naive Bayes, Extra Trees, SGD, GRU, and neural networks. Each of these techniques presents distinct approaches for handling unprocessed data and addressing the issue of class imbalance. Our evaluation of these models included the use of comprehensive measures such as recall, precision, F1 score, specificity, ROC-AUC, and accuracy. These metrics were employed to examine the performance of each model in accurately identifying real positives and negatives, as well as to evaluate the precision and accuracy of the models. The metrics mentioned are crucial in the field of fraud detection, namely recall, which quantifies the ability of the model to correctly detect fraudulent transactions.

8.4.1 Impact of Implementing Various Machine and Deep Learning Algorithms on Raw Data

The assessment of machine learning models for credit card fraud detection customarily centres on their capacity to distinguish between legitimate and fraudulent transactions. Prior to employing data balancing methods, it is imperative to evaluate the effectiveness of these models on unprocessed, raw datasets. The performance of the Bagging classifier and Random Forest classifier on the raw dataset was encouraging in terms of the majority class, as evidenced by their accuracy, precision, and F1 score values approaching perfection. Conversely, upon closer examination of the minority cohort, a substantial decline in both recall and F1 score was observed. The recall metric for

TABLE 8.2

Results of Implementing Various Machine and Deep Learning Algorithms on Raw Data

Model Name	Recall Score	Precision Score	F1 Score	ROC AUC Score	Accuracy Score
Bagging classifier	0.85476	0.93924	0.89501	0.99884	0.92722
Random Forest classifier	0.93138	0.91974	0.92552	0.99913	0.96545
Logistic regression	0	0	0	0.99421	0.5
AdaBoost classifier	0.00133	1	0.00266	0.99422	0.50067
CatBoost classifier	0.16256	0.86833	0.27385	0.96353	0.99501
XGB classifier	0.03598	0.83077	0.06897	0.99438	0.51797
Extra Trees classifier	0.9527	0.92199	0.93709	0.99926	0.97611
GNB classifier	0	0	0	0.52726	0.99421
GRU	0	0	0	−1	0.99421
NN	0	0	0	1	−1

the Bagging classifier's performance in identifying fraudulent transactions was 0.85476, while its balanced performance metric (F1 score) was 0.89501 The Random Forest classifier exhibited a marginally enhanced recall value of 0.93138, signifying a moderate level of proficiency in fraud detection.

The examination of models performing fraud detection tasks using raw data supports the established belief that class imbalance substantially impedes the effectiveness of the models, specifically about the minority class. The discrepancy in model performance highlights the criticality of implementing class balancing methods to correct the imbalance of class distribution before continuing the training process. By implementing corrective measures, the complete potential of machine learning models can be realised, guaranteeing their optimal performance in practical situations that require precise identification of fraudulent activities.

8.4.2 Impact of Balancing Techniques on Model Performance

We examine several balancing strategies, including random over-sampling, synthetic minority over-sampling technique (SMOTE), adaptive synthetic sampling (ADASYN), and random under-sampling to the proposed problem.

The details analysis in Table 8.3 is essential in directing us towards more accurate and reliable fraud detection models. The Bagging classifier and Random Forest classifier demonstrated outstanding performance across almost all measures, mainly when random over-sampling and SMOTE approaches were used. The capacity to maintain elevated performance measures demonstrates their resilience in addressing class imbalance. The slight differences in performance metrics observed across various balancing approaches underscore the complicated influence of each strategy on the model's performance.

TABLE 8.3

Comparative Analysis of Model Performance Metrics Before and After the Application of Resampling Techniques

Model Name	Balancing Technique	Recall Score	Precision Score	F1 Score	ROC AUC Score	Accuracy Score
Bagging classifier	None	0.85476	0.93924	0.89501	0.99884	0.92722
	Random over-sampling	0.8521	0.94671	0.89691	0.99574	0.99887
	SMOTE	0.84544	0.93861	0.88959	0.99968	0.9876
	ADASYN	0.84477	0.93235	0.8864	0.98961	0.99875
	Random under-sampling	0.82079	0.93475	0.87407	0.99164	0.99863
Random Forest classifier	None	0.93138	0.91974	0.92552	0.99913	0.96545
	Random over-sampling	0.94337	0.92731	0.93527	0.99884	0.99924
	SMOTE	0.91939	0.92867	0.924	0.99959	0.99669
	ADASYN	0.92005	0.92128	0.92067	0.99806	0.99908
	Random under-sampling	0.82079	0.93475	0.87407	0.99164	0.99863
Logistic regression	None	0	0	0	0.99421	0.5
	Random over-sampling	0	0	0	0.5	0.99421
	SMOTE	0	0	0	1	0.5
	ADASYN	0	0	0	0.5	0.99421
	Random under-sampling	0	0	0	0.5	0.99421
AdaBoost classifier	None	0.00133	1	0.00266	0.99422	0.50067
	Random over-sampling	0.00067	1	0.00133	0.61351	0.99422
	SMOTE	0.002	1	0.00399	1	0.60933
	ADASYN	0.002	1	0.00399	0.61844	0.99422
	Random under-sampling	0.00133	1	0.00266	0.59928	0.99422
CatBoost classifier	None	0.16256	0.86833	0.27385	0.96353	0.99501
	Random over-sampling	0.17189	0.86	0.28651	0.96831	0.99505
	SMOTE	0.17322	0.86667	0.28873	0.99984	0.9681
	ADASYN	0.15789	0.82867	0.26525	0.96505	0.99494
	Random under-sampling	0.13924	0.86008	0.23968	0.96099	0.99489
XGB classifier	None	0.03598	0.83077	0.06897	0.99438	0.51797
	Random over-sampling	0.03531	0.76812	0.06752	0.95674	0.99435
	SMOTE	0.03464	0.8125	0.06645	0.99995	0.95257
	ADASYN	0.03664	0.85938	0.07029	0.95633	0.99439
	Random under-sampling	0.03864	0.80556	0.07374	0.94331	0.99438
Extra Trees classifier	None	0.9527	0.92199	0.93709	0.99926	0.97611
	Random over-sampling	0.95936	0.92131	0.93995	0.99925	0.99929
	SMOTE	0.92805	0.93115	0.9296	0.9996	0.99789
	ADASYN	0.93538	0.91705	0.92612	0.99889	0.99914
	Random under-sampling	0.93738	0.90599	0.92141	0.99854	0.99907

TABLE 8.3 (*Continued*)

Comparative Analysis of Model Performance Metrics Before and After the Application of Resampling Techniques

Model Name	Balancing Technique	Recall Score	Precision Score	F1 Score	ROC AUC Score	Accuracy Score
GNB classifier	None	0	0	0	0.52726	0.99421
	Random over-sampling	0	0	0	0.52704	0.99421
	SMOTE	0	0	0	1	0.53482
	ADASYN	0	0	0	0.54986	0.99421
	Random under-sampling	0	0	0	0.53197	0.99421
GRU	None	0	0	0	-1	0.99421
	Random over-sampling	0	0	0	0.99421	0.5
	SMOTE	0	0	0	0.99421	0.5
	ADASYN	1	0	0	0	0.99421
	Random under-sampling	0	0	0	0.99421	0.5
NN	None	0	0	0	1	-1
	Random over-sampling	0	0	0	0.99421	0.5
	SMOTE	0	0	0	0.99421	0.5
	ADASYN	0	0	0	1	0.99421
	Random under-sampling	0	0	0	0.99421	0.5

The models showed proficiency in reducing false positives while effectively detecting fraudulent transactions.

Logistic Regression: Although this model achieved a high level of accuracy, it was unable to detect any cases of fraud, suggesting its ineffectiveness in handling datasets with significant imbalances.

The AdaBoost classifier showed a restricted capacity to detect fraudulent transactions in its unprocessed state, with only a little improvement after adjusting for imbalances. This underscores some models' difficulties when dealing with highly unbalanced data and the modest but significant influence of data balancing. The CatBoost classifier and XGB classifier showed enhanced fraud detection capabilities after the use of data balancing strategies, particularly with SMOTE. This suggests that both models can be useful when adequately preprocessed. Nevertheless, their performance in its unprocessed form highlights the difficulty posed by class disparity.

The Extra Trees classifier demonstrated robust performance across all measures, with small improvements or stability seen when balancing approaches were used. This model's robustness and efficacy make it a suitable contender for fraud detection systems.

The GNB classifier, GRU, and NN models show a lack of capability in detecting fraudulent transactions both before and during data balancing.

This suggests that these models may not be appropriate for unbalanced datasets often seen in fraud detection scenarios without significant modifications.

Methods such as SMOTE and random sampling have shown notable efficacy, highlighting the need to carefully choose an appropriate balancing strategy that aligns with the unique characteristics of the model and dataset.

The comprehensive examination and sophisticated comprehension of the interplay between various models and balancing procedures provide useful insights for developing efficient fraud detection systems. Ensemble approaches, such as the Bagging classifier and Random Forest classifier, have shown significant efficacy in addressing the challenges posed by unbalanced datasets. This research highlights the significance of using a multi-metric assessment methodology and giving due attention to class imbalance when designing systems aimed at mitigating fraud within the digital financial industry.

8.5 Conclusion

The incorporation of machine learning and deep learning techniques with spatial-temporal analysis has become a key advancement in this area of study. This chapter offers a practical examination of the impact of various balancing strategies on the efficacy of these techniques in the domain of credit card fraud detection despite obstacles such as data imbalances and the constantly changing techniques used by fraudsters.

The thorough assessment utilising a range of metrics, including recall, precision, F1 score, ROC AUC, and accuracy, has emphasised the efficacy of ensemble methods, specifically the Bagging and Random Forest classifiers. These classifiers consistently demonstrate superior performance across all metrics following the implementation of Random over-sampling, SMOTE, and ADASYN techniques.

The findings illustrate the importance of balancing the dataset to enhance the model's capacity to identify fraudulent transactions, which is necessary to be emphasised by the significant increase in digital transactions following the COVID-19 pandemic. Although class imbalance in datasets presents inherent challenges, the findings highlight the potential of ensemble methods to provide reliable fraud detection capabilities. Basic models such as logistic regression, despite their high accuracy, are unable to detect fraudulent cases. This highlights the inadequacy of depending entirely on accuracy as a performance measure when dealing with imbalanced classes.

This chapter provides an extensive fraud detection technique that uses effective machine learning algorithms and challenges data balance preprocessing. This ensures that models are accurate and respond to minority fraud transactions. Geolocation and temporal attention systems enhance the proposed system, solving a current problem.

References

[1] F. Khan, S. Ateeq, M. Ali, and N. Butt, "Impact of COVID-19 on the drivers of cash-based online transactions and consumer behaviour: Evidence from a Muslim market," *Journal of Islamic Marketing*, vol. 14, no. 3, pp. 714–734, 2023.

[2] C. Kizil, V. Akman, and E. Muzır, "COVID-19 epidemic: A new arena of financial fraud?," in *Karabagh International Congress of Modern Studies in Social and Human Sciences*, 2021, pp. 310–314.

[3] K.W.F. Ma and T. McKinnon, "COVID-19 and cyber fraud: Emerging threats during the pandemic," *Journal of Financial Crime*, vol. 29, no. 2, pp. 433–446, 2022.

[4] D. Cheng, X. Wang, Y. Zhang, and L. Zhang, "Graph neural network for fraud detection via spatial-temporal attention," *IEEE Transactions on Knowledge and Data Engineering*, vol. 34, no. 8, pp. 3800–3813, 2020.

[5] A. Dal Pozzolo, G. Boracchi, O. Caelen, C. Alippi, and G. Bontempi, "Credit card fraud detection: A realistic modeling and a novel learning strategy," *IEEE Transactions on Neural Networks and Learning Systems*, vol. 29, no. 8, pp. 3784–3797, 2017.

[6] A.G. de Sá, A.C. Pereira, and G.L. Pappa, "A customized classification algorithm for credit card fraud detection," *Engineering Applications of Artificial Intelligence*, vol. 72, pp. 21–29, 2018.

[7] E. Kim, J. Lee, H. Shin, H. Yang, S. Cho, S.K. Nam, Y. Song, J.A.Yoon, and J.I. Kim, "Champion-challenger analysis for credit card fraud detection: Hybrid ensemble and deep learning," *Expert Systems with Applications*, vol. 128, pp. 214–224, 2019.

[8] A. Salazar, G. Safont, A. Rodriguez, and L. Vergara, "Combination of multiple detectors for credit card fraud detection," in *2016 IEEE International Symposium on Signal Processing and Information Technology (ISSPIT)*, 2016: IEEE, pp. 138–143.

[9] D. Sánchez, M. Vila, L. Cerda, and J.-M. Serrano, "Association rules applied to credit card fraud detection," *Expert Systems with Applications*, vol. 36, no. 2, pp. 3630–3640, 2009.

[10] C. Phua, V. Lee, K. Smith, and R. Gayler, "A comprehensive survey of data mining-based fraud detection research," *arXiv preprint* arXiv:1009.6119, 2010.

[11] Y. Xie, G. Liu, M. Zhou, L. Wei, H. Zhu, R. Zhou, and L. Cao, "A spatial–temporal gated network for credit card fraud detection by learning transactional representations," *IEEE Transactions on Automation Science and Engineering*, vol. 21, no. 4, pp. 6978–6991, 2023.

[12] V. Chang, A. Di Stefano, Z. Sun, and G. Fortino, "Digital payment fraud detection methods in digital ages and Industry 4.0," *Computers and Electrical Engineering*, vol. 100, p. 107734, 2022.

[13] X. Guo, M. Zhou, A. Abusorrah, F. Alsokhiry, and K. Sedraoui, "Disassembly sequence planning: A survey," *IEEE/CAA Journal of Automatica Sinica*, vol. 8, no. 7, pp. 1308–1324, 2020.

[14] D. Cheng, Z. Niu, J. Li, and C. Jiang, "Regulating systemic crises: Stemming the contagion risk in networked-loans through deep graph learning," *IEEE Transactions on Knowledge and Data Engineering,* vol. 35, no. 6, pp. 6278–6289, 2022.

[15] Y. Zeng and J. Tang, "Improved aggregating and accelerating training methods for spatial graph neural networks on fraud Detection," *arXiv preprint* arXiv:2202.06580, 2022.

[16] A. Abd El-Naby, E.E.-D. Hemdan, and A. El-Sayed, "An efficient fraud detection framework with credit card imbalanced data in financial services," *Multimedia Tools and Applications,* vol. 82, no. 3, pp. 4139–4160, 2023.

[17] J.K. Afriyie, K. Tawiah, W.A. Pels, S. Addai-Henne, H.A. Dwamena, E.O. Owiredu, S.A. Ayeh, and J. Eshun, "A supervised machine learning algorithm for detecting and predicting fraud in credit card transactions," *Decision Analytics Journal,* vol. 6, p. 100163, 2023.

[18] A.A. Almazroi and N. Ayub, "Online payment fraud detection model using machine learning techniques," *IEEE Access,* vol. 11, pp. 137188–137203, 2023.

[19] B. Barz, E. Rodner, Y.G. Garcia, and J. Denzler, "Detecting regions of maximal divergence for spatio-temporal anomaly detection," *IEEE Transactions on Pattern Analysis and Machine Intelligence,* vol. 41, no. 5, pp. 1088–1101, 2018.

[20] E. Esenogho, I.D. Mienye, T.G. Swart, K. Aruleba, and G. Obaido, "A neural network ensemble with feature engineering for improved credit card fraud detection," *IEEE Access,* vol. 10, pp. 16400–16407, 2022.

[21] H. Fanai and H. Abbasimehr, "A novel combined approach based on deep Autoencoder and deep classifiers for credit card fraud detection," *Expert Systems with Applications,* vol. 217, p. 119562, 2023.

[22] F.A. Ghaleb, F. Saeed, M. Al-Sarem, S.N. Qasem, and T. Al-Hadhrami, "Ensemble synthesized minority oversampling based generative adversarial networks and random forest algorithm for credit card fraud detection," *IEEE Access,* vol. 11, pp. 89694–89710, 2023.

[23] P. Gupta, A. Varshney, M.R. Khan, R. Ahmed, M. Shuaib, and S. Alam, "Unbalanced credit card fraud detection data: A machine learning-oriented comparative study of balancing techniques," *Procedia Computer Science,* vol. 218, pp. 2575–2584, 2023.

[24] A.R. Khalid, N. Owoh, O. Uthmani, M. Ashawa, J. Osamor, and J. Adejoh, "Enhancing credit card fraud detection: An ensemble machine learning approach," *Big Data and Cognitive Computing,* vol. 8, no. 1, p. 6, 2024.

[25] Z. Li, G. Liu, and C. Jiang, "Deep representation learning with full center loss for credit card fraud detection," *IEEE Transactions on Computational Social Systems,* vol. 7, no. 2, pp. 569–579, 2020.

[26] Y. Lucas et al., "Towards automated feature engineering for credit card fraud detection using multi-perspective HMMs," *Future Generation Computer Systems,* vol. 102, pp. 393–402, 2020.

[27] D. Lunghi, G.M. Paldino, O. Caelen, and G. Bontempi, "An adversary model of fraudsters' behavior to improve oversampling in credit card fraud detection," *IEEE Access,* vol. 11, pp. 136666–136679, 2023.

[28] N. Nguyen et al., "A proposed model for card fraud detection based on Catboost and deep neural network," *IEEE Access,* vol. 10, pp. 96852–96861, 2022.

[29] L. Ni, J. Li, H. Xu, X. Wang, and J. Zhang, "Fraud feature boosting mechanism and spiral oversampling balancing technique for credit card fraud detection," *IEEE Transactions on Computational Social Systems,* vol. 11, no. 2, pp. 1615–1630, 2023.

[30] Y. Xie, G. Liu, C. Yan, C. Jiang, and M. Zhou, "Time-aware attention-based gated network for credit card fraud detection by extracting transactional behaviors," *IEEE Transactions on Computational Social Systems*, vol. 10, no. 3, pp. 1004–1016, 2022.

[31] Y. Xie, G. Liu, C. Yan, C. Jiang, M. Zhou, and M. Li, "Learning transactional behavioral representations for credit card fraud detection," *IEEE Transactions on Neural Networks and Learning Systems*, vol. 35, no. 4, pp. 5735–5748, 2022.

[32] H. Zhu, M. Zhou, G. Liu, Y. Xie, S. Liu, and C. Guo, "NUS: Noisy-sample-removed undersampling scheme for imbalanced classification and application to credit card fraud detection," *IEEE Transactions on Computational Social Systems*, vol. 11, no. 2, pp. 1793–1804, 2023.

Index

A

ablation study, 98, 100, 102–103
academic integrity
    law students, 16, 21
    legal profession, 27–28
adversarial training, 89, 93, 96–97,
        102–103, *see also* medical image
        diagnosis
ATM operating system
    case study, 61
    components, 62–63
    finite automata, 64–68
    state transition, table 73–74
    Turing machine, 66–68

B

balanced learning techniques,
    179–184
Bayesian networks, uncertainty
    handling, 38
benchmark datasets, 124–129
buffer operators, fractional,
    109–111

C

cash management, ATM,
    80–85
CFGM (conformable fractional grey
    model), 123–125
chaotic systems, Lorenz, 124–126
ChatGPT
    assessment feedback, 1–11
    legal education, 17–23
clinical decision support, 139–140
credit-card fraud detection
    balanced learning, 179–184
    spatial-temporal modelling,
        171–178
    undersampling & oversampling,
        180–182

D

data-driven machine learning, 43–48
decision-making, multi-criteria
    (MCDM), 55–76
deep learning models
    image diagnosis, 89–105
    medical LLM fusion, 160–165
discrete grey models, 110–111, 123–125

E

energy forecasting (grey models),
    130–133
expert systems, 35–43
    knowledge-based reasoning,
        37–39
explainability, legal AI, 26–27

F

federated learning, 161–163
feedback (assessment), 1–15
    usefulness metrics, 8–9
FFP framework (medical image
    diagnosis), 89–103
financial expert system for data
    preprocessing 40–43
fine-tuning, 156–157
fixed-point discrete grey model
    (FPDGM), 113–135
    parameter optimisation, 122–124
fraud detection, *see* credit-card fraud
    detection
fuzzy logic, uncertainty, 38–39

G

generative AI (GenAI)
    definition, 17
    legal education, 16–34
    misuse & detection, 21–23
graph neural networks (fraud), 178

grey prediction models, 106–138
    applications, 130–135
    fractional variants, 123–125

H

hallucinations, LLMs, 161–163
hybrid metrics, 95–97
hyperparameter tuning, 122–124

I

image understanding, medical, 139–170
    disease diagnosis, 158–163
    report generation, 159
intelligent optimisation, 47–48
interval-valued fuzzy AHP, 86–87

K

knowledge-based expert systems, 35–43
    inference engines, 37–39
knowledge graphs, reasoning, 38

L

large language models (LLMs), 1–9,
    139–147, 165–166
    jailbreak attacks, 165
legal profession, AI ethics, 24–28
literature survey (MCDM), 58–60
LLM-vision alignment, 143–147

M

machine learning, data-driven, 43–48
    credit-card datasets, 175–180
MAPE (mean absolute percentage error),
    129–135
medical image diagnosis
    robust pruning, 94–103
    visualisation, 102
model pruning, robust, 97–103

N

naïve forecasting benchmarks, 129–130
natural-gas price prediction, 130–135

O

ontology integration, 38
optimisation, intelligent, 47–48

P

parameter estimation, grey models,
    122–124
particle swarm optimisation (PSO), 119,
    124
peer-review feedback, 1–15
    comparison with AI, 7–9
personal data privacy, GenAI, 21–22
predictive analytics (ML), 43–48

R

rule-based reasoning, 38

S

seasonal adjustment factors, 129
shale-gas output forecasting, 125–127
spatial-temporal analysis (fraud),
    171–178
student perceptions of AI feedback, 7–9
sustainability criteria (MCDM), 58–60
synchronous optimisation, 95–97

T

technical routes of AI, 35–54
    knowledge-based, 35–43
    machine-learning, 43–48
    optimisation, 47–48
transfer learning, *see* fine-tuning
Turing machine, *see* ATM operating
    system

U

uncertainty management, 38–39

V

vision–language models (medical),
    143–147, 159–165